GLENCOE
LITERATURE

The Reader's Choice

Selection and Theme Assessment

Course 5

Glencoe
McGraw-Hill

New York, New York   Columbus, Ohio   Woodland Hills, California   Peoria, Illinois

Glencoe/McGraw-Hill

*A Division of The **McGraw·Hill** Companies*

Copyright © The McGraw-Hill Companies, Inc. All rights reserved. Permission is granted to reproduce
material contained herein on the condition that such material be reproduced only for classroom use; be
provided to students, teachers, and families without charge; and be used solely in conjunction with
Glencoe Literature. Any other reproduction, for use or sale, is prohibited without written permission of
the publisher.

Send all inquiries to:
Glencoe/McGraw-Hill
936 Eastwind Drive
Westerville, Ohio 43081

ISBN 0-02-817652-9

Printed in the United States of America.

1 2 3 4 5 6 7 8 9 10 024 04 03 02 01 00 99

Table of Contents

Selection Test

Score

Everyday Use (page 6)

Recalling and Interpreting (49 points total; 7 points each)
Write the letter of the best answer.

_____ 1. How does the narrator look and behave during the televised reunion with Dee that the narrator dreams about?
    a. as she does in real life
    b. as she would like to be in real life
    c. as she thinks Dee would like her to
    d. as she thinks Maggie would like her to

_____ 2. While Maggie awaits her sister's visit, her behavior indicates that she feels
    a. bored.   **c.** happy.
    b. nervous.   **d.** irritated.

_____ 3. The narrator expects Dee to react to the new house with
    a. scorn.   **c.** amazement.
    b. delight.   **d.** amusement.

_____ 4. Why, according to Dee, did she change her name to Wangero?
    a. The name *Dee* came from white people.
    b. She wanted a name that was less common.
    c. All of her friends were changing their names.
    d. There are too many women in the family named Dee.

_____ 5. What does the story suggest is the reason for Dee's interest in her heritage?
    a. She wants to please her mother.
    b. She feels guilty about past behavior.
    c. This has become a popular area of interest.
    d. Being away from home has awakened a need for family ties.

_____ 6. When, according to the narrator, did Dee begin to accept Maggie and Mama for who they are?
    a. never
    b. right after the fire
    c. when Dee left home for college
    d. when Dee developed an interest in her heritage

_____ 7. The narrator believes that Maggie says Dee can have the quilts because Maggie
    a. wants to be polite.
    b. would prefer newer, sturdier quilts.
    c. wasn't as close to Grandma Dee as Dee was.
    d. is used to having her desires come second to Dee's.

Selection Test

Using Vocabulary (15 points total; 3 points each)
Write the letter of the best answer.

_____ 8. A priceless item is one that is
        a. free.   b. worthless.   c. very valuable.

_____ 9. A word that means almost exactly the same things as *furtive* is
        a. *sneaky*.   b. *playful*.   c. *miserable*.

_____ 10. If someone oppresses a group, the group is likely to feel
        a. grateful.   b. resentful.   c. respectful.

_____ 11. A person who sidles is usually trying to
        a. show off.   b. avoid notice.   c. take it easy.

_____ 12. The doctrines of a religion are its
        a. symbols.   b. members.   c. teachings.

Interpreting and Evaluating (21 points total; 7 points each)
In the boxes below, note how the handmade quilts are viewed by Mama only (the narrator), by Dee only, and by both women.

How the Quilts Are Viewed

13. by Mama only

14. by Dee only

15. by both Mama and Dee

Evaluating and Connecting (15 points)
Use a separate sheet of paper to answer the following essay question.

16. What are some of the most important ways in which this story would probably be different if Dee were the narrator telling it from the first-person point of view? Explain your ideas.

Selection Test

Chee's Daughter (page 22)

Recalling and Interpreting (50 points total; 10 points each)
Write the letter of the best answer.

_____ 1. According to the story, Chee and his wife broke with tradition when they
  a. became farmers.
  b. married each other.
  c. moved in with his people.
  d. moved in with her people.

_____ 2. To Old Man Fat, being "progressive" means being free of
  a. family ties.
  b. ties to white people.
  c. the need to make money.
  d. the need to depend on the land.

_____ 3. When Chee lived with his wife's people, his greatest disagreement with them concerned
  a. his attitude toward the land.
  b. their treatment of his wife.
  c. their attitude toward his people.
  d. their treatment of the Little One.

_____ 4. When it appears that he has lost his daughter forever, Chee begins to question
  a. his desire to live.
  b. his faith in the land.
  c. his ties to his family.
  d. the depth of his love for her.

_____ 5. The success of Chee's plan to get the Little One back is LEAST dependent on
  a. the Little One's wishes.
  b. the location of the new cutoff.
  c. Chee's relationship with the land.
  d. Chee's understanding of his wife's people.

Using Vocabulary (15 points total; 3 points each)
Write the letter of the best answer. This exercise is continued on the next page.

_____ 6. You would be most likely to flaunt a possession if you were
  a. proud of it.   b. ashamed of it.   c. afraid of losing it.

_____ 7. A gaudy outfit would be likely to be described as
  a. loud.   b. elegant.   c. ill-fitting.

Selection Test

_____ **8.** If you approach a task zealously, you do it with
     a. fear.   **b.** passion.   **c.** carelessness.

_____ **9.** A person who demonstrates indolence might be called a
     a. bully.   **b.** chicken.   **c.** lazybones.

_____ **10.** When you surmise, you are always making
     a. a joke.   **b.** a mistake.   **c.** an assumption.

Interpreting and Evaluating (18 points total; 9 points each)

In each box below, note THREE reasons that the Little One goes to live where she does. Consider the events that occur, the roles played by Navajo traditions, and the motives, actions, and decisions of Chee and Old Man Fat and his wife.

11. What leads to the Little One's going to live with her mother's parents?	**12.** What leads to the Little One's going back to live with her father?

Evaluating and Connecting (17 points)

Use a separate sheet of paper to answer the following essay question.

13. What would you say is the main theme of this story? How is that theme communicated to the reader?

Selection Test

Civil Peace (page 38)

Recalling and Interpreting (54 points total; 9 points each)
Write the letter of the best answer.

_____ 1. Jonathan was reluctant to part with his bicycle when a man seized it "for urgent military action" because Jonathan
    a. did not support the military.
    b. was afraid it would be destroyed.
    c. thought the man was an enemy soldier.
    d. doubted that the man was really a soldier.

_____ 2. When Jonathan discovers his damaged house in Enugu, he is overcome with feelings of
    a. fury.   **c.** depression.
    b. gratitude.   **d.** helplessness.

_____ 3. Jonathan stops going to the Coal Corporation when he realizes that
    a. no one knows if the mine will reopen.
    b. he is safer and more comfortable at home.
    c. owning a bar is more profitable than mining.
    d. there are too many other applicants for mining jobs.

_____ 4. The variety of ways Jonathan and his family try to make money suggests that they are
    a. not very competent.
    b. extremely hardworking.
    c. unable to stick to any one task for long.
    d. searching for the easiest way to gain wealth.

_____ 5. The thieves are able to get what they want from Jonathan by
    a. humiliating him.
    b. blackmailing him.
    c. threatening to use violence.
    d. promising protection from other criminals.

_____ 6. The morning after the robbery, Jonathan's attitude could best be described as
    a. amazed.   **c.** accepting.
    b. thankful.   **d.** embarrassed.

Using Vocabulary (15 points total; 3 points each)
Write the letter of the best answer. This exercise is continued on the next page.

_____ 7. If government officials commandeer a possession, they
    a. take it.   **b.** destroy it.   **c.** condemn it.

_____ 8. How many days are in a fortnight?
    a. seven   **b.** fourteen   **c.** forty

_____ 9. An example of an edifice is
    a. Mt. Rainier.   **b.** the Pentagon.   **c.** Arlington Cemetery.

_____ 10. To retail a car is to
    a. sell it.   **b.** steal it.   **c.** repair it.

_____ 11. A word that means the opposite of *amenable* is
    a. *cheerful.*   **b.** *careful.*   **c.** *rebellious.*

Interpreting and Evaluating (16 points total; 8 points each)
Read each passage below and answer the questions.

"My frien," said [the leader of the thieves] at long last, "we don try our best for call dem but I tink say dem all done sleep-o . . . So wetin we go do now? Sometaim you wan call soja? Or you wan make we call dem for you? Soja better pass police. No be so?"	**12.** What is suggested or indirectly revealed by this dialogue? What suggests or reveals this?
"To God who made me; if you come inside and find one hundred pounds, take it and shoot me and shoot my wife and children. I swear to God. The only money I have in this life is this twenty-pounds *egg rasher* they gave me today . . ."	**13.** What is suggested or indirectly revealed by this dialogue? What suggests or reveals this?

Evaluating and Connecting (15 points)
Use a separate sheet of paper to answer the following essay question.

14. Why do you think the statement that "nothing puzzles God" is especially meaningful to Jonathan?

Selection Test

Two Kinds (page 48)

Recalling and Interpreting (49 points total; 7 points each)
Write the letter of the best answer.

_____ 1. At first, Jing-mei thinks that being recognized as a child genius would be
   a. fun.   **c.** embarrassing.
   b. impossible.   **d.** too much work.

_____ 2. Jing-mei's mother constantly tests her in order to
   a. teach her new things.
   b. discover where her talent lies.
   c. see if she has learned anything.
   d. keep her from becoming too proud.

_____ 3. Jing-mei's mother and Auntie Lindo complain to each other as a way to
   a. brag.   **c.** control their daughters.
   b. get sympathy.   **d.** relieve their frustrations.

_____ 4. Jing-mei believes that she was prevented from becoming a good pianist by
   a. a complete lack of talent.
   b. her teacher's deafness.
   c. her mother's foolish pride.
   d. her determination not to try.

_____ 5. Jing-mei's mother arranges for her to perform in the talent show in order to
   a. force her to practice.
   b. increase her self-confidence.
   c. show off her musical ability.
   d. discover once and for all whether she has musical talent.

_____ 6. Jing-mei approaches the talent show with a feeling of
   a. terror.   **c.** nervousness.
   b. excitement.   **d.** embarrassment.

_____ 7. Jing-mei's mother believes that what has kept her daughter from success is a lack of
   a. hope.   **c.** effort.
   b. talent.   **d.** confidence.

Using Vocabulary (15 points total; 3 points each)
Write the letter of the best answer. This exercise is continued on the next page.

_____ 8. A mesmerizing movie is one that
   a. amuses you.   **b.** frightens you.   **c.** holds your attention.

Selection Test

_____ **9.** A lament is an expression of
    a. sorrow.   **b.** criticism.   **c.** celebration.

_____ **10.** If you describe an outfit as having discordant colors, you mean that they
    a. clash.   **b.** are depressing.   **c.** are too bright.

_____ **11.** If you are engaged in a reverie, you are
    a. arguing.   **b.** performing.   **c.** daydreaming.

_____ **12.** You would be most likely to describe a game as a fiasco if your team
    a. lost badly.   **b.** almost won.   **c.** won very easily.

Interpreting and Evaluating (18 points total; 6 points each)
Choose one conflict from the story. Then answer the questions in the boxes below.

13. What kind of conflict is it?   ☐ External   ☐ Internal
- If EXTERNAL, who is it between?
- If INTERNAL, whose is it?

14. Why does the conflict exist?

15. Is the conflict resolved?   ☐ Yes   ☐ No
- If YES, how is it resolved?
- If NO, why isn't it resolved?

Evaluating and Connecting (18 points)
Use a separate sheet of paper to answer the following essay question.

16. After the talent show, what do you think Jing-mei wants most from her mother, and what do you think her mother wants most from her? Support your answers with details from the story.

Selection Test

Catch the Moon (page 62)

Recalling and Interpreting (48 points total; 8 points each)
Write the letter of the best answer.

_____ 1. At the beginning of the story, Luis's main motivation for working at his father's junkyard is
- a. the desire for freedom.
- b. the opportunity to make money.
- c. a wish to win back his father's trust.
- d. a sense of obligation toward his father.

_____ 2. At the beginning of the story, Luis sees the pile of hubcaps as his
- a. duty.
- b. destiny.
- c. salvation.
- d. punishment.

_____ 3. Luis's experiences in high school indicate that he enjoyed
- a. taking risks.
- b. being a loner.
- c. destroying things.
- d. humiliating others.

_____ 4. Since the death of his mother, Luis's relationship with his father has been
- a. closer than ever.
- b. angry and violent.
- c. awkward and tense.
- d. pleasant but distant.

_____ 5. At the beginning of the story, who has gotten over the death of Luis's mother and moved on with his life?
- a. Luis only
- b. Luis's father only
- c. both Luis and his father
- d. neither Luis nor his father

_____ 6. The story suggests that Luis's main reason for working so hard to find a hubcap for Naomi is his desire to
- a. please her.
- b. impress her.
- c. prove his father wrong.
- d. increase business for the junkyard.

Using Vocabulary (15 points total; 3 points each)
Write the letter of the best answer. This exercise is continued on the next page.

_____ 7. You would be most likely to find relics at a
- a. prison.
- b. museum.
- c. hospital.

_____ 8. Something that was once used to decapitate people was the
- a. lance.
- b. dungeon.
- c. guillotine.

_____ 9. No matter what else is true of a vintage item, it is always
- a. old.
- b. fragile.
- c. expensive.

Selection Test

_____ **10.** A word that has a milder but similar meaning to *harass* is

       a. *scold.*   **b.** *pester.*   **c.** *damage.*

_____ **11.** A makeshift item is something that you would

       a. make do with.   **b.** make up with.   **c.** make way for.

Interpreting and Evaluating (15 points total; 5 points each)

In the boxes, note THREE feelings or ideas that are conveyed by the imagery in each passage. Then, to the right of each box, identify the senses the imagery appeals to.

Feelings or ideas   Sense(s)

"Luis grunts and stands up on top of his silver mountain. He yells at no one, 'Someday, son, all this will be yours,' and sweeps his arms like the Pope blessing a crowd over the piles of car sandwiches and mounds of metal parts that cover this acre of land . . ."

12.

☐ Sight
☐ Touch
☐ Taste
☐ Smell
☐ Hearing

"Luis put some ice cubes in a Baggie and handed it to Mr. Cintrón, who had made the little bump on his head worse by rubbing it. It had GUILTY written on it, Luis thought."

13.

☐ Sight
☐ Touch
☐ Taste
☐ Smell
☐ Hearing

"Finally, when it seemed that it was a hopeless search, when it was almost midnight and Luis's hands were cut and bruised from his work, he found it. It was the perfect match for Naomi's drawing, the moon-shaped wheel cover for her car, Cinderella's shoe."

14.

☐ Sight
☐ Touch
☐ Taste
☐ Smell
☐ Hearing

Evaluating and Connecting (22 points)

Use a separate sheet of paper to answer the following essay question.

15. In a paragraph or two, describe the transformation that Luis undergoes in this story, and explain why you think he changes as he does.

Selection Test

Through the Tunnel (page 75)

Recalling and Interpreting (45 points total; 9 points each)
Write the letter of the best answer.

_____ 1. During their vacation, Jerry's mother is concerned about
       a. losing her son's affection.
       b. depending on her son too much.
       c. being overly protective of her son.
       d. how to express her love for her son.

_____ 2. Clowning around and making faces at the older boys makes Jerry feel
       a. ashamed of himself.
       b. accepted by the boys.
       c. happier and more carefree.
       d. less threatened by the boys.

_____ 3. Jerry's main goal in swimming through the tunnel is to prove something to
       a. himself.
       b. his mother.
       c. his friends at home.
       d. the older boys at the beach.

_____ 4. In order to prepare for the challenge he faces, Jerry spends days working on increasing
       a. his courage.
       b. his swimming speed.
       c. his ability to hold his breath.
       d. the depth to which he can dive.

_____ 5. Jerry rejects the idea of waiting another year, or even another day, to attempt his swim because he realizes that
       a. he will never get another chance.
       b. if he gives in to fear now, he will give in later.
       c. his mother may well discover what he has been doing.
       d. he could never be more physically ready for it than he already is.

Using Vocabulary (15 points total; 3 points each)
Write the letter of the best answer. This exercise is continued on the next page.

_____ 6. A common expression of contrition is to say,
       a. "I quit."   **b.** "I'm sorry."   **c.** "Thank you!"

_____ 7. Which of the following is convulsive?
       a. a sneeze   **b.** a whisper   **c.** a smile

Selection Test

_____ 8. You would be incredulous if you heard of someone doing something
   a. brave.   b. unkind.   c. impossible.

_____ 9. You would be likely to use a beseeching tone of voice if you
   a. were amused.   b. were irritated.   c. wanted something.

_____ 10. There are myriads of
   a. fish in the sea.   b. eggs in a carton.   c. pigs that can fly.

Interpreting and Evaluating (16 points total; 4 points each)
In the boxes, follow the directions and answer the questions.

---

11. On the plot line, make a mark to show where in the story the climax occurs.

   BEGINNING   END

---

12. What do you think is the climax of this story?

| 13. Why do you consider this event to be the climax of the story? | ⇒ | 14. What effect does the climax have on any of the conflicts in the story? |

Evaluating and Connecting (24 points total; 12 points each)
Use a separate sheet of paper to answer BOTH of the following questions.

15. Why do you think that, at the end of the story, it is no longer of the least importance to Jerry that he go to the rocky bay? Explain your ideas.

16. Is the goal that Jerry sets for himself reasonable or foolish? Explain your answer.

Selection Test

The Vision Quest (page 88)

Recalling and Interpreting (56 points total; 8 points each)
Write the letter of the best answer.

_____ 1. The young man goes on the vision quest mainly to
    a. gain power.
    b. please his uncle.
    c. worship the spirits.
    d. make his people proud of him.

_____ 2. The young man hopes to become a
    a. god.   **c.** warrior.
    b. hunter.   **d.** medicine man.

_____ 3. How do the young man's relatives feel about his vision quest?
    a. They are fearful for his safety.
    b. They think he is too young for such an attempt.
    c. They support his desire and are confident that he will succeed.
    d. They support his desire but doubt that he can possibly succeed.

_____ 4. The purpose of the sweat lodge is to
    a. provide shelter.
    b. provide a holy place for worship.
    c. test the young man's determination.
    d. remove the young man's impurities.

_____ 5. The goal of the voice that the young man hears is to get him to
    a. sleep.   **c.** dream.
    b. leave.   **d.** come closer.

_____ 6. Before the boulder attacks him, the young man's attitude toward the voice is one of
    a. awe.   **c.** respect.
    b. curiosity.   **d.** boldness.

_____ 7. The young man's uncle believes the young man failed because he was
    a. immature.   **c.** too proud.
    b. impatient.   **d.** unwilling to endure suffering.

Using Vocabulary (12 points total; 3 points each)
Write the letter of the best answer. This exercise is continued on the next page.

_____ 8. A person would be most likely to look gaunt as a result of
    a. fear.   **b.** starvation.   **c.** weight training.

Selection Test

_____ **9.** Someone who lacks humility would be inclined to

        a. brag.   **b.** rejoice.   **c.** copy other people.

_____ **10.** If you behave in a brash manner, people are most likely to consider you

        a. rude.   **b.** silly.   **c.** overly cautious.

_____ **11.** A word that means the opposite of *obliterate* is

        a. *hide*.   **b.** *create*.   **c.** *prevent*.

Interpreting and Evaluating (18 points total; 6 points each)
In each box on the left, note something that this legend conveys about the culture from which it comes. This might be a value, custom, piece of wisdom, or something else. In each box on the right, explain how the legend conveys that information about the culture.

12.   ⇒

13.   ⇒

14.   ⇒

Evaluating and Connecting (14 points)
Use a separate sheet of paper to answer the following essay question.

16. What, in your opinion, is the main lesson or message of this legend? How is it communicated to the reader?

Selection Test

By the Waters of Babylon (page 94)

Recalling and Interpreting (56 points total; 7 points each)
Write the letter of the best answer.

_____ 1. This story takes place in the
      a. future.   **c.** recent past.
      b. present.   **d.** distant past.

_____ 2. At the beginning of the story, the priests of John's people go to the Dead Places mainly in search of
      a. food.   **c.** technology.
      b. metal.   **d.** enlightenment.

_____ 3. The food in the Dead Places that "brings death" is probably dangerous to eat because it is
      a. enchanted.   **c.** not actual food.
      b. uncooked.   **d.** contaminated.

_____ 4. Even after his vision of the city as it had been, John wonders about
      a. how the gods died.
      b. whether the gods had magic.
      c. whether the gods were happy.
      d. why the Place of the Gods is abandoned.

_____ 5. When John finds the dead god, he is struck by the god's expression of
      a. fury.   **c.** sadness.
      b. terror.   **d.** frustration.

_____ 6. John believes that the dead god was, in some sense, "unconquered," because
      a. he had never lost his spirit.
      b. he had been a great scholar.
      c. his body had been preserved.
      d. he had survived the Destruction.

_____ 7. When John returns to his people, to whom does he tell the full truth about his experiences?
      a. no one   **c.** only the priests
      b. only his father   **d.** all of his people

_____ 8. At the end of the story, what has changed about John?
      a. his desire for knowledge
      b. his respect for his father
      c. his ideas of what is possible
      d. his determination not to lose his spirit.

Selection Test

Using Vocabulary (9 points total; 3 points each)
Write the letter of the best answer.

_____ **9.** One who does what he or she is bade to do is

     a. rude.   **b.** obedient.   **c.** rebellious.

_____ **10.** When you are perplexed, you feel

     a. envious.   **b.** confident.   **c.** confused.

_____ **11.** A word that is very similar in meaning to *anteroom* is

     a. *parlor*.   **b.** *pantry*.   **c.** *vestibule*.

Interpreting and Evaluating (21 points total; 7 points each)
Answer the questions in the boxes below.

12. What is John's main goal in this story?

⇓

13. Give TWO reasons why it is important to John that he achieve this particular goal.

⇒

14. What consequences does John's achievement of this goal have for him and his people?

Evaluating and Connecting (14 points)
Use a separate sheet of paper to answer the following essay question.

15. Do you agree with the moral of this story? In a paragraph or two, support your answer with references to the story and your life experiences.

Selection Test

Score

What I Have Been Doing Lately (page 108)

Recalling and Interpreting (48 points total; 8 points each)
Write the letter of the best answer.

_____ 1. At what point in the story is the narrator in her bed?
   a. only at the end
   b. only at the beginning
   c. only at the beginning and the end
   d. at the beginning, the end, and during the picnic scene

_____ 2. The narrator gets out of the hole she jumps into by
   a. calling for help.
   b. climbing back up.
   c. deciding to go the other way.
   d. eventually falling out the other end.

_____ 3. When the narrator tells the woman what she has been doing, the events she describes
   a. are exactly the same as those she has already related.
   b. are in a different order than those she has already related.
   c. are the same events as those she has already related but with more details.
   d. begin similarly to those she has already related but then change significantly.

_____ 4. At first, the narrator's reaction to the picnicking people is one of
   a. worry.
   b. horror.
   c. boredom.
   d. fascination.

_____ 5. As the narrator approaches the picnicking people, they
   a. change.
   b. disappear.
   c. look more familiar.
   d. move away from her.

_____ 6. The narrator decides that she doesn't like what she is doing when she realizes
   a. how hungry she is.
   b. how much she would like to be home.
   c. how much danger she is in.
   d. how repetitive her activities are.

Selection Test   (continued)

Using Vocabulary (12 points total; 4 points each)
Write the letter of the best answer.

_____ 7. Which of the following words is most similar in meaning to *interlaced*?
   a. *tangled*   **b.** *braided*   **c.** *clasped*

_____ 8. A verandah is a type of
   a. roof.   **b.** patio.   **c.** porch.

_____ 9. One would be most likely to hear a psalm during
   a. a parade.   **b.** a church service.   **c.** an elevator ride.

Interpreting and Evaluating (16 points total; 8 points each)
Read the descriptions from the story. Then follow the directions in the boxes.

"Either it was drizzling or there was a lot of dust in the air and the dust was damp. I stuck out my tongue and the drizzle or the damp dust tasted like government school ink."

10. Identify ONE sensory detail from this description.   ⇒

Identify the sense(s) to which this detail appeals.
☐ Sight
☐ Touch
☐ Taste
☐ Smell
☐ Hearing

"The fourth time I threw the stone, the monkey caught it and threw it back at me. The stone struck me on my forehead over my right eye, making a deep gash. The gash healed immediately but now the skin on my forehead felt false to me."

11. Identify ONE sensory detail from this description.   ⇒

Identify the sense(s) to which this detail appeals.
☐ Sight
☐ Touch
☐ Taste
☐ Smell
☐ Hearing

Evaluating and Connecting (24 points)
Use a separate sheet of paper to answer the following essay question.

12. What can you tell from this story about the narrator's hopes and fears? Support your ideas.

Selection Test

With All Flags Flying (page 114)

Recalling and Interpreting (49 points total; 7 points each)
Write the letter of the best answer.

_____ 1. Mr. Carpenter sees his life up to the present as having been
    a. wasted.   c. tragic.
    b. satisfying.   d. too long.

_____ 2. Riding on the back of the motorcycle makes Mr. Carpenter feel
    a. free.   c. old and feeble.
    b. terrified.   d. silly and embarrassed.

_____ 3. During his stay with his daughter Clara, Mr. Carpenter is determined not to reveal his
    a. real plans.   c. love for his family.
    b. financial situation.   d. physical weaknesses.

_____ 4. Mr. Carpenter most fears being viewed as
    a. wrong.   c. selfish.
    b. pathetic.   d. stubborn.

_____ 5. More than anything else, Mr. Carpenter wants to avoid
    a. worrying his children.
    b. disappointing his children.
    c. being a burden to his children.
    d. being involved in his children's lives.

_____ 6. Clara and her family fail to convince Mr. Carpenter that they
    a. love him.
    b. want him to live with them.
    c. would be better off if he lived with them.
    d. are being honest with him about their feelings.

_____ 7. Mr. Carpenter would be most likely to describe his children as
    a. kind.   c. wasteful.
    b. foolish.   d. thoughtless.

Using Vocabulary (15 points total; 3 points each)
Write the letter of the best answer. This exercise is continued on the next page.

_____ 8. You would be most likely to wince in response to a
    a. pinch.   b. greeting.   c. compliment.

_____ 9. Which of the following is a monosyllabic word?
    a. *youth*   b. *adolescent*   c. *teeny-bopper*

Selection Test   *(continued)*

_____ **10.** A disease that is usually chronic is
   a. the flu.   **b.** arthritis.   **c.** chicken pox.

_____ **11.** A word that means the opposite of *subtle* is
   a. *big*.   **b.** *stiff*.   **c.** *obvious*.

_____ **12.** Someone described as being doddering would be most likely to need a
   a. cane.   **b.** hearing aid.   **c.** translator.

Interpreting and Evaluating (18 points total; 9 points each)
In the boxes, answer the questions below.

	Mr. Carpenter	Clara, his daughter
13. Is the character a main or minor one? Explain.	☐ Main ☐ Minor	☐ Main ☐ Minor
14. Is the character a flat or round one? Explain.	☐ Flat ☐ Round	☐ Flat ☐ Round

Evaluating and Connecting (18 points)
Use a separate sheet of paper to answer the following essay question.

15. Given what you know about the characters in this story and their situations, do you think that Mr. Carpenter's move into the old folks' home is best for everyone involved? Explain your answer.

Selection and Theme Assessment

Selection Test

A Child, a Dog, The Night (page 128)

Recalling and Interpreting (49 points total; 7 points each)
Write the letter of the best answer.

_____ 1. Which of the following best describes Little Juan before Black arrived?
  a. shy   **c.** lonely
  b. quiet   **d.** cheerful

_____ 2. The story suggests that Mr. Davies owns Black primarily
  a. to impress others.
  b. to guard the mines.
  c. to counteract loneliness.
  d. for personal protection.

_____ 3. Mr. Davies chooses Mr. Labra to watch Black while he is gone because Mr. Labra
  a. has a small child.
  b. needs the money.
  c. is known for being a loyal friend.
  d. is known for being kind to animals.

_____ 4. How does Mr. Labra feel when Mr. Davies asks him to care for Black?
  a. lucky   **c.** worried
  b. proud   **d.** resentful

_____ 5. Mr. Labra discourages Little Juan from hoping to own Black by pointing out that the dog
  a. is valuable.
  b. is loyal to Mr. Davies.
  c. is loved by Mr. Davies.
  d. would cost too much to feed.

_____ 6. Why does Little Juan refuse payment for caring for Black?
  a. He doesn't want to offend Mr. Davies.
  b. He wants to make Mr. Davies feel bad.
  c. He believes this is the polite thing to do.
  d. He hopes Mr. Davies will see that he deserves the dog.

_____ 7. The story suggests that, when Mr. Davies understands the cause of Black's howling, his response is one of
  a. anger.   **c.** irritation.
  b. sadness.   **d.** frustration.

Selection Test

Using Vocabulary (15 points total; 3 points each)
Write the letter of the best answer.

_____ 8. An example of a plaintive noise is a
     a. cough.   **b.** giggle.   **c.** whimper.

_____ 9. A word that means the opposite of *disperse* is
     a. *save.*   **b.** *gather.*   **c.** *compromise.*

_____ 10. When a sight intrigues you, you are most likely to
     a. stare at it.   **b.** avoid notice.   **c.** turn away from it.

_____ 11. The residue of a campfire is
     a. ashes.   **b.** flames.   **c.** kindling.

_____ 12. If you were given a gift, a reciprocal gesture would be to
     a. refuse it.   **b.** express thanks.   **c.** give one in return.

Interpreting and Evaluating (21 points total; 7 points each)
Think about how this story would be different if it had been told from a first-person point of view instead of from an omniscient point of view. Then, in each box, indicate TWO questions that might NOT have been answered if the story had been presented from the point of view of each character.

13. Little Juan	14. Juan Labra	15. Mr. Davies

Evaluating and Connecting (15 points)
Use a separate sheet of paper to answer the following essay question.

16. The story ends with the line, "In that miraculous moment, a new warmth tempered the night of Chuqui." In a paragraph or two, discuss why this moment might seem "miraculous" in the setting of this story.

     Selection and Theme Assessment

Selection Test

A White Heron (page 143)

Recalling and Interpreting (48 points total; 8 points each)
Write the letter of the best answer.

_____ 1. The main reason that Sylvia had been unhappy living in the city was that
    a. her home was crowded.
    b. she was afraid of people.
    c. she missed her grandmother.
    d. there were few plants and animals.

_____ 2. Why does Mrs. Tilley allow the young man to stay at her house?
    a. He offers to pay.
    b. He reminds her of her son, Dan.
    c. She thinks he will entertain Sylvia.
    d. She is a friendly and helpful person.

_____ 3. Which of the following is something that Sylvia and the young man have in common?
    a. self-confidence   **c.** deep interest in nature
    b. financial hardship   **d.** doubts about shooting birds

_____ 4. What is it about the young man that Sylvia finds impossible to understand?
    a. why he kills birds he admires
    b. why he lets her go hunting with him
    c. why he wants to find the white heron
    d. why he cannot find the white heron on his own

_____ 5. Why doesn't Sylvia tell anyone that she plans to climb the pine tree?
    a. She wants her discovery to be a surprise.
    b. She is afraid her grandmother would forbid it.
    c. She fears that the young man would insist on coming along.
    d. She doesn't want to have to admit failure if she cannot do it.

_____ 6. Sylvia searches for the white heron's nest because she wants to
    a. warn the bird.
    b. please the young man.
    c. please her grandmother.
    d. be able to see the bird up close.

Using Vocabulary (15 points total; 3 points each)
Write the letter of the best answer. This exercise is continued on the next page.

_____ 7. You would likely respond in a vexed way to something
    a. funny.   **b.** irritating.   **c.** frightening.

_____ **8.** Advice to behave discreetly would most likely include

      a. "Be careful."   **b.** "Go for it!"   **c.** "Keep trying."

_____ **9.** Which person has the most perilous job?

      a. an actor   **b.** a surgeon   **c.** a firefighter

_____ **10.** A parent is most likely to rebuke a child who is

      a. sick.   **b.** hungry.   **c.** naughty.

_____ **11.** A word that means the opposite of *wary* is

      a. *hearty*.   **b.** *reckless*.   **c.** *energetic*.

Interpreting and Evaluating (21 points total; 7 points each)

Think about the inner conflict Sylvia deals with in this story. Then answer the questions in the boxes below to reflect your thoughts about this conflict.

12. Sylvia's main inner conflict is between

_____ and _____

which is resolved by

13. Name TWO things Sylvia gains as a result.

14. Name TWO things she loses as a result.

Evaluating and Connecting (16 points)

Use a separate sheet of paper to answer the following essay question.

15. Consider all the aspects of the setting of this story—the time, the general place, and the details of the specific place. Which aspect or aspects do you consider most important to the story? Could any aspects of the setting change without changing the story in important ways? Explain your answer.

Selection and Theme Assessment

Selection Test

Score

The Boar Hunt (page 157)

Recalling and Interpreting (49 points total; 7 points each)
Write the letter of the best answer.

_____ 1. The men in this story usually go on hunting parties for reasons having most to do
with
     a. hunger   **c.** finances.
     b. pleasure.   **d.** tradition.

_____ 2. The men expect the boar hunt to be all of the following EXCEPT
     a. fun.   **c.** challenging.
     b. rewarding.   **d.** life-threatening.

_____ 3. When the men first see the boars, their reaction is one of
     a. awe.   **c.** delight.
     b. terror.   **d.** disappointment.

_____ 4. At first, the narrator views the slaughter of the boars as
     a. routine.   **c.** wonderful.
     b. revolting.   **d.** a necessary evil.

_____ 5. The men do not flee the danger they are in because
     a. they are too proud.
     b. they are too exhausted.
     c. they aren't aware of their danger.
     d. there is no obvious, safe way to run away.

_____ 6. The narrator concludes that the boars' attack on the men was motivated by
     a. hunger.   **c.** self-defense.
     b. revenge.   **d.** blind instinct.

_____ 7. The narrator's experience leads him to believe that hunting for pleasure is a bad
idea because it is
     a. immoral.   **c.** wasteful.
     b. dangerous.   **d.** unpredictable.

Using Vocabulary (15 points total; 3 points each)
Write the letter of the best answer. This exercise is continued on the next page.

_____ 8. People often exhibit lethargy by
     a. gasping.   **b.** yawning.   **c.** bragging.

_____ 9. A word that means the opposite of *sporadic* is
     a. *rapid*.   **b.** *admirable*.   **c.** *continual*.

Selection Test   (continued)

_____ 10. You would most likely be interested in atonement for something you felt
     a. proud of.   **b.** guilty about.   **c.** amused by.

_____ 11. A person who works at something tenaciously is one who will not
     a. give up.   **b.** try hard.   **c.** follow directions.

_____ 12. A word that means the opposite of *impotent* is
     a. *minor*.   **b.** *cheerful*.   **c.** *powerful*.

Interpreting and Evaluating (16 points total; 8 points each)
Think about how the narrator is changed by the boar hunt, and why. Then, in each box on the left, jot down a word or phrase that describes how the narrator feels about the boar hunt. In each box on the right, explain why he feels that way.

13. Before the boar hunt

Feeling ⇒	Reason

14. After the boar hunt

Feeling ⇒	Reason

Evaluating and Connecting (20 points)
Use a separate sheet of paper to answer the following essay question.

15. Why do you think the writer of this story chose to use a first-person point of view instead of third-person? (Remember that a third-person narrator does not participate in the action of a story.) Give at least one reason and support it with references to the story.

Selection and Theme Assessment

Open-Book Selection Test

Score

Delicious Death (page 167)

Recalling and Interpreting (60 points total; 10 points each)
Write the letter of the best answer.

_____ 1. The mother's reluctance to let her son go hunting is based mainly on
   a. worries about his safety.
   b. unwillingness to be apart from him.
   c. dismay at his growing independence.
   d. doubts about the morality of hunting.

_____ 2. In line 13, the mother is mainly attempting to
   a. make up with her son.
   b. affect her son's attitude.
   c. change her son's decision.
   d. support her son's decision.

_____ 3. Which of the following best describes the mother's overall view of her son?
   a. "killer"
   b. "boy/man"
   c. "the hunter"
   d. "winged soul"

_____ 4. Both the mother and son associate hunting with
   a. danger.
   b. injustice.
   c. maturity.
   d. spirituality.

_____ 5. Which of the following does the mother pray for in lines 25–33?
   a. wisdom
   b. patience
   c. harmony
   d. forgiveness

_____ 6. Which of the following is the best example of colloquial language?
   a. "autumn day-sky of steel / and rifles," (lines 4 and 5)
   b. "like / am I some kind of wimp or what," (lines 8 and 9)
   c. " 'Guard / this human who goes / in search of / lives.' " (lines 15–18)
   d. "The wonder of the hunt is on my tongue," (line 43)

Open-Book Selection Test

Interpreting and Evaluating (16 points total; 8 points each)

In each box on the left, jot down a word or phrase that describes how the person feels about the four quail that the son kills. In each box on the right, explain why the person might feel that way about them.

Feelings

Reasons

7. The son

Feelings

Reasons

8. The mother

Evaluating and Connecting (24 points)

Use a separate sheet of paper to answer the following essay question.

9. What is the mother's general attitude toward hunting? How does she react to her son's first hunting trip, and how does she make use of that occasion? Support your ideas with references to the poem.

Selection Test

Score

The Monkey's Paw (page 172)

Recalling and Interpreting (56 points total; 8 points each)
Write the letter of the best answer.

_____ 1. The White family's initial response to Sergeant Major Morris's claims about the monkey's paw is mainly
    a. excited.   **c.** frightened.
    b. doubtful.   **d.** uninterested.

_____ 2. Morris's own attitude toward the monkey's paw could best be described as
    a. angry.   **c.** respectful.
    b. terrified.   **d.** disappointed.

_____ 3. People to whom Morris has offered to sell the monkey's paw have been unwilling to buy it because they
    a. feared its magical powers.
    b. doubted that it could grant their wishes.
    c. did not have enough money to pay the price he asked.
    d. were unwilling to limit themselves to sensible wishes.

_____ 4. What does the story suggest about Morris's personal experiences with the monkey's paw?
    a. His wishes had mixed results.
    b. All of his wishes had terrible results.
    c. All of his wishes had pleasant results.
    d. He, himself, never wished on the monkey's paw.

_____ 5. What attitude does Herbert display toward his father's wish on the monkey's paw?
    a. fearful   **c.** disgusted
    b. amazed   **d.** lighthearted

_____ 6. When the monkey's paw moves in his hand, Mr. White's response could best be described as
    a. reassured.
    b. fascinated.
    c. excited and hopeful.
    d. frightened and disgusted.

_____ 7. What is Mr. White's third wish?
    a. that Herbert is dead
    b. that the knocking stop
    c. that Herbert had never died
    d. that he had never wished on the monkey's paw

Selection Test

(continued)

Using Vocabulary (15 points total; 3 points each)
Write the letter of the best answer.

_____ 8. An avaricious person finds it difficult to
      a. share.   **b.** stay awake.   **c.** feel confident.

_____ 9. A person who deals with a task doggedly demonstrates
      a. insecurity.   **b.** resentment.   **c.** persistence.

_____ 10. You are most likely to speak amiably to someone you
      a. like.   **b.** fear.   **c.** hate.

_____ 11. A presumptuous person is likely to be thought of as
      a. shy.   **b.** rude.   **c.** mysterious.

_____ 12. A word that means the opposite of *enthralled* is
      a. *lively*.   **b.** *bored*.   **c.** *encouraged*.

Interpreting and Evaluating (14 points total; 7 points each)
In each left-hand box below, identify ONE particularly suspenseful moment in the story, and in each right-hand box, explain what made that moment suspenseful.

13. A suspenseful moment was	What made it suspenseful was

14. A suspenseful moment was	What made it suspenseful was

Evaluating and Connecting (15 points)
Use a separate sheet of paper to answer the following essay question.

15. Do you think the Whites deserved what happened to them? Why or why not?

Selection Test

Score

Tuesday Siesta (page 188)

Recalling and Interpreting (60 points total; 10 points each)
Write the letter of the best answer.

_____ 1. What does the story suggest is unusual about the mother and daughter's visit to
the parish house?
  a. They arrive during siesta.
  b. They have no appointment.
  c. They want keys to the cemetery.
  d. They are not residents of the town.

_____ 2. What does the story suggest is the reason that the mother does not cry?
  a. She is relieved that her son is dead.
  b. She thinks this would be embarrassing behavior.
  c. She does not want anyone to guess why she is in town.
  d. She does not want anyone to know that she loved her son.

_____ 3. Who or what does the mother seem to blame for her son's death?
  a. bad luck
  b. the townspeople
  c. the old woman, Rebecca
  d. a terrible misunderstanding

_____ 4. The story suggests that people have gathered to see the woman and her daughter
because they are
  a. unusual-looking.
  b. strangers in town.
  c. the family of a thief.
  d. visitors at the parish house.

_____ 5. Throughout the story, the mother's attitude is
  a. calm.   c. anxious.
  b. harsh.   d. mournful.

_____ 6. Throughout the story, the girl's attitude is one of
  a. fear.
  b. embarrassment.
  c. quiet obedience.
  d. impatient excitement.

Using Vocabulary (15 points total; 3 points each)
Write the letter of the best answer. This exercise is continued on the next page.

_____ 7. If a speech is interminable, it seems
  a. too long.   b. unplanned.   c. overly dramatic.

Selection Test

_____ **8.** If you scrutinize something, you

       a. avoid it.   **b.** repair it.   **c.** examine it.

_____ **9.** An inscrutable person is one who is difficult or impossible to

       a. like.   **b.** understand.   **c.** escape from.

_____ **10.** If you are skeptical about something someone says, you feel

       a. unsure.   **b.** amused.   **c.** jealous.

_____ **11.** A feeling that is associated with serenity is

       a. rage.   **b.** sadness.   **c.** contentment.

Interpreting and Evaluating (7 points total)

Read the following passage from the story and think about how the author feels about the scene he is describing. Then answer the questions in the boxes.

There was no one at the station. On the other side of the street, on the sidewalk shaded by the almond trees, only the pool hall was open. The town was floating in the heat. The woman and the girl got off the train and crossed the abandoned station—the tiles split apart by the grass growing up between—and over to the shady side of the street.

12. What is the tone of this passage?

Why do you think this is the tone?

Evaluating and Connecting (18 points)

Use a separate sheet of paper to answer the following essay question.

13. Why do you think the mother makes the journey? How do you think she is feeling, and why does she feel this way?

| Selection Test | Score |

Contents of the Dead Man's Pocket (page 198)

Recalling and Interpreting (49 points total; 7 points each)
Write the letter of the best answer.

_____ 1. Why does Tom want to spend the evening working?
    a. His boss has asked him to do so.
    b. He is eager to finish his proposal.
    c. He wants to be paid for overtime work.
    d. He doesn't care to see the movie his wife wants to see.

_____ 2. Clare's response to Tom's desire to stay home is one of
    a. relief.   **c.** regret.
    b. anger.   **d.** suspicion.

_____ 3. When Tom first goes out on the ledge, he sees his action as mainly
    a. heroic.   **c.** brave.
    b. foolish.   **d.** practical.

_____ 4. When Tom reaches the paper and bends to retrieve it, he suddenly realizes
    a. that his life is truly at risk.
    b. that his life is worth living.
    c. why he has done what he has done.
    d. what a good story the effort will make.

_____ 5. Walking back to the window is more difficult than walking away from it mainly because of a change in
    a. the temperature.
    b. the wind direction.
    c. Tom's attitude.
    d. Tom's desire to retrieve the paper.

_____ 6. When Tom imagines the report of "the contents of the dead man's pockets," he realizes that
    a. he doesn't deserve to go on living.
    b. he is no different from anyone else.
    c. his wife will not be well provided for.
    d. his priorities in life have been foolish.

_____ 7. Tom decides to take the risk involved in trying to break the window because
    a. he is too terrified to think clearly.
    b. he knows he will fall unless he can get inside.
    c. he dreads the humiliation of being found on the ledge.
    d. he fears that the cigarette he left burning may start a fire.

Selection Test   *(continued)*

Using Vocabulary (10 points total; 2 points each)
For each underlined word, write the letter of the word that means the OPPOSITE.

_____ 8. taut   **a.** straight

_____ 9. deftness   **b.** loose

_____ 10. unimpeded   **c.** rehearsed

_____ 11. improvised   **d.** hindered

_____ 12. convoluted   **e.** clumsiness

Interpreting and Evaluating (27 points total; 9 points each)
Think about what the yellow sheet of paper means to Tom—what it represents or symbolizes to him—at the beginning of the story and at the end. Then answer the questions in the boxes.

What does the yellow paper mean to Tom . . .

13. as he considers going after it?	14. as he replaces it on the desk?

15. Why does he laugh as it sails out the broken window?

Evaluating and Connecting (14 points)
Use a separate sheet of paper to answer the following questions.

16. Why do you think the author of this story chose to use a third-person point of view, limited to Tom? Do you think it would have worked as well if told another way? Explain your answer.

Selection Test

The Censors (page 217)

Recalling and Interpreting (45 points total; 9 points each)
Write the letter of the best answer.

_____ 1. At the beginning of the story, Juan is worried about his letter to Mariana for all of
the following reasons EXCEPT that the letter
   a. will be censored.
   b. could get her into trouble.
   c. could get him into trouble.
   d. contains statements against the government.

_____ 2. Which of the following motivates Juan to write to Mariana?
   a. fear   c. sense of duty
   b. happiness   d. political considerations

_____ 3. Juan applies for a job as a censor because he
   a. desperately needs a job.
   b. wants to impress Mariana.
   c. wants a chance to intercept his letter.
   d. wants to do whatever he can to bring an end to censorship.

_____ 4. The real reason that Juan begins to find more material to censor in the letters he
reads is that
   a. his job is beginning to consume him.
   b. the government authorities are testing him.
   c. more anti-government material is being written.
   d. he is getting better at recognizing anti-government statements.

_____ 5. The story indicates that Juan's feelings about censoring his own letter are
   a. proud.   c. depressed.
   b. anxious.   d. matter-of-fact.

Using Vocabulary (15 points total; 3 points each)
Write the letter of the best answer. This exercise is continued on the next page.

_____ 6. One expects to find a certain degree of staidness in the behavior of
   a. a judge.   b. an actor.   c. an athlete.

_____ 7. An ulterior purpose for doing something is one that is
   a. clear.   b. disgraceful.   c. kept hidden.

_____ 8. If someone is smart albeit trusting, that person is
   a. smart and not trusting.
   b. both smart and trusting.
   c. smarter and more trusting than others.

Selection Test

_____ 9. A word that means the opposite of *irreproachable* is

     a. *distant.*   **b.** *obvious.*   **c.** *shameful.*

_____ 10. What kind of effects are subversive acts designed to have?

     a. helpful   **b.** harmful   **c.** invisible

Interpreting and Evaluating (24 points total; 8 points each)
Answer the questions in the boxes below. Consider Juan's personality as well as his goals, motivations, and values.

11. What do you think is a major turning point in Juan's life?

12. What FOUR words or phrases could describe Juan before this turning point?

13. What FOUR words or phrases could describe Juan after this turning point?

Evaluating and Connecting (16 points)
Use a separate sheet of paper to answer the following essay question.

14. In a paragraph or two, identify TWO things that you think the author uses satire to criticize. Explain how she goes about poking fun at these things.

Selection Test

The Ring (page 224)

Recalling and Interpreting (48 points total; 8 points each)
Write the letter of the best answer.

_____ 1. Which of the following best describes Lise and Sigismund's moods at the beginning of the story?
    a. calm   **c.** anxious
    b. gloomy   **d.** cheerful

_____ 2. Who agrees with Mathias when he says that he "would like to string up the murderer"?
    a. only Lise   **c.** both Lise and Sigismund
    b. only Sigismund   **d.** neither Lise nor Sigismund

_____ 3. Lise enters the glen because she wants to
    a. feel safe.   **c.** have some peace and quiet.
    b. imagine another life.   **d.** prove something to Sigismund.

_____ 4. Which of the following best describes what happens to Lise's wedding ring?
    a. It is deliberately dropped and lost.
    b. It is offered and accepted as a gift.
    c. It is offered, rejected, and then left behind.
    d. It is taken away by force and then discarded.

_____ 5. Wolves and sheep in this story have symbolic meaning. Which of the following characters is most wolf-like?
    a. Lise   **c.** Mathias
    b. the thief   **d.** Sigismund

_____ 6. Wolves and sheep have symbolic meaning in this story. Which of the following characters is most sheep-like?
    a. the thief
    b. Lise, at the end of the story
    c. Lise, at the beginning of the story
    d. Sigismund, at the end of the story

Using Vocabulary (15 points total; 3 points each)
Write the letter of the best answer. This exercise is continued on the next page.

_____ 7. Which of the following would you most expect to find in a rustic environment?
    a. farms   **b.** soldiers   **c.** junkyards

_____ 8. If you conceive an idea, you
    a. copy it.   **b.** reject it.   **c.** think of it.

Selection Test   *(continued)*

_____ 9. An unconditional answer would never begin with

   a. "If."   **b.** "No."   **c.** "Of course."

_____ 10. An example of a definitive reply to a question is

   a. "No."   **b.** "Maybe."   **c.** "Please explain that."

_____ 11. A void is always

   a. cold.   **b.** empty.   **c.** dangerous.

Interpreting and Evaluating (21 points total; 7 points each)
In the boxes on the right, explain what is revealed in the quotations from the story.

What is revealed about what each person is like?

It was not a long time since she had played with dolls; as now she dressed her own hair, looked over her linen press and arranged her flowers she again lived through an enchanting and cherished experience: one was doing everything gravely and solicitously, and all the time one knew one was playing.

> **12.** What THREE character traits of Lise does the quotation reveal?

Sigismund, the young husband, had promised himself that from now there should be no stone in his bride's path, nor should any shadow fall across it.

> **13.** What THREE character traits of Sigismund does the quotation reveal?

He was no longer just run to earth and crouching for a spring, but he was wondering, trying to know. At that she seemed to see herself with the eyes of the wild animal at bay in his dark hiding-place; her silently approaching white figure, which might mean death.

> **14.** What THREE character traits of the thief does the quotation reveal?

Evaluating and Connecting (16 points)
Use a separate sheet of paper to answer ONE of the following essay questions.

15. In a paragraph or two, discuss what you think Lise loses and gains in the glen. Support your ideas with reference to the story.

16. Why do you think Lise doesn't tell Sigismund about the thief? Do you think she does the right thing? Explain your answer.

Selection Test

The Happy Man's Shirt (page 240)

Recalling and Interpreting (42 points total; 7 points each)
Write the letter of the best answer.

_____ 1. The prince's unhappiness could best be described as a result of
    a. boredom.   **c.** jealousy of others.
    b. heartbreak.   **d.** general discontent.

_____ 2. How does the king respond to the prince's unhappiness?
    a. He ignores it.
    b. He makes fun of it.
    c. He refuses to accept it.
    d. He considers it normal for someone his son's age.

_____ 3. From the story, you can tell that the king is the kind of person who never
    a. gives up.
    b. asks for help.
    c. makes up his mind.
    d. accepts responsibility.

_____ 4. What does the story suggest about happy people?
    a. They are extremely hard to find.
    b. They do not realize they are happy.
    c. They are happy for the wrong reasons.
    d. They are unwilling to be helpful to unhappy people.

_____ 5. The king's attention is drawn to the happy man by the young man's
    a. smile.   **c.** reputation.
    b. singing.   **d.** claims of happiness.

_____ 6. The happy man's initial response to the king is one of
    a. suspicion.   **c.** worried concern.
    b. formal respect.   **d.** cheerful good will.

Using Vocabulary (15 points total; 3 points each)
Write the letter of the best answer. This exercise is continued on the next page.

_____ 7. A decree is a type of
    a. joke.   **b.** order.   **c.** measurement.

_____ 8. If a song has a refrain, it is the part that is
    a. repeated.   **b.** sung loudest.   **c.** just instrumental.

_____ 9. A king's retinue are the people who
    a. oppose him.   **b.** accompany him.   **c.** give him advice.

Selection Test

_____ **10.** If you did not like the hue of a shirt, you would object to its

     a. cost.   **b.** color.   **c.** fabric.

_____ **11.** A word that means the opposite of *slew* is

     a. *few.*   **b.** *glee.*   **c.** *threat.*

Interpreting and Evaluating (18 points total; 9 points each)
Think about how the moral, or lesson, of this story would be different if the story ended differently. Then answer the questions in the boxes.

12. How does the story end?	What moral does this ending communicate to the reader? Explain your reasoning.
13. What is another way this story might have ended?	What moral would this ending communicate to the reader? Explain your reasoning.

Evaluating and Connecting (25 points)
Use a separate sheet of paper to answer the following essay question.

14. What are the main differences between the happy young man and the two men who seem at first to be happy—the priest and the neighboring king? How do these differences connect to the moral of the story? In your answer, consider the symbolism of these characters.

           Selection and Theme Assessment

Selection Test

The Californian's Tale (page 247)

Recalling and Interpreting (56 points total; 8 points each)
Write the letter of the best answer.

_____ 1. Although the narrator describes the countryside in various ways, his strongest reaction to it centers on its
      a. beauty.   **c.** peacefulness.
      b. loneliness.   **d.** spaciousness.

_____ 2. What is unusual about the cottage the narrator visits?
      a. It is well-kept.
      b. It is far from a town.
      c. It is covered with roses.
      d. There are no other houses nearby.

_____ 3. Why does the narrator agree to stay with Henry longer than he had first planned?
      a. He feels sorry for Henry.
      b. He does not want to be rude.
      c. He is weary from his travels.
      d. He is eager to meet Henry's wife.

_____ 4. Which is an important clue to the ending that is ignored by the narrator?
      a. Joe's command to take the other drink
      b. the lack of other women in the area
      c. the miners' request to hear the wife's letter
      d. the fact that everything in the house is neat and tidy

_____ 5. As the time for the wife's arrival draws closer, Henry becomes more and more
      a. joyful.   **c.** hospitable.
      b. worried.   **d.** vague and rambling.

_____ 6. The narrator wants someone to stay with him after Henry goes to sleep because he
      a. has become afraid of Henry.
      b. has begun to suspect the truth.
      c. doesn't want to startle Henry's wife.
      d. thinks Henry will be upset that the miners have gone.

_____ 7. What turned out to be odd about the letter that Henry read aloud?
      a. Henry just pretended to read it.
      b. Henry actually wrote it himself.
      c. It was actually written many years ago.
      d. It contains parts that Henry had not read aloud.

Selection Test   *(continued)*

Using Vocabulary (15 points total; 3 points each)
Write the letter of the best answer.

_____ 8. If you are filled with apprehension, you feel
      a. guilty.   **b.** nervous.   **c.** confused.

_____ 9. To sever a relationship is to
      a. end it.   **b.** begin it.   **c.** truly enjoy it.

_____ 10. A gesture that is usually meant to provide solace is a
      a. raised fist.   **b.** pat on the back.   **c.** nudge in the ribs.

_____ 11. A word that means the opposite of *sedate* is
      a. *lively*.   **b.** *glorious*.   **c.** *temporary*.

_____ 12. Which person would you expect to be LEAST concerned with materialistic matters?
      a. a lawyer   **b.** a shopkeeper   **c.** a philosopher

Interpreting and Evaluating (14 points)
Think about how the ending of the story affects one's understanding of events in the story. Answer the questions in the boxes.

13. What is something in the story that you interpreted differently after finishing the story than you did when you first read about that thing?	
How did you originally interpret this?	How did you interpret it later?

Evaluating and Connecting (15 points)
Use a separate sheet of paper to answer the following essay question.

14. Do you think this story would work as well if the story were written in a very different style—if, for example, it contained no dialogue or were very formal? Defend your opinion.

         Selection and Theme Assessment

Selection Test

Score

An Astrologer's Day (page 259)

Recalling and Interpreting (63 points total; 9 points each)
Write the letter of the best answer. This exercise is continued on the next page.

_____ 1. According to the narrator, the astrologer's success in his profession is primarily due to
  a. luck.
  b. the bargains he drives.
  c. the location of his business.
  d. his understanding of people.

_____ 2. The story suggests that the astrologer's comments and observations please people by
  a. promising them success and good fortune.
  b. proving, as time passes, to have been true.
  c. flattering them or supporting their own views.
  d. helping them learn to solve their own problems.

_____ 3. Guru Nayak consults the astrologer because Nayak wants
  a. to understand the past.
  b. to find out who the astrologer is.
  c. to make some money through a bet.
  d. to get the answer to a specific question.

_____ 4. Why is Guru Nayak looking for the man who tried to kill him?
  a. to get revenge
  b. to get an apology
  c. to demand an explanation
  d. to prove the man was unsuccessful

_____ 5. The astrologer's remarks make Guru Nayak feel all of the following EXCEPT
  a. relieved.
  b. suspicious.
  c. impressed.
  d. disappointed.

_____ 6. Which of the following quotations is a clue to the surprise ending?
  a. " . . . even a half-wit's eyes would sparkle in such a setting."
  b. "He had a working analysis of mankind's troubles: marriage, money and
     the tangles of human ties."
  c. "He had to leave home without telling anyone, and he could not rest until
     he left it behind a couple of hundred miles."
  d. "He sensed a possible client and said: 'You look so careworn. It will do you
     good to sit down for a while and chat with me.'"

_____ 7. The astrologer's wife's reaction to his news suggests that she
  a. was unaware of his past.
  b. has been worried about his safety.
  c. has known him since he was young.
  d. is concerned about her future with him.

Selection Test

Using Vocabulary (15 points total; 3 points each)
Write the letter of the best answer.

_____ 8. A doctor's paraphernalia includes
        a. a hospital.   **b.** a stethoscope.   **c.** an answering service.

_____ 9. If you dally on your way to school, you are likely to
        a. be late.   **b.** get tired.   **c.** ruin your clothes.

_____ 10. A word that means the opposite of *impetuous* is
        a. *lucky*.   **b.** *honest*.   **c.** *cautious*.

_____ 11. To enhance his or her skill at baseball, a person might
        a. brag.   **b.** practice.   **c.** hit a home run.

_____ 12. One example of a piqued response is
        a. "All right!"   **b.** "Maybe later."   **c.** "How dare you!"

Interpreting and Evaluating (10 points)
In the box, note something that the sensory details in the quotation suggest about the astrologer, the setting, or the other merchants. Then circle ONE part of the quotation that suggests this.

13.	The astrologer transacted his business by the light of a flare which crackled and smoked up above the groundnut heap nearby. Half the enchantment of the place was due to the fact that it did not have the benefit of municipal lighting. The place was lit up by shop lights. One or two had hissing gaslights, some had naked flares stuck on poles, some were lit up by old cycle lamps and one or two, like the astrologer's, managed without lights of their own. It was a bewildering criss-cross of light rays and moving shadows.

Evaluating and Connecting (12 points)
Use a separate sheet of paper to answer the following essay question.

14. How do you react to the astrologer? Do you feel positively or negatively about him, and why?

Selection Test

The Interlopers (page 268)

Recalling and Interpreting (60 points total; 12 points each)
Write the letter of the best answer.

_____ 1. The major reason for the conflict between Ulrich and Georg is that each of them
   a. needs the land to survive.
   b. values the beauty of the land.
   c. believes that, by right, the land is his.
   d. wants the social status that owning the land provides.

_____ 2. Ulrich and Georg do not shoot immediately upon encountering each other because
   a. they are startled.
   b. they are too civilized.
   c. each feels sympathy for the other.
   d. their rifles are not loaded and ready.

_____ 3. What is the main reason that Ulrich considers ending the feud with Georg?
   a. sympathy and respect for his enemy
   b. a desire to surprise and shock their neighbors
   c. the realization that he may need Georg's help
   d. the realization that they have a common enemy

_____ 4. One reason that Georg refuses Ulrich's offer to share the wine is that he
   a. suspects Ulrich's motives.
   b. wants to remain clear-headed.
   c. thinks Ulrich needs it more than he does.
   d. is too proud to receive a favor from Ulrich.

_____ 5. Near the end of the story, each trapped man hopes his men will arrive first because that will allow him to
   a. be sure of his survival.
   b. be the first to be freed.
   c. demonstrate his friendship.
   d. guarantee his control of the land.

Using Vocabulary (15 points total; 3 points each)
Write the letter of the best answer. This exercise is continued on the next page.

_____ 6. An expression that recommends reconciliation is
   a. "play it by ear."
   b. "forgive and forget."
   c. "keep your nose to the grindstone."

_____ 7. Which of the following is something a pious person would be expected to do more often than one who was not?
   a. pray   **b.** work   **c.** argue

Selection Test

_____ **8.** A word that means the opposite of *acquiesce* is

      a. *give.*   **b.** *object.*   **c.** *ignore.*

_____ **9.** A person often suffers from languor when he or she is

      a. ill.   **b.** shy.   **c.** upset.

_____ **10.** An endeavor always involves

      a. secrecy.   **b.** courage.   **c.** serious effort.

Interpreting and Evaluating (10 points)

Make a mark next to ONE quotation that you think presents a view that is reflected in this story. In the box at the bottom, explain how you could use "The Interlopers" to support the view expressed in the quotation you chose.

11.

☐ He that diggeth a pit shall fall into it. —Ecclesiastes
☐ Anger is never without a reason, but seldom with a good one. —Benjamin Franklin
☐ Hating people is like burning down your own house to get rid of a rat. —H. E. Fosdick

Evaluating and Connecting (15 points)

Use a separate sheet of paper to answer the following essay question.

12. Ulrich and Georg maintain that no interlopers can interfere with their decision to give up their conflict. What makes this statement clearly untrue? What do you think will happen with regard to the conflict between the families?

Selection Test

As It Is with Strangers (page 278)

Recalling and Interpreting (55 points total; 11 points each)
Write the letter of the best answer.

_____ 1. Over the course of this story, whom does Tiffany perceive as a stranger?
- **a.** Jack only
- **b.** Linda only
- **c.** both Jack and Linda
- **d.** neither Jack nor Linda

_____ 2. When she sees what her mother has prepared for dinner, Tiffany feels
- **a.** proud.
- **b.** disappointed.
- **c.** embarrassed.
- **d.** somewhat jealous.

_____ 3. Why does Tiffany tell Jack that her mother does terrible things to her?
- **a.** to lighten the mood
- **b.** to get her mother's attention
- **c.** to make Jack feel sorry for her
- **d.** to make Jack feel better about being given up for adoption

_____ 4. Tiffany finds it tiring to talk to Jack because
- **a.** he is boring.
- **b.** he is unfriendly.
- **c.** the situation is awkward.
- **d.** she isn't much of a conversationalist.

_____ 5. Tiffany's mother tries to convince Tiffany that it is a big mistake to
- **a.** try to make up for the past.
- **b.** refuse to leave well enough alone.
- **c.** listen to advice from other people.
- **d.** give up anything that truly matters to her.

Using Vocabulary (15 points total; 5 points each)
Write the letter of the best answer.

_____ 6. If someone asked you whether a friend of yours was absent due to illness, and you said, "Presumably," you would mean,
- **a.** "Don't ask me; how would I know?"
- **b.** "That seems logical, but I don't know for sure."
- **c.** "That's what most people think, but they're wrong."

_____ 7. Which of the following is designed to protect the sanctity of one's home?
- **a.** a sturdy roof and weather-proofing measures
- **b.** structural supports, such as beams and weight-bearing walls
- **c.** the need for police to obtain a search warrant before demanding entry

_____ 8. A word that means the opposite of *prodigal* is
- **a.** *thrifty*.
- **b.** *ordinary*.
- **c.** *argumentative*.

Selection Test

Interpreting and Evaluating (10 points)

9. Circle the letter of the quotation that contains an example of understatement. Then, in the boxes, answer the questions about that quotation.

a.	"I'm sure I've told you about him," Mom said. "You must have forgotten." I figured I probably had. I'm always forgetting little things like my homework and being elected President of the United States.
b.	I went straight home from school, and was surprised, first to find the place spotless, and then to see Mom in the kitchen cooking away. "I took a sick day," she informed me. "So I could prepare better."
c.	"Did Dad know?" I asked. "I told him," Mom said. "He said it didn't matter to him. And it didn't.

What is understated in the quotation?

What is accomplished by the use of understatement? In other words, why might it have been used here?

Evaluating and Connecting (20 points)
Use a separate sheet of paper to answer the following essay question.

10. Why, do you think, does Tiffany make no attempt to comfort her mother at the end of the story?

Selection Test

The False Gems (page 288)

Recalling and Interpreting (45 points total; 9 points each)
Write the letter of the best answer.

_____ 1. The story suggests that Monsieur Lantin is attracted to his first wife for all of the following reasons EXCEPT her
    a. charm.
    b. beauty.
    c. air of modesty.
    d. love of good times.

_____ 2. During his first marriage, Monsieur Lantin believes that the couple lives well because his wife
    a. has made wise investments.
    b. is unusually good at managing money.
    c. adds to his income with money of her own.
    d. gets special prices from shopkeepers and merchants.

_____ 3. The major reason that Monsieur Lantin decides to sell an item of his wife's jewelry is because
    a. the jewelry reminds him of her.
    b. he is in desperate need of money.
    c. he has always disliked the jewelry.
    d. he has no use for the jewelry anymore.

_____ 4. When he realizes that the gems are real, Monsieur Lantin's first reaction is
    a. confusion about how this can be.
    b. joy that he will, at last, be wealthy.
    c. sadness that his wife had deceived him.
    d. fear that he will be suspected of stealing them.

_____ 5. After selling the gems, Monsieur Lantin does all of the following EXCEPT
    a. brag about his wealth.
    b. exaggerate his wealth.
    c. spend money on luxuries.
    d. find another wife like his first.

Using Vocabulary (15 points total; 3 points each)
Write the letter of the best answer. This exercise is continued on the next page.

_____ 6. You would be most likely to remonstrate with someone whose behavior you
    a. admired.   **b.** disapproved of.   **c.** found amusing.

_____ 7. If you perceive something, you
    a. share it.   **b.** create it.   **c.** notice it.

_____ 8. A word that means the opposite of *disdain* is
    a. *charm.*   **b.** *honesty.*   **c.** *admiration.*

Selection Test

_____ 9. If you find someone droll, that person is likely to make you
  a. gasp.   **b.** laugh.   **c.** shudder.

_____ 10. What does food assuage?
  a. hunger   **b.** dieting   **c.** physical growth

Interpreting and Evaluating (20 points total; 10 points each)
Use of a limited third-person point of view, like use of first-person, allows information to be withheld from the reader. Follow the directions in the boxes to reflect your thoughts.

11. Write down TWO pieces of information withheld (temporarily or permanently) by the use of limited third-person narration that are eventually revealed.	12. Write down TWO pieces of information withheld (temporarily or permanently) by the use of limited third-person narration that are never revealed.

Evaluating and Connecting (20 points)
Use a separate sheet of paper to answer the following essay question.

13. To what, besides jewelry, do you think the title of this story might refer? Explain your answer.

Selection Test

The Saleswoman (page 298) and Mrs. James (page 304)

Recalling and Interpreting (49 points total; 7 points each)
Write the letter of the best answer.

_____ 1. The saleswoman uses every possible opportunity to
    a. lie to her customer.
    b. get on her customer's good side.
    c. make her customer feel insecure.
    d. make sure her customer is pleased.

_____ 2. When the saleswoman says, "I wasn't suggesting it [the navy-blue hat] to you because I didn't think I was talented enough to sell hats like that one," she is suggesting that the hat
    a. is absolutely dreadful.
    b. requires special skill in fitting.
    c. would strain the customer's budget.
    d. would not be as flattering to the customer as others.

_____ 3. Mrs. James suggests that a depression would
    a. make her life harder.
    b. teach Mildred a lesson.
    c. level out the economy.
    d. create a need for domestic help.

_____ 4. The purpose of Mildred's comment to Mrs. James that "some folks might be doin' their own housework." is to
    a. try to make Mrs. James feel guilty.
    b. point out that Mrs. James is a snob.
    c. explain Mildred's feelings about her work.
    d. respond to a subtle threat with a subtle threat.

_____ 5. All of the following could be used in describing the tone of "Mrs. James" EXCEPT
    a. bitter.   **c.** mocking.
    b. casual.   **d.** humorous.

_____ 6. In each of these stories, the main character's attitude toward the woman she serves is a feeling of
    a. affection.   **c.** superiority.
    b. inferiority.   **d.** intense dislike.

_____ 7. Which of the following characteristics is exhibited by the main character in both stories?
    a. wit   **c.** charm
    b. grace   **d.** sincerity

Selection Test

Using Vocabulary (15 points total; 3 points each)
Write the letter of the best answer.

_____ 8. The word *chic* would usually be used to compliment a person's

      a. appearance.   **b.** conversation.   **c.** intelligence.

_____ 9. A store's clientele are those people who

      a. work there.   **b.** shop there.   **c.** make its products.

_____ 10. A person who mortifies himself or herself is most likely to

      a. brag.   **b.** yawn.   **c.** blush.

_____ 11. You might encourage someone to indulge himself or herself by saying,

      a. "No pain, no gain!"

      b. "I wouldn't if I were you."

      c. "Go on; you know you want to."

_____ 12. Someone who sashays is walking in a way that is very

      a. bold.   **b.** casual.   **c.** sneaky.

Interpreting and Evaluating (16 points total; 8 points each)
Read the following examples of dialogue from "The Saleswoman." Think about what they reveal about the saleswoman and about her customer. Then answer the questions in the boxes.

> "I can see it's not a hit. Besides, you're right, it's not your style. On you, it looks a little . . . a little too ladylike. It's funny, I just sold the same hat to Mrs. W. She is ravishing in it, Mrs. W, with her long neck, and especially here, you see, her chin, her cheeks, so fresh and the ear . . ."

> "Try on this one here, just for me. It's not at all excessive, but I think it's both rich and discreet, because of this polished cotton fantasia which gives it all its cachet . . . No? Ah, I'm not having any luck at all . . ."

13. What FOUR character traits does the dialogue reveal about the saleswoman?

_____

_____

_____

_____

14. What FOUR character traits does the dialogue reveal about the customer?

_____

_____

_____

_____

Evaluating and Connecting (20 points)
Use a separate sheet of paper to answer the following essay question.

15. Compare and contrast the saleswoman and Mildred. In what ways, if any, are they alike? In what ways, if any, are they different?

Selection Test

Score

A Sound of Thunder (page 315)

Recalling and Interpreting (48 points total; 8 points each)
Write the letter of the best answer.

_____ 1. Time Safari hunts animals that are about to die anyway because
      a. it is easier to justify killing those animals.
      b. those animals are the least dangerous ones.
      c. those animals are the most dangerous ones.
      d. killing those animals is least likely to affect history.

_____ 2. At what point is Eckels convinced that the *Tyrannosaurus* cannot be killed?
      a. from the very beginning of the story
      b. when Travis explains how to kill a dinosaur
      c. when Eckels sees the *Tyrannosaurus* the first time
      d. when the men begin shooting at the *Tyrannosaurus*

_____ 3. Travis insists that Eckels retrieve the bullets because
      a. Eckels is the only one who can do it.
      b. Travis is angry and wants Eckels to suffer.
      c. Travis thinks it may help Eckels feel better.
      d. it is part of the company's agreement with Eckels.

_____ 4. Lesperance, Travis's assistant, seems to think that Travis's treatment of Eckels is
      a. too harsh.   c. perfectly reasonable.
      b. too risky to the others. d. none of his business.

_____ 5. The final sound of thunder that Eckels hears is from the sound of
      a. a gun being shot in the past.
      b. a gun being shot in the present.
      c. the *Tyrannosaurus* falling down dead.
      d. the men passing themselves on their way back to the future.

_____ 6. When does Eckels take full responsibility for the effects of his actions?
      a. never
      b. as soon as he realizes that he stepped off the Path
      c. when he sees the *Tyrannosaurus*
      d. when Travis explains how his actions could change history

Using Vocabulary (15 points total; 3 points each)
Write the letter of the best answer. This exercise is continued on the next page.

_____ 7. One material that is known for being resilient is
      a. rubber.   b. plaster.   c. aluminum.

Selection Test

_____ 8. A paradox is something that may be true even though it involves
  a. a deliberate lie.
  b. a seeming contradiction.
  c. an unpleasant or horrifying fact.

_____ 9. A word that means the opposite of *expendable* is
  a. *tight*.   b. *logical*.   c. *required*.

_____ 10. A primeval forest would be one that was
  a. lush.   b. ancient.   c. dangerous.

_____ 11. You would correlate your arrival at a place with someone else's arrival if you wanted to
  a. get there first.
  b. avoid the person.
  c. meet the person without waiting.

Interpreting and Evaluating (21 points total; 7 points each)
In the boxes, explain what the similes or metaphors in the quotations emphasize.

12. The Machine howled. Time was a film run backward. Suns fled and ten million moons fled after them.	
13. Step on a mouse and you crush the Pyramids. Step on a mouse and you leave your print, like a Grand Canyon, across Eternity.	
14. Each lower leg was a piston, a thousand pounds of white bone, sunk in thick ropes of muscle, sheathed over in a gleam of pebbled skin like the [armor] of a terrible warrior.	

Evaluating and Connecting (16 points)
Use a separate sheet of paper to answer the following essay question.

15. What question, or unknown element, do you think provides the most suspense in this story? What is the answer to that question, and is it foreshadowed? Support your answers with details from the story.

Selection Test

Lullaby (page 329)

Recalling and Interpreting (49 points total; 7 points each)
Write the letter of the best answer.

_____ 1. The main feeling Ayah remembers when Chato told her that Jimmie wouldn't be coming home anymore is
    a. rage.   **c.** disbelief.
    b. guilt.   **d.** acceptance.

_____ 2. There were several reasons that Ayah signed the papers allowing the doctors to take the children away. These included all of the following EXCEPT that
    a. she couldn't read what she was signing.
    b. she thought it would make the doctors leave.
    c. she didn't realize what the consequences were.
    d. she trusted the doctors to know what was best for her children.

_____ 3. How does Ayah feel about Chato's behavior when the doctors and the policeman come to take Danny and Ella away?
    a. proud   **c.** betrayed
    b. guilty   **d.** embarrassed

_____ 4. The story indicates that the children never return to live with Ayah and Chato because
    a. the children die of tuberculosis.
    b. Ayah and Chato cannot afford to support them.
    c. Ayah and Chato decide the children are better off where they are.
    d. government officials decide the children are better off where they are.

_____ 5. Ayah's attitude toward Chato's drinking could best be described as
    a. angry.   **c.** embarrassed.
    b. scornful.   **d.** matter-of-fact.

_____ 6. At the end of the story, how does Ayah feel toward Chato?
    a. jealous   **c.** respectful
    b. protective   **d.** unconcerned

_____ 7. The story suggests that if Chato were to freeze to death under the night sky at the end of the story, Ayah would most probably view his death as
    a. a tragedy.
    b. a blessing.
    c. a betrayal of her.
    d. an act of vengeance.

Selection Test   *(continued)*

Using Vocabulary (8 points total; 2 points each)
Write the letter of the best answer.

_____ **8.** A crevice is a type of
   a. hole.   **b.** ridge.   **c.** covering.

_____ **9.** One place that almost always has sparse vegetation is a
   a. farm.   **b.** desert.   **c.** jungle.

_____ **10.** An arroyo is most like a
   a. hill.   **b.** ditch.   **c.** prairie.

_____ **11.** A dress would suffer from distortion if it were
   a. dyed.   **b.** stained.   **c.** stretched.

Interpreting and Evaluating (27 points total; 9 points each)
On the left, write down an event from the story that occurs in flashback. On the right, note TWO things that each flashback adds to your understanding of Ayah.

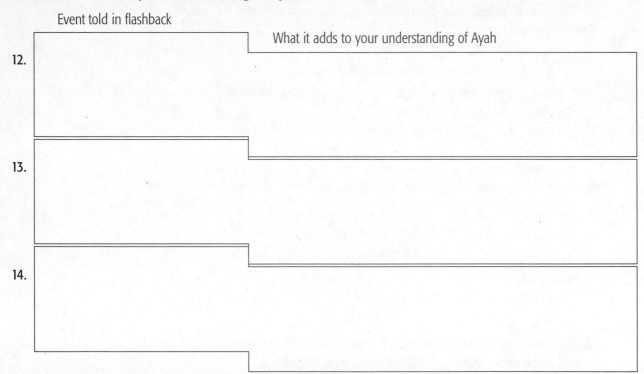

Event told in flashback

What it adds to your understanding of Ayah

12.

13.

14.

Evaluating and Connecting (16 points)
Use a separate sheet of paper to answer the following essay question.

15. In your opinion, does this story have a hero? Does it have a villain? Support your answers with details from the story.

Name _____ Date _____ Class _____

And of Clay Are We Created (page 342)

Recalling and Interpreting (54 points total; 9 points each)
Write the letter of the best answer.

_____ 1. As a reporter, Rolf has a reputation for all of the following EXCEPT
    a. taking unnecessary risks.
    b. doing live, on-the-scene reports.
    c. keeping his cool when others are panicking.
    d. getting emotionally involved with his subjects.

_____ 2. During his first few hours at the scene of the disaster, Rolf focuses on
    a. trying to free Azucena.
    b. getting to know Azucena.
    c. saving as many people as he possibly can.
    d. reporting Azucena's story to the TV viewers.

_____ 3. Why can't Rolf "look at [Azucena] through a lens any longer"?
    a. He feels too guilty.
    b. She has touched his heart.
    c. Doing so frightens him too much.
    d. Doing so makes her suffering too clear.

_____ 4. The story indicates that all of the TV reporters use Azucena as a symbol of
    a. hope.   **c.** dignity.
    b. horror.   **d.** compassion.

_____ 5. What is the main feeling that Azucena inspires in the narrator?
    a. jealousy   **c.** compassion
    b. curiosity   **d.** bewilderment

_____ 6. Azucena possesses all of the following qualities EXCEPT
    a. dignity.   **c.** modesty.
    b. patience.   **d.** fearlessness.

Using Vocabulary (15 points total; 3 points each)
Write the letter of the best answer. This exercise is continued on the next page.

_____ 7. A person who demonstrates equanimity appears to be
    a. shy.   **b.** lonely.   **c.** calm.

_____ 8. One would expect to find conditions of pandemonium during a
    a. riot.   **b.** fancy ball.   **c.** final exam.

_____ 9. A presentiment is a feeling of
    a. pity.   **b.** outrage.   **c.** expectancy.

Selection Test
(continued)

_____ **10.** A word that means the opposite of *fortitude* is
        a. *misery.*   **b.** *weakness.*   **c.** *embarrassment.*

_____ **11.** Which of the following is the best example of a cataclysm?
        a. erosion   **b.** extinction   **c.** an avalanche

Interpreting and Evaluating (15 points total; 5 points each)
As you read the following passage, circle FIVE words and phrases that convey mood and think about how the mood shifts during the passage. Then draw a slash mark between TWO sentences where you think the most dramatic mood shift occurs. In the boxes, describe the mood at the beginning and then after the shift.

12. Circle words and phrases that convey mood. Then mark the shift in mood.

> It was impossible to reach [Azucena] from the approach [Rolf] was attempting, so he retreated and circled around where there seemed to be firmer footing. When finally he was close enough, he took the rope and tied it beneath her arms, so they could pull her out. He smiled at her with that smile that crinkles his eyes and makes him look like a little boy; he told her that everything was fine, that he was here with her now, that soon they would have her out. He signaled the others to pull, but as soon as the cord tensed, the girl screamed. They tried again, and her shoulders and arms appeared, but they could move her no farther; she was trapped. Someone suggested that her legs might be caught in the collapsed walls of her house, but she said it was not just rubble, that she was also held by the bodies of her brothers and sisters clinging to her legs.

13. Mood at the beginning of the passage	**14.** Mood after the shift you noted

Evaluating and Connecting (16 points)
Use a separate sheet of paper to answer the following essay question.

15. In a paragraph or two, explain in your own words what Rolf needs saving from and how Azucena saves him.

Selection Test

Colombia's Mortal Agony (page 354)

Recalling and Interpreting (55 points total; 11 points each)
Write the letter of the best answer.

_____ 1. The main problem caused by the blast of the volcano to the cargo jet that Manuel
Cervero was flying had to do with
   a. visibility.
   b. turbulence.
   c. damage to the engines.
   d. a sudden loss of air pressure.

_____ 2. According to the author, the eruption of Nevado del Ruiz was about as destructive
as the
   a. typical California earthquake.
   b. 1985 Mexico City earthquake.
   c. 1980 eruption of Mount St. Helens.
   d. eruption of Mount Vesuvius in A.D. 79.

_____ 3. Most of the people of Armero who survived the eruption of Nevado del Ruiz did
so by
   a. seeking shelter.
   b. reaching high ground.
   c. forming human chains.
   d. holding onto things that would float.

_____ 4. Most of the people who died as a result of the eruption died of
   a. burns.
   b. infection.
   c. suffocation or injury.
   d. starvation and dehydration.

_____ 5. According to the author, what was the primary concern of the rescue squads that
went to Armero after the eruption?
   a. saving lives
   b. getting out alive
   c. keeping accurate records
   d. recovering the bodies of the dead

Using Vocabulary (15 points total; 3 points each)
Write the letter of the best answer. This exercise is continued on the next page.

_____ 6. The phrase "a pall of smoke" is a way of describing smoke as a
   a. signal.   b. covering.   c. consequence.

Selection Test   *(continued)*

_____ **7.** A tentative gesture is

       a. bold.   **b.** kind.   **c.** hesitant.

_____ **8.** To spawn a flood is to

       a. flee it.   **b.** dread it.   **c.** produce it.

_____ **9.** An animal known for its ferocity is the

       a. owl.   **b.** lion.   **c.** mouse.

_____ **10.** One example of the phenomena of nature is

       a. a bolt of lightning.

       b. a weather prediction.

       c. a memory of summer.

Interpreting and Evaluating (16 points total; 8 points each)
Read the descriptive passage below. Then answer the questions about the tone, or attitude of the author, that the description helps to convey.

> [The] superheated magma within Nevado del Ruiz began to melt the thick blanket of snow and ice that caps the top 2,000 ft. of the peak. Filthy water started to flow down the sides of the mountain. The trickle swiftly turned into a torrent of viscous mud, stones, ashes and debris with a crest of 15 ft. to 50 ft. The liquid avalanche, known as a lahar, was soon hurtling down the steep slopes at speeds of up to 30 m.p.h. With irresistible force, it roared down the flanks of Nevado del Ruiz in the most natural of channels: the beds of the Guali, Azufrado and Lagunilla rivers, which flow east and south from the base of the volcano.

11.	What is the tone of this passage?
12.	How did you come to this conclusion?

Evaluating and Connecting (14 points)
Use a separate sheet of paper to answer the following essay question.

13. How would you describe the attitude taken by the author toward Omaira Sanchez, "13, who remained up to her neck in ooze two days following the disaster"? Do you think this attitude is appropriate?

Selection Test

Winter Night (page 362)

Recalling and Interpreting (50 points total; 10 points each)
Write the letter of the best answer.

_____ 1. At the beginning of the story, as Felicia waits in the living room, she feels
    a. tired.   **c.** excited.
    b. insecure.   **d.** resentful.

_____ 2. The story suggests that this night's sitter is different from most in that she
    a. tells Felicia a story.
    b. doesn't need the job.
    c. is sincerely interested in Felicia.
    d. is used to being around children.

_____ 3. What does Felicia see in the woman's face when she first comes into the kitchen
and throughout much of the night?
    a. fear   **c.** pity
    b. shame   **d.** sorrow

_____ 4. Felicia reacts with interest but without much sympathy to the story of the other little girl because Felicia
    a. thinks the sitter is making it up.
    b. thinks her own life is much worse.
    c. doesn't care about other children.
    d. doesn't understand the realities of the story.

_____ 5. On most nights, what prevents Felicia's mother from being with her?
    a. her job   **c.** an active social life
    b. night classes   **d.** volunteer war work

Using Vocabulary (15 points total; 3 points each)
Write the letter of the best answer.

_____ 6. A room would be in obscurity if it were
    a. dark.   **b.** messy.   **c.** lonely.

_____ 7. If you say something in a tone of derision, you are indicating
    a. fear.   **b.** scorn.   **c.** cheerfulness.

_____ 8. One kind of reprieve from schoolwork is
    a. recess.   **b.** a test.   **c.** a report card.

_____ 9. A word that means the opposite of *singular* is
    a. *odd*.   **b.** *friendly*.   **c.** *ordinary*.

Selection Test

_____ **10.** Construction work is in abeyance while the workers are

       a. hammering.   **b.** pouring cement.   **c.** on a coffee break.

Interpreting and Evaluating (20 points total; 10 points each)
Choose ONE of the following passages and write its letter in the space below. Then answer the questions in the boxes about the passage you chose.

A.

"Did—did the little girl cry when she was hungry?" Felicia asked, and the woman shook her head.

"Sometimes she cried," she said, "but not very much. She was very quiet. One night when she heard the other children crying, she said to me, 'You know, they are not crying because they want something to eat. They are crying because their mothers have gone away.'"

"Did the mothers have to go out to supper?" Felicia asked, and she watched the woman's face for the answer.

"No," said the woman. She stood up from her chair. . . . "Shall we go into the other room, and you will do your pirouette for me?"

B.

"And then," said Felicia softly, persistently, "what happened to the little girl?"

"I do not know. I cannot say," the woman said. But now the brush and comb had ceased to move, and in the silence Felicia turned her thin, small body on the chair, and she and the woman suddenly put their arms around each other. "They must all be asleep now, all of them," the woman said, and in the silence that fell on them again, they held each other closer.

Passage _____

11. Do you think the passage contains dramatic irony? Explain.
12. Do you think the passage contains verbal irony? Explain.

Evaluating and Connecting (15 points)
Use a separate sheet of paper to answer the following essay question.

13. Reread the final sentence of the story: "And then, as startling as a slap across her delicately tinted face, she saw the woman lying sleeping on the divan, and Felicia, in her school dress still, asleep within the woman's arms."

    How do you account for Felicia's mother's reaction to this scene? Do you think she will want the woman to take care of Felicia again? Explain your opinions.

Selection Test

Score

Waltz of the Fat Man (page 376)

Recalling and Interpreting (54 points total; 9 points each)
Write the letter of the best answer.

_____ 1. How do the townspeople, in general, respond to Noé?
   a. They try to avoid him.
   b. They are afraid of him.
   c. They find him amusing.
   d. They take advantage of him.

_____ 2. When Noé kisses mourners at wakes, he does so mainly out of
   a. duty.
   b. personal need.
   c. respect for the dead.
   d. concern for the mourners.

_____ 3. In Noé's mind, when he shakes hands with a woman in the town, he is
   a. getting revenge.
   b. risking his reputation.
   c. taking part in an act of intimacy.
   d. demonstrating his good intentions.

_____ 4. To the townspeople, the clocks in Noé's shop make the shop seem
   a. weird.   c. cheerful.
   b. charming.   d. disorganized.

_____ 5. When Noé hears the blue clock falter, his first reaction is one of
   a. despair.   c. irritation.
   b. concern.   d. hurt feelings.

_____ 6. The story indicates that the soldiers' main objective is to
   a. take revenge on Noé.
   b. steal the clock for their own use.
   c. frighten Noé into changing his behavior.
   d. make a fool of Noé for their own entertainment.

Using Vocabulary (10 points total; 2 points each)
Write the letter of the best answer. This exercise is continued on the next page.

_____ 7. Which of the following would you be most likely to handle gingerly?
   a. a heavy book   b. a velvet pillow   c. a broken glass

_____ 8. A person who patronizes a store is someone who
   a. shops there.   b. works there.   c. steals from it.

Selection Test

_____ 9. One would expect to find bereaved people at a
      a. party.   **b.** funeral.   **c.** clearance sale.

_____ 10. A word that means the opposite of *manifest* is
      a. *hide*.   **b.** *save*.   **c.** *enjoy*.

_____ 11. In order to behave with propriety, you must have
      a. courage.   **b.** kindness.   **c.** good manners.

Interpreting and Evaluating (24 points total; 6 points each)
Think about this story as one man's search for something. Then answer the questions in the boxes about Noé's lifelong search.

12. At the beginning of the story, what is Noé looking for?

13. Does he seem to find what he is looking for in the townspeople? Why or why not?

14. Does he seem to find what he needs in the clocks? Why or why not?

15. Does he seem to find what he needs in the circus people? Why or why not?

Evaluating and Connecting (12 points)
Use a separate sheet of paper to answer the following essay questions.

16. Think about this story as an example of magical realism. Then, in a paragraph or two, explain what the "thin girl" adds to your understanding of Noé. How does she affect your attitude toward him? Why?

Name _____ Date _____ Class _____

Score

The Masque of the Red Death (page 388)

Recalling and Interpreting (54 points total; 9 points each)
Write the letter of the best answer.

_____ 1. The people in this story have avoided the Red Death's victims mainly because
    a. the disease is disgusting.
    b. the disease is contagious.
    c. they don't want to be bothered.
    d. they believe the victims deserve their fate.

_____ 2. The people at the masque eat, drink, and party because they
    a. are afraid to insult their host.
    b. are celebrating the Red Death's end.
    c. want to live their last days to the fullest.
    d. have largely convinced themselves that they are safe.

_____ 3. The sound of the ebony clock tolling the hour seems to make the guests feel
    a. amazed.   **c.** impatient.
    b. insecure.   **d.** courageous.

_____ 4. It is LEAST likely that the tolling of the ebony clock is meant to symbolize
    a. fate.   **c.** death.
    b. time.   **d.** happiness.

_____ 5. The guests seem to feel that the masked figure's costume is
    a. amusing.   **c.** tasteless.
    b. mysterious.   **d.** fascinating.

_____ 6. Which of the following best describes what the characters in this story are trying
    to do?
    a. cheat or defy death   **c.** make peace with death
    b. teach death a lesson   **d.** make a bargain with death

Using Vocabulary (10 points total; 2 points each)
Write the letter of the best answer. This exercise is continued on the next page.

_____ 7. An animal that is often used to represent sagacious qualities is the
    a. owl.   **b.** wolf.   **c.** buzzard.

_____ 8. If an event appals you, you are likely to
    a. grin.   **b.** gasp.   **c.** shrug.

_____ 9. A word that means the opposite of *dauntless* is
    a. *wealthy*.   **b.** *cowardly*.   **c.** *cheerful*.

Selection Test

_____ **10.** A person might be said to have a spectral appearance if he or she is quite

       a. pale.   **b.** muscular.   **c.** attractive.

_____ **11.** Blasphemous behavior is most offensive to people who are

       a. religious.   **b.** soft-hearted.   **c.** easily disgusted.

Interpreting and Evaluating (20 points total; 5 points each)
**Poe's descriptions help the reader not only to picture the setting, but also to under-
stand the characters' situation, personalities, and frame of mind. Read the passage
below. Then complete the ideas in the boxes.**

> It was [Prince Prospero's] own guiding taste which had given character to the masqueraders. Be sure they were grotesque. . . . There were delirious fancies such as the madman fashions. There were much of the beautiful, much of the wanton, much of the *bizarre,* something of the terrible, and not a little of that which might have excited disgust. To and fro in the seven chambers there stalked, in fact, a multitude of dreams. And these—the dreams—writhed in and about, taking hue from the rooms, and causing the wild music of the orchestra to seem as the echo of their steps. And, anon, there strikes the ebony clock which stands in the hall of the velvet. And then, for a moment, all is still, and all is silent save the voice of the clock. The dreams are stiff-frozen as they stand. But the echoes of the chime die away—they have endured but an instant—and a light, half-subdued laughter floats after them as they depart. And now again the music swells, and the dreams live, and writhe to and fro more merrily than ever, taking hue from the many-tinted windows through which stream the rays from the tripods.

The description in this passage . . .

12.	makes the setting seem
13.	makes the situation of Prince Prospero and his guests seem
14.	suggests that Prince Prospero and his guests are the kind of people who
15.	encourages the reader to feel

Evaluating and Connecting (16 points)
Use a separate sheet of paper to answer the following essay question.

16. In your opinion, are the deaths of Prince Prospero and his guests tragic? Why or why not?

Selection Test

To Da-duh, in Memoriam (page 398)

Recalling and Interpreting (45 points total; 9 points each)
Write the letter of the best answer.

_____ 1. When the narrator visits Barbados as a child, her first impression is that it is
      a. oddly familiar.   **c.** amazingly beautiful.
      b. dangerously wild.   **d.** hopelessly backward.

_____ 2. Da-duh and the narrator are most alike in their
      a. stubbornness.
      b. cultural beliefs.
      c. attitude toward nature.
      d. attitude toward machines.

_____ 3. In her conversations with Da-duh, the narrator most wants to
      a. impress her.
      b. not be caught lying.
      c. be careful of her feelings.
      d. show her the proper respect.

_____ 4. Over the course of the story, which of the following undergoes the greatest change?
      a. the narrator's opinion of Barbados
      b. the narrator's opinion of New York
      c. Da-duh's attitude toward the narrator
      d. Da-duh's sense of the world and her place in it

_____ 5. The LEAST important conflict in this story is that between
      a. nature and technology.
      b. lower and upper classes.
      c. older and younger generations.
      d. Caribbean and Western cultures.

Using Vocabulary (15 points total; 3 points each)
Write the letter of the best answer. This exercise is continued on the next page.

_____ 6. A word that means nearly the opposite of *hurtle* is
      a. *cry*.   **b.** *throw*.   **c.** *crawl*.

_____ 7. An arrogant person is most likely to be described as acting
      a. goofy.   **b.** stuck up.   **c.** like a baby.

_____ 8. A decrepit chair would probably be
      a. wobbly.   **b.** comfortable.   **c.** easy to lift.

Selection Test

_____ 9. Malicious behavior is always
   a. illegal.   b. unkind.   c. hesitant.

_____ 10. The more formidable team in a game is the one that is more likely to
   a. win.   b. lose.   c. cheat.

Interpreting and Evaluating (24 points total; 6 points each)
For each turning point in the story listed below, explain its significance for Da-duh, the narrator, and/or their relationship.

11. Da-duh stares into the narrator's eyes when they are introduced.

12. Da-duh takes the narrator "out into the ground" for the first time.

13. The narrator tells Da-duh about the Empire State Building.

14. Da-duh dies.

Evaluating and Connecting (16 points)
Use a separate sheet of paper to answer the following essay question.

15. Think about the author's use of local color and then, in a paragraph, discuss the importance of the setting to this story. Support your opinions with reference to the story.

Selection Test

from **Travels with Charley** (page 426)

Recalling and Interpreting (50 points total; 10 points each)
Write the letter of the best answer.

_____ 1. In the truck, Charley pants because of
    a. heat.   **c.** exhaustion.
    b. nerves.   **d.** excitement.

_____ 2. Steinbeck says, "They were favored animals, not starved, but well furred, the golden hair tempered with black guard hairs." By "favored animals," he means that
    a. coyotes tend to be lucky.
    b. these two have had advantages.
    c. he has always been interested in coyotes.
    d. he particularly enjoys seeing these two coyotes.

_____ 3. Steinbeck first feels a reluctance to shoot the coyotes when
    a. they show no fear of him.
    b. he is able to see them clearly.
    c. he considers the range of his rifle.
    d. one behaves in a dog-like fashion.

_____ 4. The coyotes respond to Steinbeck with
    a. fear.   **c.** mild curiosity.
    b. anger.   **d.** great friendliness.

_____ 5. Steinbeck leaves food for the coyotes because he
    a. realizes they need it.
    b. wants to keep them from eating chickens.
    c. feels guilty about planning to kill them.
    d. feels some responsibility for their welfare.

Using Vocabulary (15 points total; 3 points each)
Write the letter of the best answer. This exercise is continued on the next page.

_____ 6. A person who exhibits constancy might be described as being
    a. true-blue.   **b.** free as a bird.   **c.** a stick-in-the-mud.

_____ 7. One common example of vermin is a
    a. rat.   **b.** duck.   **c.** butterfly.

_____ 8. When your arms loll, they might be
    a. waving.   **b.** folded.   **c.** dangling.

Selection Test

_____ 9. Many people temper their coffee with
   a. cream.   **b.** a filter.   **c.** breakfast.

_____ 10. If a neighbor spent an hour helping you fix a broken faucet, what would serve as a token gesture of appreciation?
   a. criticism of the help
   b. a batch of homemade cookies
   c. payment of the standard plumber's rate for one hour

Interpreting and Evaluating (20 points)
In the boxes, complete the statements about this selection's main internal conflict.

11. The selection's main INTERNAL conflict is between Steinbeck's . . .

and his . . .

This conflict exists because . . .

and is resolved by . . .

Evaluating and Connecting (15 points)
Use a separate sheet of paper to answer the following essay question.

12. As you read the following excerpt from the selection, look for what Steinbeck implies about his feelings in this situation. Then, in a paragraph or two, explain what you can infer (that is, understand without being directly told) about Steinbeck's attitudes and feelings and how you can tell.

> The cross was steady on the breast just below the panting tongue. I could imagine the splash and jar of angry steel, the leap and struggle until the torn heart failed, and then, not too long later, the shadow of a buzzard, and another. By that time I would be long gone—out of the desert and across the Colorado River. And beside the sage-bush there would be a naked, eyeless skull, a few picked bones, a spot of black dried blood and a few rags of golden fur.

Selection Test

A Child's Christmas in Wales (page 432)

Recalling and Interpreting (54 points total; 9 points each)
Write the letter of the best answer.

_____ 1. How do the boys feel about the fire at the Protheros' house?
    a. guilty   **c.** excited
    b. scared   **d.** uninterested

_____ 2. In Thomas's memories, all of the following were part of every Christmas EXCEPT
    a. aunts.   **c.** mistletoe.
    b. caroling.   **d.** Useful Presents.

_____ 3. What the narrator means by a "Useless Present" is one that
    a. doesn't fit.
    b. he doesn't want.
    c. is quickly lost or broken.
    d. is fun rather than practical.

_____ 4. References such as "We were so still, Eskimo-footed arctic marksmen in the muf-
fling silence . . ." and "Now we were snow-blind travellers lost on the north hills . . ."
suggest that as children, Thomas and his friends were
    a. liars.   **c.** neglected.
    b. brave.   **d.** imaginative.

_____ 5. Thomas describes how he recalls past Christmases by saying, "I plunge my hands
into the snow and bring out whatever I can find." This suggests that
    a. he never knows what memories will come to mind.
    b. he finds it difficult and unpleasant to try to remember.
    c. he can remember his youth only by experiencing snow again.
    d. all he can remember clearly is that these times were snowy.

_____ 6. It is clear from this selection that Thomas's memories are quite
    a. fond.   **c.** accurate.
    b. bitter.   **d.** unhappy.

Using Vocabulary (10 points total; 2 points each)
Write the letter of the best answer. This exercise is continued on the next page.

_____ 7. A word that means the opposite of *daft* is
    a. *clumsy.*   **b.** *cheerful.*   **c.** *sensible.*

_____ 8. One might lurk if he or she were preparing for
    a. a trip.   **b.** an ambush.   **c.** a performance.

Selection Test

_____ 9. What kind of walking makes a person seem quite hale?
     a. striding   **b.** limping   **c.** tiptoeing

_____ 10. Which kind of bird often utters sounds stridently?
     a. a dove   **b.** a chick   **c.** a parrot

_____ 11. A word that means the opposite of *judiciously* is
     a. *firmly.*   **b.** *foolishly.*   **c.** *unevenly.*

Interpreting and Evaluating (18 points total; 6 points each)
In the small boxes, make checkmarks to indicate to which senses the imagery in each quotation appeals. Then, in the large boxes, answer the question about imagery for each quotation.

		To which sense(s) does the imagery appeal?	What feelings and ideas does the imagery communicate?
12.	"[S]now grew overnight on the roofs of the houses like a pure and grandfather moss, minutely white-ivied the walls and settled on the postman, opening the gate, like a dumb, numb thunderstorm of white, torn Christmas cards."	Sight Touch Taste Smell Hearing	
13.	"And [the church bells] rang their tidings over the bandaged town, over the frozen foam of the powder and ice-cream hills, over the crackling sea."	Sight Touch Taste Smell Hearing	
14.	"[A]nd some few small Aunts, not wanted in the kitchen, nor anywhere else for that matter, sat on the very edges of their chairs, poised and brittle, afraid to break, like faded cups and saucers."	Sight Touch Taste Smell Hearing	

Evaluating and Connecting (18 points)
Use a separate sheet of paper to answer the following essay question.

15. What do you find appealing or pleasant about the way of life that Thomas presents in this memoir? What do you think you would find least pleasant about that life if you lived it? Explain your opinions.

Selection Test

from **Kaffir Boy** (page 444)

Recalling and Interpreting (42 points total; 7 points each)
Write the letter of the best answer.

_____ 1. At first, Mathabane thinks that the life led by the street gang members is
     a. sad.   **c.** comfortable.
     b. exciting.   **d.** quite dangerous.

_____ 2. Mathabane's mother manages to get him to school for the first time by
     a. pleading with him.   **c.** demanding obedience.
     b. using physical force.   **d.** persuading him to cooperate.

_____ 3. It has taken a long time for Mathabane's mother to get him into school because she had to
     a. obtain the proper papers.
     b. raise the money for tuition.
     c. persuade his father to allow it.
     d. talk the principal into accepting him.

_____ 4. The principal hesitates about admitting Mathabane because of his
     a. age.   **c.** heritage.
     b. attitude.   **d.** behavior.

_____ 5. Mathabane's mother feels tied to her husband because of
     a. her marriage vows.
     b. her feelings for him.
     c. the fact that he purchased her.
     d. concern for her children's welfare.

_____ 6. Mathabane suggests that what is most unusual about his mother is
     a. that her marriage was arranged.
     b. how she is treated by her husband.
     c. how she feels about her son's attending school.
     d. her attitudes about the traditional rules for women.

Using Vocabulary (15 points total; 3 points each)
Write the letter of the best answer. This exercise is continued on the next page.

_____ 7. You are most likely to hear a tirade from your parents if you have
     a. misbehaved.   **b.** received an A+.   **c.** said something funny.

_____ 8. A group that would be called a coterie is most similar to a
     a. mob.   **b.** crew.   **c.** club.

Selection Test

_____ **9.** You might admonish someone if you found his or behavior to be

    a. amusing.   **b.** dangerous.   **c.** praiseworthy.

_____ **10.** A word that means the opposite of *vehemently* is

    a. *mildly.*   **b.** *safely.*   **c.** *quickly.*

_____ **11.** You would peruse a book or article if you wanted to

    a. skim it.   **b.** study it.   **c.** check its length.

Interpreting and Evaluating (28 points total; 14 points each)

Think of TWO persons or groups who support Mathabane's going to school. In answer to the question below, write the names of these persons or groups in the first boxes. Then, in the next boxes, give the reason for their support.

12. Who supports Mathabane's going to school and why do they support it?

Person or group:	Person or group:
because:	because:

Think of TWO persons or groups who oppose Mathabane's going to school. In answer to the question below, write the names of these persons or groups in the first boxes below. Then, in the next boxes, give the reason for their opposition.

13. Who opposes Mathabane's going to school, and why do they oppose it?

Person or group:	Person or group:
because:	because:

Evaluating and Connecting (15 points)

Use a separate sheet of paper to answer the following essay question.

14. In a paragraph or two, discuss the effects that Mathabane's mother's monologue has on him. Why do you think Mathabane is affected by this monologue as he is?

Name _____ Date _____ Class _____

Selection Test

Score

from **Farewell to Manzanar** (page 459)

Recalling and Interpreting (56 points total; 8 points each)
Write the letter of the best answer.

_____ 1. The government's treatment of Japanese-Americans seems to have been caused mainly by a
    a. suspicion of them.   **c.** desire for profit.
    b. hatred of them.   **d.** desire to protect them.

_____ 2. Japanese-Americans are moved off Terminal Island because
    a. they are in danger there.
    b. there is no more work for them there.
    c. the area is needed for wartime industry.
    d. the area is near an American naval base.

_____ 3. The narrator suggests that her Boyle Heights teacher's unfriendliness is caused by
    a. shame.   **c.** shyness.
    b. distrust.   **d.** a dislike of teaching.

_____ 4. Mrs. Wakatsuki breaks her prized dishes for all of the following reasons EXCEPT to
    a. show how angry she is at the dealer.
    b. express frustration about the family's situation.
    c. destroy a reminder of the happier times of the past.
    d. keep the dealer from making a huge and unfair profit.

_____ 5. Difficulties in fixing the living quarters at Manzanar are mainly the result of
    a. a lack of time.   **c.** rules in the camp.
    b. a lack of supplies.   **d.** limited experience.

_____ 6. What part of camp life does Mrs. Wakatsuki seem to dislike the most?
    a. the cold weather   **c.** the dirty barracks
    b. the overcrowding   **d.** the lack of privacy

_____ 7. The Japanese saying *Shikata ga nai* expresses an attitude of
    a. optimism.   **c.** acceptance.
    b. bitterness.   **d.** good humor.

Using Vocabulary (10 points total; 2 points each)
Write the letter of the best answer. This exercise is continued on the next page.

_____ 8. To alleviate a problem is to
    a. cause it.   **b.** describe it.   **c.** decrease it.

Copyright © by The McGraw-Hill Companies, Inc.

_____ **9.** The patriarch of a family is most often the
      a. father.   **b.** mother.   **c.** oldest son.

_____ **10.** A whimsical story is usually
      a. tragic.   **b.** light-hearted.   **c.** about family life.

_____ **11.** A word that means the opposite of *irrational* is
      a. *kind*.   **b.** *secretive*.   **c.** *reasonable*.

_____ **12.** People who often subordinate their own desires are usually seen as being
      a. greedy.   **b.** unselfish.   **c.** wishful thinkers.

Interpreting and Evaluating (20 points total; 10 points each)

Think about what this excerpt from her autobiography reveals about Jeanne Wakatsuki Houston, both as a child and as an adult. Then, complete the questions in the boxes below.

13. What word or phrase describes Houston as a child?	How does the autobiography tell you this?

14. What word or phrase describes Houston as an adult?	How does the autobiography tell you this?

Evaluating and Connecting (14 points)

Use a separate sheet of paper to answer the following essay question.

15. Which members of the Wakatsuki family do you think found Manzanar easier to bear than others did? Why did they find it easier?

Selection Test

Score

By Any Other Name (page 478)

Recalling and Interpreting (56 points total; 8 points each)
Write the letter of the best answer.

_____ 1. What worries Santha's mother about English schools is
   a. the subjects taught.
   b. the teachers' abilities.
   c. her daughters' safety.
   d. the attitudes of the English.

_____ 2. The selection suggests that the headmistress changes the girls' names because she
   a. wants to embarrass them.
   b. wants to avoid confusion.
   c. thinks that English culture is superior.
   d. thinks this will make them feel comfortable.

_____ 3. Santha does poorly at the schoolyard games because
   a. the other children don't play fairly.
   b. she has never played outdoor games before.
   c. she doesn't understand their competitive nature.
   d. she is smaller and younger than the other children.

_____ 4. At first, Premila's concerns about school seem to be based on her
   a. desire to fit in.
   b. worry about Santha's happiness.
   c. trouble in keeping up with her studies.
   d. anger at the way Indian students are treated.

_____ 5. Santha's attitude toward Cynthia—the girl she is at school—is mainly one of
   a. guilt.
   b. pride.
   c. worry.
   d. lack of interest.

_____ 6. Premila leaves school and does not want to return because she feels
   a. left out.
   b. insulted.
   c. ignorant.
   d. superior to the other students.

_____ 7. The selection suggests that the idea of not returning to school makes Santha feel
   a. happy.   c. disappointed.
   b. ashamed.   d. nervous and confused.

Selection Test

Using Vocabulary (10 points total; 2 points each)
Write the letter of the best answer.

_____ 8. A person with insular views could be called
      a. nosy.   **b.** open-minded.   **c.** narrow-minded.

_____ 9. One example of a detached reaction is a
      a. grin.   **b.** shrug.   **c.** scowl.

_____ 10. A word that means the opposite of *incomprehensible* is
      a. *clear*.   **b.** *capable*.   **c.** *intelligent*.

_____ 11. Which sign is most likely to intimidate a visitor?
      a. "Welcome"   **b.** "Gone Fishing"   **c.** "Beware of Dog"

_____ 12. Which of the following is usually consumed while tepid?
      a. soup   **b.** lemonade   **c.** a baby's formula

Interpreting and Evaluating (20 points total; 10 points each)
Think about the contrasts that are drawn in this selection between the atmosphere at the Anglo-Indian school and the atmosphere at Santha and Premila's home. Then complete the information in the boxes.

	List FOUR activities, people, or feelings that are closely associated with . . .	What word or phrase best describes the atmosphere at . . .
13.	the school.	the school?
14.	the home.	the home?

Evaluating and Connecting (14 points)
Use a separate sheet of paper to answer the following essay question.

15. The selection's title was taken from these lines in William Shakespeare's *Romeo and Juliet:* "What's in a name? that which we call a rose / By any other name would smell as sweet." Do you think the author of "By Any Other Name" would agree or disagree with the idea presented in these famous lines? Explain.

Selection Test

Score

Living Well. Living Good. (page 488)

Recalling and Interpreting (48 points total; 8 points each)
Write the letter of the best answer.

_____ 1. Aunt Tee suggests that having the keys to rich houses made her feel
        a. trusted.   **c.** resentful.
        b. envious.   **d.** burdened.

_____ 2. The food that Aunt Tee would cook on Saturdays was meant for
        a. her employers.
        b. the household staff.
        c. herself and her friends.
        d. whoever happened to stop by.

_____ 3. Why do Aunt Tee's employers want to observe her party?
        a. to find out how to play whist
        b. to make sure everyone behaves well
        c. to see how poor people amuse themselves
        d. to have something of interest in their lives

_____ 4. Angelou says that the necessary "basic talents" that allow one to live well include
all of the following EXCEPT
        a. tolerance.   **c.** appreciation.
        b. intelligence.   **d.** a cheerful outlook.

_____ 5. When her employers interrupt Aunt Tee's party, at first she feels
        a. irritated.   **c.** guilty.
        b. nervous.   **d.** embarrassed.

_____ 6. Angelou indicates that being able to develop the art of living well is mainly a matter of
        a. luck.   **c.** hard work.
        b. attitude.   **d.** material advantage.

Using Vocabulary (10 points total; 2 points each)
Write the letter of the best answer. This exercise is continued on the next page.

_____ 7. A meticulous person might be described as
        a. fussy.   **b.** sympathetic.   **c.** short-tempered.

_____ 8. A word that means the opposite of *commodious* is
        a. *messy.*   **b.** *cramped.*   **c.** *unfriendly.*

_____ 9. One would expect a convivial person to do a lot of
        a. shopping.   **b.** housework.   **c.** entertaining.

Selection Test

_____ **10.** A person who insists on sticking to his or her scenario for an event is someone who doesn't like

     a. surprises.   **b.** other people.   **c.** responsibility.

_____ **11.** If someone often inhibits you, you might say that person makes you feel

     a. stupid.   **b.** smothered.   **c.** successful.

Interpreting and Evaluating (27 points total; 9 points each)
Think about the contrasts that are drawn in this essay between Aunt Tee and her friends and Aunt Tee's employers. Then, complete the information requested in the boxes below.

12. List THREE words that describe Aunt Tee and her friends.	**13.** List THREE words that describe Aunt Tee's employers.

14. What theme or main message is conveyed through the contrast of the characters named above?

Evaluating and Connecting (15 points)
Use a separate sheet of paper to answer the following essay question.

15. How does Angelou account for the situation in which Aunt Tee's employers find themselves near the end of their lives?

Selection Test

A Swimming Lesson (page 494)

Recalling and Interpreting (45 points total; 9 points each)
Write the letter of the best answer.

_____ 1. At nine, Gomez saw her grandmother, Lydia, as all of the following EXCEPT
    a. strong.   **c.** courageous.
    b. confident.   **d.** hard to please.

_____ 2. Gomez's reference to the "peculiar institution" is a reference to
    a. slavery.
    b. college.
    c. mainstream culture.
    d. Boston's ethnic neighborhoods.

_____ 3. As a child, Gomez assumed that spectators at the beach viewed her grandmother
    with
    a. suspicion.   **c.** confusion.
    b. sympathy.   **d.** admiration.

_____ 4. As an adult, Gomez believes that being able to swim gives her a
    a. purpose in life.
    b. connection to the past.
    c. sense of pride in herself.
    d. greater understanding of others.

_____ 5. What did Gomez realize upon finding out that her grandmother was not actually a
    good swimmer?
    a. that one can easily teach a skill one does not possess
    b. that no one can ever fully understand another person
    c. that Lydia had been even braver than Gomez had thought
    d. that many abilities that seem impressive are merely make-believe

Using Vocabulary (15 points total; 3 points each)
Write the letter of the best answer. This exercise is continued on the next page.

_____ 6. A word that means the opposite of *benevolence* is
    a. *cruelty.*   **b.** *anxiety.*   **c.** *sympathy.*

_____ 7. To indicate that something is invaluable, you might refer to it as being a
    a. bargain.   **b.** treasure.   **c.** piece of junk.

_____ 8. A hairbrush is a superfluous item for a
    a. barber.   **b.** bald person.   **c.** long-haired person.

Selection Test

_____ **9.** Shoes are usually torturous if they are
        a. buckled.   **b.** unlaced.   **c.** too small.

_____ **10.** A vulnerable child is one who needs to be
        a. scolded.   **b.** protected.   **c.** given an education.

Interpreting and Evaluating (24 points total; 6 points each)
In the boxes, answer the questions about the sea motif in this essay.

11. Why was the sea a fearful place for West Africans during the time of slavery?
12. Why wasn't the sea a fearful place for Lydia in the late 1950s?
13. Why was the sea once a fearful place for Gomez?
14. Why did the sea stop being a fearful place for Gomez?

Evaluating and Connecting (16 points)
Use a separate sheet of paper to answer the following essay question.

15. What do you think was the most important lesson about life that Lydia taught the author? Why do you think this lesson was so important?

Selection Test

Pizza in Warsaw, Torte in Prague (page 506)

Recalling and Interpreting (54 points total; 9 points each)
Write the letter of the best answer.

_____ 1. Drakulić believes that the reason Coke is popular in Poland is that it is
    a. inexpensive.   **c.** sweeter than coffee or tea.
    b. widely advertised.   **d.** symbolic of another way of life.

_____ 2. According to Drakulić, using the word *like* in discussing food suggests that the speaker
    a. is narrow-minded about eating.
    b. doesn't know what he or she is missing.
    c. has a wider than normal experience of food.
    d. has a cheerful outlook about what is available.

_____ 3. This essay suggests that what is largely to blame for the difficulties of life in Eastern Europe is
    a. World War II.   **c.** land and labor shortages.
    b. overpopulation.   **d.** communism and its aftermath.

_____ 4. According to Drakulić, what distinguishes one Eastern European city from another is
    a. what foods are in short supply.
    b. whether there are food shortages.
    c. how politically minded the residents are.
    d. how dependent on bread the residents are.

_____ 5. Drakulić's friend Evelina maintains that, in Bulgaria, all meals are accompanied by
    a. worry.   **c.** politics.
    b. humor.   **d.** gratitude.

_____ 6. According to Drakulić, what made it most clear that communism was a failure?
    a. organized protests
    b. the hardships of daily life
    c. the results of free elections
    d. widespread, voiced dissatisfaction

Using Vocabulary (15 points total; 3 points each)
Write the letter of the best answer. This exercise is continued on the next page.

_____ 7. An impeccable uniform would be
    a. spotless.   **b.** colorful.   **c.** uncomfortable.

_____ 8. Which of the following can be described as palpable?
    a. an idea   **b.** an instinct   **c.** a raindrop

Selection Test

_____ 9. A word that means the opposite of *abstract* is
   a. *simple.*   b. *concrete.*   c. *intelligent.*

_____ 10. An affluent person has more than enough
   a. money.   b. friends.   c. intelligence.

_____ 11. Which of the following is an example of an ideology?
   a. gravity   b. democracy   c. a sense of humor

Interpreting and Evaluating (16 points total; 4 points each)
In the boxes below, jot down the thesis of each anecdote, or story, Drakulić uses to develop the main thesis of her essay. Then, in the last box, note what you think is the main thesis of the essay.

12. The anecdote about getting a pizza in Warsaw

Thesis:

13. The anecdote about the old man eating a whole banana

Thesis:

14. The anecdote about looking for torte in Prague

Thesis:

15. The essay as a whole

Thesis:

Evaluating and Connecting (15 points)
Use a separate sheet of paper to answer the following essay question.

16. Besides some basic facts about living with food shortages, what did you learn from reading this essay?

Selection Test

I've Seen the Promised Land (page 516)

Recalling and Interpreting (45 points total; 9 points each)
Write the letter of the best answer.

_____ 1. In King's description of his imagined view of all human history, what does he conclude about the time he is living in?
   a. It is the most challenging and dangerous time of all.
   b. It is better than ancient times but worse than the Renaissance.
   c. Although troubled, it holds great promise for the triumph of justice.
   d. Despite progress, it is a time of greater injustice than any other time.

_____ 2. In this speech, King emphasizes his listeners' ability to change policy through their use of
   a. negotiation.
   b. the right to vote.
   c. economic pressure.
   d. educational opportunity.

_____ 3. When King says, "Somewhere I read of the freedom of speech," he is making an allusion to
   a. the Bible.
   b. the U.S. Constitution.
   c. his own letters and essays.
   d. newspaper articles about the strike.

_____ 4. King's description of the struggle in Birmingham makes it clear that Bull Connor's tactics were
   a. brutal.   c. successful.
   b. illegal.   d. sly and sneaky.

_____ 5. King suggests that his trip to Memphis was delayed because
   a. the pilot didn't want him on the plane.
   b. local leaders discouraged him from coming.
   c. he was, at first, unwilling to travel in the South.
   d. threats to his life required extra security measures.

Using Vocabulary (15 points total; 3 points each)
Write the letter of the best answer. This exercise is continued on the next page.

_____ 6. An agenda is most similar to a
   a. plan.   b. meeting.   c. representative.

_____ 7. A word that means the opposite of *compassionate* is
   a. *efficient*.   b. *misunderstood*.   c. *unsympathetic*.

Selection Test

_____ **8.** You would grapple with a problem if you wanted to

      a. avoid it.   **b.** describe it.   **c.** overcome it.

_____ **9.** You would be most likely to speculate about the contents of

      a. a paper you had written.

      b. a gift you had not yet opened.

      c. a carton of eggs you had purchased.

_____ **10.** To articulate an idea is to

      a. debate it.   **b.** express it.   **c.** consider it carefully.

Interpreting and Evaluating (20 points total; 10 points each)

The more you know about the character, place, or situation referred to in an allusion, the better you can understand the point that is being made. Think about what King is saying and what he might be suggesting with the allusion in the box below. Then, in each empty box below, note one idea that the allusion emphasizes or suggests about the situation facing King's audience in 1968.

> You know, whenever Pharaoh wanted to prolong the period of slavery in Egypt, he had a favorite, favorite formula for doing it. What was that? He kept the slaves fighting among themselves. But whenever the slaves get together, something happens in Pharaoh's court, and he cannot hold the slaves in slavery. When the slaves get together, that's the beginning of getting out of slavery.

This allusion communicates the idea or suggests that . . .

11.	12.

Evaluating and Connecting (20 points)

Use a separate sheet of paper to answer the following essay question.

13. What is the "promised land" that King speaks of at the end of the speech, and why is it a _promised_ land? What are two other words or phrases that he might use to describe it, and why might those descriptions be accurate?

       Selection and Theme Assessment

Selection Test

Exploring Antartic Ice (page 531)

Recalling and Interpreting (50 points total; 10 points each)
Write the letter of the best answer.

_____ 1. The greatest worry these workers face away from the ship is the threat of
        a. getting lost.
        b. wind exposure.
        c. disintegrating ice.
        d. attack by wildlife.

_____ 2. On this trip, the workers are mainly studying
        a. wildlife behavior.
        b. snow and ice thickness.
        c. wind direction and speed.
        d. heat flow in the Weddell Sea.

_____ 3. What makes up the "pasture" that forms the basis of the food chain in the
Antarctic region?
        a. algae
        b. larvae
        c. tiny fish in the seawater
        d. dust particles containing iron

_____ 4. Scientists on the first Antarctic research ship were surprised to discover that
        a. whales could survive on krill.
        b. the entire region was blocked by ice.
        c. the winter sea supported life in abundance.
        d. open areas could freeze rapidly, trapping a ship.

_____ 5. The author and her coworkers use power tools only occasionally because
        a. they break down in the cold.
        b. they pollute the environment.
        c. working without them is faster.
        d. the noise is frightening to local wildlife.

Using Vocabulary (10 points total; 2 points each)
Write the letter of the best answer. This exercise is continued on the next page.

_____ 6. One place that is usually devoid of people is
        a. an abandoned building.
        b. a doctor's waiting room.
        c. a stadium during a game.

_____ 7. A word that means the opposite of *ephemeral* is
        a. *plain.*   **b.** *fragile.*   **c.** *permanent.*

Selection Test

_____ **8.** A person is likely to consider his or her work to be tedious if it involves

   a. risk and danger.

   b. mental challenges.

   c. doing the same thing over and over.

_____ **9.** A transient emotion is one that is

   a. deeply felt.   **b.** briefly felt.   **c.** based on fear.

_____ **10.** A word that means the opposite of *disconcerting* is

   a. *soothing*.   **b.** *shameful*.   **c.** *important*.

Interpreting and Evaluating (24 points total; 8 points each)

Fill in the bar chart to show how important you think each purpose was to the author in writing this essay. Then explain why you rated each purpose as you did.

11. To inform

Not Important   **Very Important**

12. To persuade

Not Important   **Very Important**

13. To entertain

Not Important   **Very Important**

Evaluating and Connecting (16 points)

Use a separate sheet of paper to answer the following essay question.

14. The author says, "No humans can ever live here [in the Antarctic]. We can't conquer it, settle it, even own it." What reasons are there to believe that she is right? Do you see any reasons to doubt the accuracy of this statement? Explain.

Selection Test

from **A Match to the Heart** (page 543)

Recalling and Interpreting (48 points total; 8 points each)
Write the letter of the best answer.

_____ 1. The part of this passage that is called the "exposition" provides information about
    a. Ehrlich's medical treatment.
    b. where the events in the story take place.
    c. Ehrlich's concerns when she first awoke.
    d. why it took so long for the ambulance to reach the hospital.

_____ 2. After being struck, Ehrlich tries to get into a position that will
    a. relieve her pain.
    b. reduce the strain on her heart.
    c. offer some protection from the storm.
    d. follow the Buddhist instructions for dying.

_____ 3. Ehrlich suggests that, at the first hospital, the treatment she receives is limited mainly by
    a. a lack of supplies.
    b. the staff's incompetence.
    c. overcrowding in the emergency room.
    d. an insistence on following old-fashioned rules.

_____ 4. Ehrlich quotes (in italic print) the standard medical procedures for treating electrical injuries in order to
    a. describe how she is being treated.
    b. give her writing a professional feeling.
    c. show that her treatment is completely inadequate.
    d. show that recommended procedures are too complicated for most medical workers to understand.

_____ 5. Ehrlich doesn't kill the rattlesnake she sees in her house because
    a. it hasn't harmed her.
    b. she is too sick to deal with it.
    c. she no longer cares if she lives or dies.
    d. she thinks it is a vision brought on by illness.

_____ 6. During the time described in this selection, Ehrlich is most cheered by the attention she receives from
    a. her dogs.
    b. her husband.
    c. her regular doctor.
    d. the doctor who sees her "aura."

Name _____ Date _____ Class _____

Selection Test   *(continued)*

Using Vocabulary (10 points total; 2 points each)
Write the letter of the best answer.

_____ **7.** You could expend your energy by
     a. resting.   **b.** exercising.   **c.** eating well.

_____ **8.** A word that means the opposite of *fortuitous* is
     a. *unfortunate.*   **b.** *responsible.*   **c.** *defenseless.*

_____ **9.** A person who speaks incoherently might be
     a. yelling.   **b.** babbling.   **c.** gossiping.

_____ **10.** You would most likely be inert if you were
     a. dizzy.   **b.** nervous.   **c.** unconscious.

_____ **11.** One is most likely to muse while
     a. taking a difficult test.
     b. weighing the evidence in a court case.
     c. imagining what it would be like to inherit a million dollars.

Interpreting and Evaluating (24 points total; 8 points each)
Consider what THREE personality traits this selection reveals about the author and how it reveals them. Then, list ONE trait in each of the left-hand boxes below. In the right-hand boxes, note how the selection reveals each trait.

The author seems to be . . .	which is revealed by . . .
12.	
13.	
14.	

Evaluating and Connecting (18 points)
Use a separate sheet of paper to answer the following essay question.

15. Besides the actual fact of the author's being struck by lightning, what TWO things do you find most extraordinary about her experience? Explain.

     Selection and Theme Assessment

Selection Test

The Angry Winter (page 556)

Recalling and Interpreting (56 points total; 8 points each)
Write the letter of the best answer.

_____ 1. To Wolf, the bone seems to represent
      a. love.
      b. a plaything.
      c. self-preservation.
      d. all that is of value to him.

_____ 2. Which of the following is most surprising to the narrator?
      a. that Wolf threatens him to keep a bone
      b. that Wolf wants to go out during a blizzard
      c. that Wolf seems upset by an internal conflict
      d. that Wolf chews on a bone that has no food value

_____ 3. The internal conflict that Wolf suffers during this incident is between
      a. his desire for the bone and his desire for a walk.
      b. his instinctual reaction and his love for his owner.
      c. his desire to protect his owner and his desire to obey him.
      d. what he feels about the bone and what he knows about it.

_____ 4. When the narrator refers to Wolf and himself as being affected by "the shadows,"
he means they are affected by
      a. their imaginations.
      b. ignorance and confusion.
      c. the cruel realities of life.
      d. the grip of the ancient past.

_____ 5. The narrator's main reactions to the incident are feelings of
      a. concern and fear.   c. shock and outrage.
      b. surprise and interest.   d. horror and disbelief.

_____ 6. The narrator returns fully to the present when he
      a. leaves the house.
      b. understands Wolf's reaction.
      c. allows himself to be guided home.
      d. puts the bone on a shelf and turns out the light.

_____ 7. The essay suggests that in the future, the narrator will
      a. think only about the present.
      b. keep old bones away from Wolf.
      c. train Wolf to be more reliably obedient.
      d. try to repeat the evening's events as an experiment.

Selection Test   (continued)

Using Vocabulary (9 points total; 3 points each)
Write the letter of the best answer.

_____ **8.** You could show that you feel indifferently about a suggestion by
      a. nodding.   **b.** shrugging.   **c.** shaking your head.

_____ **9.** A word that means the opposite of *augment* is
      a. *reduce*.   **b.** *surrender*.   **c.** *understand*.

_____ **10.** While you are reading a novel, you might be diverted by
      a. the author.   **b.** a phone call.   **c.** an unexpected ending.

Interpreting and Evaluating (20 points total; 10 points each)
Think about the contrast that is drawn in this selection between the two "winters"—the one in the present setting and the one in the past. Then, in each box below, list FIVE conflicts, issues, ideas, characters, objects, or feelings that are associated with each setting in the selection.

11. Present "Winter"

_____

_____

_____

_____

_____

12. Past "Winter"

_____

_____

_____

_____

_____

Evaluating and Connecting (15 points)
Use a separate sheet of paper to answer the following essay question.

13. What meaning does the narrator attach to this experience? Does he seem to believe that the experience will have a deep, lasting effect on him and/or his dog? Explain.

Selection Test

The Tucson Zoo (page 562)

Recalling and Interpreting (36 points total; 12 points each)
Write the letter of the best answer.

_____ 1. Which of the following best describes Thomas's voice in this essay?
    a. poetic   **c.** hard-hitting
    b. formal   **d.** conversational

_____ 2. Thomas suggests that human feelings of affection for other creatures are
    a. rare.   **c.** insincere.
    b. natural.   **d.** dangerous.

_____ 3. Thomas comes to believe that useful and helpful behavior may result from
    a. education.
    b. instinctive drives.
    c. violations of natural law.
    d. the triumph of the conscious mind over the unconscious.

Using Vocabulary (12 points total; 4 points each)
Write the letter of the best answer.

_____ 4. One attribute of a rabbit is
    a. fur.   **b.** a fox.   **c.** a carrot.

_____ 5. A word that means the opposite of *intact* is
    a. *rude*.   **b.** *broken*.   **c.** *external*.

_____ 6. Elation is a feeling of great
    a. joy.   **b.** pain.   **c.** embarrassment.

Interpreting and Evaluating (30 points total; 15 points each)
In each box below, list THREE reasons why Thomas reacts favorably to the creatures named.

7. Beavers and otters	8. Ants

Evaluating and Connecting (22 points)
Use a separate sheet of paper to answer the following essay question.

9. Thomas wonders how any single ant feels when the whole mass of ants is together on the mound. What does Thomas's wondering reveal about him? Explain.

Open-Book Selection Test

Eldorado (page 582)

Recalling and Interpreting (45 points total; 15 points each)
Write the letter of the best answer.

_____ 1. The knight assumes that he has not found what he is looking for because
   a. what he seeks does not exist.
   b. he does not deserve to find it.
   c. he has looked in the wrong places.
   d. someone else has already found it.

_____ 2. The pilgrim shadow suggests that the knight has not found what he seeks because
   a. it is too well hidden.
   b. it does not exist on earth.
   c. he has failed to recognize it.
   d. he is too easily discouraged.

_____ 3. In which stanza of the poem does the rhyme scheme vary from that in the other stanzas?
   a. the first   c. the third
   b. the second   d. the fourth

Interpreting and Evaluating (30 points total; 15 points each)
In each box on the left, jot down a word or phrase that describes the knight's personality. (Do NOT use words and phrases that are used in the poem.) In each box on the right, explain why you would describe the knight this way.

The knight is . . .	This is revealed by . . .
4.	
5.	

Evaluating and Connecting (25 points)
Use a separate sheet of paper to answer the following essay question.

6. Think about this poem as an example of narrative poetry—poetry that tells a story. What lessons of life are there to be learned from the story it tells?

Open-Book Selection Test

One Perfect Rose and
Shall I Compare Thee . . . (page 586)

Recalling and Interpreting (56 points total; 7 points each)
Write the letter of the best answer. This exercise is continued on the next page.

_____ 1. The speaker of "One Perfect Rose" indicates that she is unhappy about
   a. the beauty of the gift she receives.
   b. the monetary value of the gift she receives.
   c. the feeling expressed by the gift she receives.
   d. feeling obligated to the man who has given her the gift.

_____ 2. In "One Perfect Rose," when the speaker refers to "the language of the floweret,"
she is talking about
   a. nature's ability to communicate.
   b. a secret she shares with the man.
   c. a card that accompanies the rose.
   d. what roses symbolize in romance.

_____ 3. Which of the following song titles expresses the idea most similar to the idea
expressed in "One Perfect Rose"?
   a. "All You Need Is Love"
   b. "Diamonds Are a Girl's Best Friend"
   c. "Hey That's No Way to Say Goodbye"
   d. "You've Got to Hide Your Love Away"

_____ 4. In "Shall I Compare Thee to A Summer's Day," the speaker suggests that his
beloved is
   a. gentle.   c. fickle.
   b. young.   d. wealthy.

_____ 5. In "Shall I Compare Thee . . .," the speaker notes all of the following as flaws of
summer EXCEPT that
   a. it doesn't last.
   b. it replaces spring.
   c. not all days are sunny.
   d. the weather may be too warm.

_____ 6. Which of the following best describes the tone of "Shall I Compare Thee . . ."?
   a. tender   c. mocking
   b. hopeless   d. regretful

_____ 7. Which poem follows an *abab* rhyme scheme throughout?
   a. "One Perfect Rose"
   b. "Shall I Compare Thee . . ."
   c. both poems
   d. neither poem

Open-Book Selection Test

_____ 8. Which poem contains iambic feet?
   a. "One Perfect Rose"
   b. "Shall I Compare Thee . . ."
   c. both poems
   d. neither poem

Interpreting and Evaluating (24 points total; 12 points each)
Think about the sonnet structure or form of "Shall I Compare Thee . . ."
Then answer the questions below.

9.   What related ideas are developed in each of the three quatrains?

Quatrain 1
Quatrain 2
Quatrain 3

10. What conclusion, observation, or comment is offered in the couplet?

Evaluating and Connecting (20 points)
Use a separate sheet of paper to answer the following essay question.

11. Consider who and/or what Dorothy Parker might be making fun of in "One Perfect Rose."
   In a paragraph, explain your idea (or ideas).

Open-Book Selection Test

Simile and Well, I Have Lost You; and I Lost You Fairly (page 591)

Recalling and Interpreting (56 points total; 8 points each)
Write the letter of the best answer.

_____ 1. "Simile" suggests that the people are like deer in that they are
     a. swift.
     b. graceful.
     c. cautious.
     d. natural creatures.

_____ 2. "Simile" suggests that the speaker is feeling
     a. angry.   **c.** uncertain.
     b. guilty.   **d.** resentful.

_____ 3. All of the following adjectives could be used to describe the speaker of "Well, I Have Lost You . . ." EXCEPT
     a. sad.   **c.** dignified.
     b. bitter.   **d.** passionate.

_____ 4. "Well, I Have Lost You . . ." suggests that the speaker lost his or her beloved as a result of
     a. giving up too easily.
     b. imposing restrictions on the beloved.
     c. being truthful about his or her feelings.
     d. being too proud to love deeply and sincerely.

_____ 5. In "Well, I Have Lost You . . .," the speaker suggests that, at various times before the relationship ended, he or she experienced all of the following EXCEPT feelings of
     a. joy.   **c.** misery.
     b. fear.   **d.** betrayal.

_____ 6. In which poem does the speaker suggest that he or she feels confused?
     a. "Simile"
     b. "Well, I Have Lost You . . ."
     c. both poems
     d. neither poem

_____ 7. Which poem suggests that a relationship important to the speaker has recently changed?
     a. "Simile"
     b. "Well, I Have Lost You . . ."
     c. both poems
     d. neither poem

Open-Book Selection Test
(continued)

Interpreting and Evaluating (24 points total; 8 points each)
Think about the simile in "Simile," both how the compared things are alike and how they are different. Then answer the questions in the boxes below.

8. What do they fear?

deer
people

9. How do they behave?

deer
people

10. Do you think their behavior offers hope for them? Why or why not?

deer
people

Evaluating and Connecting (20 points)
Use a separate sheet of paper to answer the following essay question.

11. If the speaker of "Well, I Have Lost You . . ." were to make up a Code of Conduct for Lovers, what FOUR rules do you think would be included?

Open-Book Selection Test

Score

The Glory of the Day Was in Her Face
and Missing You (page 596)

Recalling and Interpreting (60 points total; 10 points each)
Write the letter of the best answer.

_____ 1. In "The Glory of the Day . . .," the speaker suggests that after losing his beloved, he is unable to
    a. feel anything.
    b. remember her clearly.
    c. notice or respond to beauty.
    d. believe in the power of love.

_____ 2. The tone of "The Glory of the Day . . ." could best be described as
    a. sad.
    b. bitter.
    c. anxious.
    d. desperate.

_____ 3. The objects in the first stanza of "Missing You" are mentioned because they
    a. cannot be explained, just as love cannot.
    b. remind the speaker of his or her beloved.
    c. are things the speaker cared about in the past.
    d. are things that physically reflect the speaker's emotions.

_____ 4. "Missing You" suggests that the speaker's tears
    a. do not fully reflect the degree of his or her pain.
    b. are forced from him or her by other people's expectations.
    c. will never stop, because an ocean of grief cannot be emptied.
    d. indicate that his or her feelings are less intense than expected.

_____ 5. Which poem uses descriptions from the natural world to communicate something about the speaker's perceptions or feelings?
    a. "The Glory of the Day . . ."
    b. "Missing You"
    c. both poems
    d. neither poem

_____ 6. Which poem communicates a sense of the personality of the beloved?
    a. "The Glory of the Day . . ."
    b. "Missing You"
    c. both poems
    d. neither poem

Open-Book Selection Test

Interpreting and Evaluating (20 points total; 10 points each)

Both of these poems make figurative comparisons, either stated or suggested. For each poem, choose ONE **of the examples listed below and identify your choice. Then, in the boxes, note what the example compares and the feeling or idea it communicates.**

"The Glory of the Day . . ."

Example A.   "And in her voice, the calling of the dove"

Example B.   "And in her smile, the breaking light of love"

7. Example _____

    compares | _____ *to* _____ |

    conveys this idea or feeling | _____ |

"Missing You"

Example C.   "An equation chalked on the board, with no solution"

Example D.   "A pair of useless oars that never cross the water"

8. Example _____

    compares | _____ *to* _____ |

    conveys this idea or feeling | _____ |

Evaluating and Connecting (20 points)

Use a separate sheet of paper to answer the following essay question.

9. In each of these poems, the speaker is separated from his or her beloved. Which of the speakers do you think expects the separation to be permanent? How can you tell?

Open-Book Selection Test

Score

First Lesson and Those Winter Sundays (page 602)

Recalling and Interpreting (60 points total; 6 points each)
Write the letter of the best answer. This exercise is continued on the next page.

_____ 1. In lines 1–5 of "First Lesson," the speaker suggests that it is important for his or her daughter to
     a. be more careful.
     b. trust the speaker.
     c. believe in herself.
     d. demonstrate more effort.

_____ 2. In lines 11 and 12 of "First Lesson," it is clear that the daughter is
     a. holding on to the speaker.
     b. being held by the speaker.
     c. floating with only the sea's support.
     d. standing with her head above water.

_____ 3. The speaker of "First Lesson" suggests that floating is a way to
     a. give up on life.
     b. restore one's strength.
     c. re-examine one's goals.
     d. avoid difficult challenges.

_____ 4. "First Lesson" suggests that one who becomes afraid should
     a. heed the warning and flee the danger.
     b. overcome the fear with concentrated effort.
     c. change the conditions causing the fearful reaction.
     d. calm the fear with faith in that which is dependable.

_____ 5. The first stanza of "Those Winter Sundays" suggests the speaker's feelings of
     a. anger.   c. resentment.
     b. confusion.   d. compassion.

_____ 6. "Those Winter Sundays" suggests that the atmosphere in the speaker's childhood home was
     a. tense.   c. violent.
     b. happy.   d. unemotional.

_____ 7. In "Those Winter Sundays," the speaker suggests that the father's efforts in the home were
     a. resented.
     b. appreciated.
     c. taken for granted.
     d. completely misunderstood.

Open-Book Selection Test

_____ 8. In the last stanza of "Those Winter Sundays," what feeling about the past does the speaker express?

      a. pride   c. regret

      b. anger   d. confusion

_____ 9. Which poem explores the idea of a child's eventual independence?

      a. "First Lesson"

      b. "Those Winter Sundays"

      c. both poems

      d. neither poem

_____ 10. Which of the following lines of "Those Winter Sundays" contain significant alliteration?

      a. lines 4 and 5   c. lines 8 and 9

      b. lines 6 and 7   d. lines 10 and 11

Interpreting and Evaluating (24 points total; 12 points each)

Think about the lessons of life that each of these poems communicates. In each left-hand box below, note one lesson that you think is taught by, or can be learned from, each poem. In each right-hand box, note how that lesson is communicated by the parent or by the poem as a whole.

11. Lesson in "First Lesson"	Revealed by

12. Lesson in "Those Winter Sundays"	Revealed by

Evaluating and Connecting (16 points)

Use a separate sheet of paper to answer the following essay question.

13. How would you describe the love that the father demonstrates in "Those Winter Sundays"? Why do you suppose the speaker failed to appreciate or understand the father's love when he was a child?

Open-Book Selection Test

Horses Graze and A Blessing (page 610)

Recalling and Interpreting (48 points total; 8 points each)
Write the letter of the best answer.

_____ 1. In "Horses Graze," how do the animals react to human concerns?
      a. They disapprove of them.
      b. They are amused by them.
      c. They misunderstand them.
      d. They are unaware of them.

_____ 2. In lines 13 and 14 of "Horses Graze," the word *your* refers to
      a. a friend of the speaker.
      b. the speaker.
      c. people in general.
      d. government officials.

_____ 3. Which statement comes closest to the meaning of lines 26 and 27 of "Horses Graze"?
      a. The earth is solid and supportive.
      b. The earth is the source of all security.
      c. Animals are limited in ways people are not.
      d. Any creature can be in only one place at a time.

_____ 4. In "A Blessing," who or what is blessed?
      a. the speaker
      b. the two ponies
      c. all of nature
      d. all humankind

_____ 5. What does "A Blessing" suggest is the reason that the ponies approach the speaker and the speaker's friend?
      a. curiosity
      b. the hope of food
      c. a need for safety
      d. a desire for human companionship

_____ 6. Which poem uses occasional rhyme to provide structure and to reinforce its theme?
      a. "Horses Graze"
      b. "A Blessing"
      c. both poems
      d. neither poem

Open-Book Selection Test

Interpreting and Evaluating (28 points total; 14 points each)

In each box left-hand box below, give one reason why the animal in the poem appeals to the speaker. In each box on the right, explain how the poem reveals this.

7. What about the horses appeals to
   the speaker of "Horses Graze"?   How can you tell?

8. What about the ponies appeals to
   the speaker of "A Blessing"?   How can you tell?

Evaluating and Connecting (24 points)

Use a separate sheet of paper to answer ONE of the following essay questions.

9. What are some of the behaviors of people and aspects of civilization that Brooks uses "Horses Graze" to criticize? Support your ideas with details from the poem.

10. Explain in your own words what the speaker is feeling in the last two lines of "A Blessing," and why the speaker is feeling that way.

Open-Book Selection Test

Score

Afro-American Fragment and Heaven (page 622)

Recalling and Interpreting (60 points total; 10 points each)
Write the letter of the best answer.

_____ 1. The speaker of "Afro-American Fragment" would be most likely to describe Africa
as a place that he feels
    a. resentful of.
    b. connected to.
    c. familiar with.
    d. responsible for.

_____ 2. In lines 7 and 8, the speaker uses the word *blood* to refer to
    a. human mortality.
    b. the source of all life.
    c. that which is brutal and violent.
    d. something inborn and part of one's nature.

_____ 3. It is most likely that the speaker of "Afro-American Fragment" refers to both
"history books" and "songs" to suggest that
    a. his ties to Africa combine knowledge and feeling.
    b. he believes the past can be best interpreted through art.
    c. he sees himself as being equally skilled in academics and art.
    d. African music can only be understood by those who understand history.

_____ 4. The "he" referred to in line 39 of "Heaven" is the speaker's
    a. son.
    b. father.
    c. brother.
    d. grandfather.

_____ 5. Why did the boy from Guangzhou fail to return to China?
    a. There was no gold in China.
    b. He preferred life in America.
    c. He died before he could return..
    d. He had became lost in America.

_____ 6. Poetry written in free verse could contain all of the following EXCEPT
    a. imagery.
    b. personification.
    c. uneven line lengths.
    d. a regular rhyme pattern.

Open-Book Selection Test

Interpreting and Evaluating (24 points total; 6 points each)
In the boxes, describe places that are important to the people in these poems.

"Afro-American Fragment"

7. The speaker thinks of **Africa** as being . . .	This is probably because . . .

"Heaven"

8. The speaker thinks of **China** as being . . .	This is probably because . . .

9. She thinks of **the place she lives in** as being . . .	This is probably because . . .

10. Her son thinks of **China** as being . . .	This is probably because . . .

Evaluating and Connecting (16 points)
Use a separate sheet of paper to answer the following essay question.

11. In a paragraph, discuss the symbolic meaning of "songs" or "singing" in each of these poems. What do you think songs represent in each?

Open-Book Selection Test

The Base Stealer and To Satch (page 628)

Recalling and Interpreting (48 points total; 12 points each)
Write the letter of the best answer.

_____ 1. The mood of "The Base Stealer" is one of
      a. fear.   **c.** triumph.
      b. dismay.   **d.** excitement.

_____ 2. "The Base Stealer" uses all of the following EXCEPT
      a. similes.   **c.** alliteration.
      b. repetition.   **d.** personification.

_____ 3. Which statement comes closest to being the message of "To Satch"?
      a. Attitude is every bit as important as skill.
      b. It's a delight to do something extremely well.
      c. To be successful, you must reach for the stars.
      d. In life, as in baseball, it's three strikes and you're out.

_____ 4. In "To Satch," the speaker's attitude in the last line is one of
      a. pride.   **c.** gratitude.
      b. surprise.   **d.** amusement.

Open-Book Selection Test

Interpreting and Evaluating (30 points total; 15 points each)
What do you see in your imagination as you read these poems? Choose one image from each poem and answer the questions in the boxes.

What is the image?	What ideas or feelings does this image communicate to you?
5. in "The Base Stealer"	
6. in "To Satch"	

Evaluating and Connecting (22 points)
Use a separate sheet of paper to answer the following essay question.

7. What is one thing about the game of baseball that you think both of these poems communicate? Support your answer with references to the poems.

Open-Book Selection Test

Score

Ex-Basketball Player and Miss Rosie (page 635)

Recalling and Interpreting (56 points total; 7 points each)
Write the letter of the best answer.

_____ 1. "Ex-Basketball Player" suggests that, since high school, Flick's life has been all of the following EXCEPT
      a. wasted.   **c.** unexciting.
      b. dangerous.   **d.** unrewarding.

_____ 2. The nickname "Flick" in "Ex-Basketball Player" probably refers to
      a. the briefness of his fame.
      b. the way he lights his cigars.
      c. the way he used to shoot the ball.
      d. his height and general appearance.

_____ 3. In "Ex-Basketball Player," which of the following is described in a way that is similar to how the speaker might describe Flick himself?
      a. Pearl Avenue
      b. Berth's garage
      c. the gasoline pumps
      d. Mae's Luncheonette

_____ 4. "Miss Rosie" suggests that Miss Rosie's clothes are all of the following EXCEPT
      a. old.   **c.** worn out.
      b. ill-fitting.   **d.** overly fancy.

_____ 5. What does line 9 of "Miss Rosie" suggest about Miss Rosie?
      a. She is not intelligent.
      b. She is living in the past.
      c. She is not in touch with reality.
      d. She thinks only about life's necessities.

_____ 6. In "Miss Rosie," the speaker suggests that people used to view Miss Rosie with
      a. sympathy.   **c.** resentment.
      b. admiration.   **d.** amusement.

_____ 7. In which poem does the speaker contrast the present and the past?
      a. "Ex-Basketball Player" **c.** both poems
      b. "Miss Rosie"   **d.** neither poem

_____ 8. In which poem does rhyme contribute to the effect?
      a. "Ex-Basketball Player" **c.** both poems
      b. "Miss Rosie"   **d.** neither poem

Open-Book Selection Test
(continued)

Interpreting and Evaluating (30 points total; 10 points each)

In the boxes, answer the questions about the speakers' attitudes toward the main characters in these poems.

	"Ex-Basketball Player"	"Miss Rosie"
9. What is the speaker's main attitude toward the title character?		
10. What are some words and phrases in the poem that reveal this attitude?		
11. How do you account for the speaker's attitude?		

Evaluating and Connecting (14 points)

Use a separate sheet of paper to answer the following essay question.

12. In your own words, tell what you think the speaker is saying in the last three lines of "Miss Rosie." What feelings do these lines communicate?

Open-Book Selection Test

Score

The Road Not Taken and We Are Many (page 642)

Recalling and Interpreting (64 points total; 8 points each)
Write the letter of the best answer. This exercise is continued on the next page.

_____ 1. In "The Road Not Taken," what does the speaker know about the two roads?
  a. how they look
  b. where they lead
  c. what people say about them
  d. who else has traveled on them

_____ 2. Given the suggestions made in "The Road Not Taken," it is most likely that the speaker is
  a. a child.   c. a middle-aged adult.
  b. a young adult.   d. an elderly person.

_____ 3. Which of the following would the speaker in "The Road Not Taken" be most likely to say "ages and ages hence" about the choice he made?
  a. I knew what lay ahead of me.
  b. I am responsible for the choice I made.
  c. I wish I could make my choice over again.
  d. I considered both options in detail before selecting one.

_____ 4. The difference between the two roads in "The Road Not Taken" is that
  a. one is prettier than the other.
  b. one bends and the other does not.
  c. one seems an easier route than the other.
  d. one has had fewer travelers than the other.

_____ 5. One of the main reasons that "The Road Not Taken" is considered a lyric poem is that
  a. it presents a contrast.
  b. it contains nature imagery.
  c. the subject matter is personal.
  d. the speaker is a character in it.

_____ 6. In line 2 of "We Are Many," the speaker uses *settle* to mean
  a. "decide."
  b. "agree with."
  c. "become quiet or calm."
  d. "remain fairly permanently."

_____ 7. The speaker of "We Are Many" suggests that he often reacts to his own behavior with
  a. pride.   c. disinterest.
  b. surprise.   d. great amusement.

Open-Book Selection Test

_____ 8. Who are the "arsonist" and the "fireman" referred to in lines 16 and 17 of
"We Are Many?"

        a. different sides of the speaker's personality

        b. the speaker in the present and in the past

        c. the speaker's real self and his imagined self

        d. a good friend of the speaker's and a bad one

Interpreting and Evaluating (20 points total; 5 points each)
In the boxes below, answer the questions about the speaker of "We Are Many."

9. What is the strongest feeling or attitude that the speaker has?	**10.** Toward whom or what is this feeling or attitude directed?
11. How is the feeling or attitude revealed in the poem?	**12.** Why might the speaker feel this way?

Evaluating and Connecting (16 points)
Use a separate sheet of paper to answer the following essay question.

13. In your own words, explain what the speaker of "The Road Not Taken" means by the
words "Yet knowing how way leads on to way, / I doubted if I should ever come back."
Why might the speaker believe that this would be the case?

Open-Book Selection Test

The Floral Apron
and My Mother Pieced Quilts (page 648)

Recalling and Interpreting (56 points total; 8 points each)
Write the letter of the best answer.

_____ 1. The "moment's barbarism" in line 14 of "The Floral Apron" refers to
  a. eating the squid.
  b. catching the squid.
  c. cutting up the squid.
  d. speaking to those watching

_____ 2. The speaker "absolves" the woman in the floral apron because the speaker
  a. realizes that the action was necessary.
  b. is caught up in wanting to eat the dinner.
  c. doesn't want to make the woman feel bad.
  d. knows how important it is to respect one's elders.

_____ 3. What the speaker learned from the woman in the floral apron mainly influenced her
  a. behavior.
  b. view of the world.
  c. attitude about her culture.
  d. expectations of the future.

_____ 4. In "My Mother Pieced Quilts," the mother is compared to all of the following
  EXCEPT
  a. a bird.   c. a painter.
  b. a river.   d. a wagon driver.

_____ 5. In which stanza does the speaker of "My Mother Pieced Quilts" describe her
  mother as two very different things?
  a. lines 13–19   c. lines 27–36
  b. lines 20–26   d. lines 37–43

_____ 6. Which of the following is a central idea in both of these poems?
  a. self-sacrifice
  b. the need for love
  c. hope and expectation
  d. keeping the past alive

_____ 7. Which poem has a joyful tone?
  a. "The Floral Apron"
  b. "My Mother Pieced Quilts"
  c. both poems
  d. neither poem

Open-Book Selection Test

Interpreting and Evaluating (24 points total; 12 points each)
What do you see in your imagination as you read these poems? Choose one image from each poem and answer the questions in the boxes.

8. "The Floral Apron"

> What is the image?

> How would you describe this image?
> (Is it, for example, *natural? colorful?*
> *tender? goofy? everyday? exotic?*)

> What ideas or feelings does the
> image communicate to you?

9. "My Mother Pieced Quilts"

> What is the image?

> How would you describe this image?

> What ideas or feelings does the
> image communicate to you?

Evaluating and Connecting (20 points)
Use a separate sheet of paper to answer the following essay question.

10. In TWO paragraphs, discuss the significance to the speakers of the objects referred to in the titles of these poems. Support your ideas with details from the poems.

Open-Book Selection Test

A Bus Along St. Clair: December
and Freeway 280 (page 654)

Recalling and Interpreting (48 points total; 12 points each)
Write the letter of the best answer.

_____ 1. What are the "monuments / of concrete slabs" referred to in lines 6 and 7 of "A Bus Along St. Clair: December"?
    a. roads   **c.** grave markers
    b. buildings   **d.** statues of historical figures

_____ 2. The tone of "A Bus . . ." could best be described as
    a. defiant.   **c.** objective.
    b. envious.   **d.** mournful.

_____ 3. The second stanza of "Freeway 280" describes the power of
    a. love.   **c.** the past.
    b. nature.   **d.** progress.

_____ 4. In line 22 of "Freeway 280," it is most likely that *it* refers to the speaker's
    a. youth.   **c.** heritage.
    b. family.   **d.** memories.

Open-Book Selection Test

Interpreting and Evaluating (32 points total; 16 points each)

Think about how the speaker of "Freeway 280" has changed in her feelings toward the freeway. In the boxes, jot down a word or phrase that describes how the speaker once felt about the freeway, how the speaker feels now, and what reasons are suggested for those feelings.

How speaker felt about the freeway BEFORE

How speaker feels about the freeway NOW

5. BEFORE	6. NOW
Reasons	Reasons

Evaluating and Connecting (20 points)
Use a separate sheet of paper to answer the following question.

7. Who do you think the speaker is in "A Bus Along St. Clair: December"? In your own words, what message do you think the speaker is communicating?

Open-Book Selection Test

Score

Making a Fist and What We Believe (page 660)

Recalling and Interpreting (36 points total; 12 points each)
Write the letter of the best answer.

_____ 1. Which of the following motivates the speaker's question in "Making a Fist"?
      a. fear   **c.** sorrow
      b. anger   **d.** impatience

_____ 2. Why, at the end of "Making a Fist," is the speaker still "clenching and opening one small hand"?
      a. to show anger at life
      b. to show anger at death
      c. to reassure himself or herself
      d. to prove something to the mother

_____ 3. Which element of poetry gives "What We Believe" a structure?
      a. rhyme   **c.** repetition
      b. rhythm   **d.** none of these

Open-Book Selection Test (continued)

Interpreting and Evaluating (40 points total; 20 points each)
Answer the questions in the left-hand boxes below. In the right-hand boxes, provide a clue from the poem or a personal interpretation that supports your answer.

Clue or personal interpretation:

4. In "Making a Fist," what does the ability to make a fist symbolize?	

5. In "What We Believe," what do horses symbolize?	

Evaluating and Connecting (24 points)
Use a separate sheet of paper to answer the following essay question.

6. How would you describe the mother's response to the speaker's question in "Making a Fist"? Explain your answer.

Selection and Theme Assessment

Open-Book Selection Test

Score

Foreign Ways and Song for My Name (page 666)

Recalling and Interpreting (45 points total; 15 points each)
Write the letter of the best answer.

_____ 1. When the speaker of "Foreign Ways" says, "Still they'd know me," she means that she would be
  a. understood.
  b. treated as a friend.
  c. recognized as a foreigner.
  d. recognized as a familiar person.

_____ 2. "Song for My Name" closely relates the speaker's name and
  a. a bird.   **c.** her home.
  b. the sun.   **d.** her people.

_____ 3. Which poem suggests that the speaker is dissatisfied with who she is?
  a. "Foreign Ways"   **c.** both poems
  b. "Song for My Name"   **d.** neither poem

Open-Book Selection Test
(continued)

Interpreting and Evaluating (40 points total; 20 points each)
Make a mark in the small box next to each sense to which the sensory details appeal in these lines from the poems. Then, on the right, note the main ideas or feelings that the sensory details communicate.

	Sense(s)	Main Idea or Feeling
4. "my voice from Duluth my lope with its prairie air"	☐ Taste ☐ Sight ☐ Touch ☐ Smell ☐ Hearing	
5. "and in her own land the mornings are pale, birds sing into the white curtains and show off their soft breasts"	☐ Taste ☐ Sight ☐ Touch ☐ Smell ☐ Hearing	

Evaluating and Connecting (15 points)
Use a separate sheet of paper to answer the following essay question.

6. How would you describe the tone, or attitude, of the speaker of "Song for My Name"? Explain your answer.

Open-Book Selection Test

Score

Night Clouds and Tiger Year (page 676)

Recalling and Interpreting (54 points total; 9 points each)
Write the letter of the best answer.

_____ 1. "Night Clouds" suggests that all of the following are true on the night being described EXCEPT that
   a. the stars are out.
   b. it is about to rain.
   c. the sky appears to be green.
   d. there are white clouds tipped with gold.

_____ 2. The image of the sky created in "Night Clouds" includes all of the following EXCEPT
   a. colors.
   b. smells.
   c. motion.
   d. textures.

_____ 3. "Tiger Year" suggests that all of the following are true on the night being described EXCEPT that
   a. stars are visible.
   b. it is just getting dark.
   c. there is a new moon.
   d. there are clouds in the sky.

_____ 4. Which of the following best describes the speaker's tone in "Tiger Year"?
   a. calm
   b. anxious
   c. sorrowful
   d. frightened

_____ 5. In which of these two poems is the speaker addressing something in nature?
   a. "Night Clouds"
   b. "Tiger Year"
   c. both poems
   d. neither poem

_____ 6. Which of these two poems compares something in nature to a tiger?
   a. "Night Clouds"
   b. "Tiger Year"
   c. both poems
   d. neither poem

Open-Book Selection Test

Interpreting and Evaluating (24 points total; 8 points each)
Read the following lines (9–15) from "Tiger Year." Then, in the boxes below, answer the questions about imagery in those lines.

> "see how the stars are blossoming
> one by one:
> as if merely to breathe.
>
> they blossom for you,
> defining your way
> through the clear night air
> with hands as pure and bright as clouds."

7. To which sense(s) does the imagery appeal?	☐ Sight ☐ Taste ☐ Hearing ☐ Touch ☐ Smell
8. What is one pair of things that the figurative language compares?	
9. What do the imagery and figurative language communicate or help you to see or understand better?	

Evaluating and Connecting (22 points)
Use a separate sheet of paper to answer the following essay question.

10. Think about the poet's use of metaphor in "Night Clouds," in which clouds are referred to as mares. What characteristics does this metaphor suggest about the clouds? That is, what adjectives might you use to describe them? Choose THREE words or phrases (such as "feeble," "worried," or "in a good mood") that could be used to describe the clouds, and support your choices with evidence from the poem.

Open-Book Selection Test

For Poets and Reapers (page 682)

Recalling and Interpreting (56 points total; 7 points each)
Write the letter of the best answer.

_____ 1. In the first stanza of "For Poets," the speaker might be warning against any of the following EXCEPT
    a. living inside your own head.
    b. going into the world of everyday life.
    c. thinking too much about your own feelings.
    d. spending too much time with books and poetry.

_____ 2. The things mentioned in lines 4–6 of "For Poets" are similar in that they are all
    a. hard.   **c.** worthless.
    b. dead.   **d.** unthinking.

_____ 3. In the second stanza of "For Poets," the speaker suggests that living is
    a. an adventure.   **c.** a struggle.
    b. an assignment.   **d.** a competition.

_____ 4. Which of the following lines from "For Poets" contains assonance?
    a. line 2   **c.** line 10
    b. line 5   **d.** line 12

_____ 5. What word could describe the action of the mower blade in "Reapers"?
    a. angry.   **c.** hateful.
    b. uncaring.   **d.** regretful.

_____ 6. "Reapers" suggests that
    a. reaping is brutal but necessary.
    b. reaping is unusually dangerous work.
    c. the reapers are concerned only with getting their job done.
    d. replacing the reapers with mowers is as cruel as harming the field rat.

_____ 7. All of the following lines from "Reapers" contain assonance EXCEPT
    a. line 1.   **c.** line 6.
    b. line 2.   **d.** line 8.

_____ 8. Which of these poems suggests that a single-minded approach to one's work can have negative effects?
    a. "For Poets"
    b. "Reapers"
    c. both poems
    d. neither poem

Open-Book Selection Test   *(continued)*

Interpreting and Evaluating (24 points total; 12 points each)
For each poem, describe one striking image, the feelings or ideas communicated by that image, and what you think is the theme of the poem.

	9. "For Poets"		10. "Reapers"
Striking Image			
Feelings and Ideas			
Theme			

Evaluating and Connecting (20 points)
Use a separate sheet of paper to answer the following essay question.

11. What do you think the speaker of "For Poets" means by the words "be the very hero of birds" (line 11)? Why might this be particularly important for a poet?

Selection and Theme Assessment

Open-Book Selection Test

Score

Three Haiku and Two Tanka (page 686)

Recalling and Interpreting (60 points total; 12 points each)
Write the letter of the best answer.

_____ 1. What is it about the autumn frost that the first haiku emphasizes?
     a. how cold it is   **c.** how little it weighs
     b. how delicate it is   **d.** how depressing it is

_____ 2. In the second haiku, the speaker suggests that he or she is
     a. sorry to see winter end.
     b. looking forward to autumn.
     c. happy for the arrival of spring.
     d. too aware that winter will come again.

_____ 3. All three of the haiku deal with
     a. a sense of loss.   **c.** the joy of feeling reborn.
     b. a season of the year.   **d.** mankind's effect on nature.

_____ 4. Which of the two tanka includes a metaphor?
     a. the first   **c.** both poems
     b. the second   **d.** neither poem

_____ 5. Which group of poems, the haiku or the tanka, expresses wonder about the world?
     a. the haiku   **c.** both groups
     b. the tanka   **d.** neither group

Open-Book Selection Test
(continued)

Interpreting and Evaluating (20 points)
Haiku and tanka use imagery to call up, or evoke, an emotional response in the reader. Choose one image from this poetry that evokes an emotional response in you. In the boxes, make notes to describe the image and your reaction to it.

6.   image

reaction

Evaluating and Connecting (20 points)
Use a separate sheet of paper to answer the following essay question.

7. After reading this poetry, what can you tell about these poets' attitude either toward nature generally or toward spring specifically? Explain your answer.

Open-Book Selection Test

A Motto from Poets: Leave Stone
and Constantly risking absurdity (page 690)

Recalling and Interpreting (64 points total; 8 points each)
Write the letter of the best answer. This exercise is continued on the next page.

_____ 1. In "A Motto from Poets: Leave Stone," what does the speaker suggest poets value most?
  a. nature
  b. permanence
  c. dignity and nobility
  d. the ability to grow and change

_____ 2. "A Motto . . ." suggests that all of the following are the "detritus" of trees EXCEPT
  a. beds.   c. campfires.
  b. acorns.   d. picnic tables.

_____ 3. In "A Motto . . . ," the speaker suggests that stone has value in that it
  a. lasts a long time.
  b. has witnessed history.
  c. becomes more beautiful over time.
  d. can be used without being changed.

_____ 4. In "Constantly risking absurdity," the speaker suggests that the poet is like an acrobat in all the following ways EXCEPT that he or she
  a. entertains.
  b. performs a delicate task.
  c. takes risks to accomplish a goal.
  d. becomes confident through practice.

_____ 5. In "Constantly . . . ," the speaker suggests that the poet approaches beauty by
  a. being theatrical.
  b. keeping a sense of proportion.
  c. seeing things for what they are.
  d. keeping the reader interested at all times.

_____ 6. Which poem has a regular rhyme pattern?
  a. "A Motto from Poets: Leave Stone"
  b. "Constantly risking absurdity"
  c. both poems
  d. neither poem

_____ 7. Which poem contains rhyme?
  a. "A Motto from Poets: Leave Stone"
  b. "Constantly risking absurdity"
  c. both poems
  d. neither poem

Open-Book Selection Test
(continued)

_____ **8.** Which poem explores the nature of art and the artist?
- **a.** "A Motto from Poets: Leave Stone"
- **b.** "Constantly risking absurdity"
- **c.** both poems
- **d.** neither poem

Interpreting and Evaluating (20 points total; 5 points each)
Think about what the extended comparison in "Constantly risking absurdity" communicates about the poet's role, job, or responsibility. On each line, identify one of these tasks or responsibilities, and in the box under it, note phrases and/or lines from the poem that support your ideas.

9. Job or responsibility: _____

> Support:

10. Job or responsibility: _____

> Support:

11. Job or responsibility: _____

> Support:

12. Job or responsibility: _____

> Support:

Evaluating and Connecting (16 points)
Use a separate sheet of paper to answer the following essay question.

13. What do you think is the message, or point, in "A Motto from Poets: Leave Stone"?

Open-Book Selection Test

let my spirit fly in time and Jazz Fantasia (page 697)

Recalling and Interpreting (56 points total; 7 points each)
Write the letter of the best answer.

_____ 1. In "let my spirit fly in time," the speaker suggests that jazz music gives him or her a sense of all of the following EXCEPT

    a. motion.   **c.** richness.
    b. anxiety.   **d.** liberation.

_____ 2. In "let my spirit . . . ," the poet uses all of the following techniques of jazz EXCEPT

    a. repetition.
    b. loose but definite rhythms.
    c. variations on certain phrases.
    d. improvisation on an already familiar song.

_____ 3. In "Jazz Fantasia" the aspect of jazz that the speaker MOST emphasizes is its

    a. cool sound.
    b. ability to express different moods.
    c. origins in African-American music.
    d. place in the development of American music.

_____ 4. The music described in lines 7 and 8 of "Jazz Fantasia" is

    a. harsh and loud.
    b. light and lively.
    c. low and mournful.
    d. peaceful and mellow.

_____ 5. The music described in lines 10–13 of "Jazz Fantasia" is

    a. harsh and loud.
    b. light and lively.
    c. low and mournful.
    d. peaceful and mellow.

_____ 6. Which of the following best describes the tone of "Jazz Fantasia"?

    a. angry   **c.** objective
    b. proud   **d.** enthusiastic

_____ 7. Which poem abandons ordinary sentence structure?

    a. "Let my spirit fly in time"
    b. "Jazz Fantasia"
    c. both poems
    d. neither poem

_____ 8. Which poem is addressed to jazz musicians?

    a. "Let my spirit fly in time"
    b. "Jazz Fantasia"
    c. both poems
    d. neither poem

Open-Book Selection Test

Interpreting and Evaluating (24 points total; 6 points each)

Imagery is used in both of these poems to communicate how the speakers are affected by the jazz music that is being played. In each left-hand box, jot down TWO effective images in the poems and in each right-hand box explain what those images reveal about the jazz music it relates to and the mood the music creates.

"let my spirit fly in time"

Image	What It Reveals
9.	

Image	What It Reveals
10.	

"Jazz Fantasia"

Image	What It Reveals
11.	

Image	What It Reveals
12.	

Evaluating and Connecting (20 points)
Use a separate sheet of paper to answer the following essay question.

13. In a paragraph, compare the attitudes of the speakers toward jazz. How do you account for their attitudes?

Selection Test

from Big River: The Adventures of Huckleberry Finn (page 716)

Recalling and Interpreting (40 points total; 10 points each)
Write the letter of the best answer.

_____ 1. Huck indicates that he has run away from home in order to
     a. find adventure.   **c.** help Jim find freedom.
     b. worry his father.   **d.** escape intolerable conditions.

_____ 2. Jim indicates that he has run away from home in order to
     a. look for Huck.   **c.** avoid being sold.
     b. find adventure.   **d.** escape cruelty there.

_____ 3. Jim has acquired the goods he has by
     a. stealing them.   **c.** borrowing them.
     b. salvaging them.   **d.** purchasing them.

_____ 4. Huck plans to be useful to Jim by
     a. claiming Jim is dead.
     b. pretending to be his owner.
     c. helping him guide the raft.
     d. helping him find the town of Cairo.

Selection Test
(continued)

Interpreting and Evaluating (40 points total; 10 points each)
In each box on the left, identify a trait that the character demonstrates in this scene.
In each box on the right, explain how that trait is revealed.

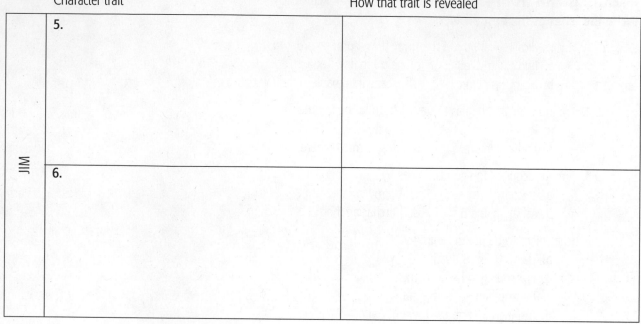

Character trait   How that trait is revealed

JIM

5.

6.

HUCK

7.

8.

Evaluating and Connecting (20 points)
Use a separate sheet of paper to answer the following essay question.

9. What do you think are the chief advantages and disadvantages to Huck of the plan of
    action he agrees to with Jim?

Selection Test

Antigone, Part 1 (page 726)

Recalling and Interpreting (48 points total; 6 points each)
Write the letter of the best answer.

_____ 1. Creon has forbidden Polyneices's burial because Creon views him as
   a. a traitor.
   b. a coward.
   c. insignificant.
   d. cursed by the gods.

_____ 2. Antigone's determination to bury Polyneices is based mainly on feelings of
   a. hatred for Creon.
   b. disloyalty to Thebes.
   c. loyalty to her brother.
   d. anger at the insult to her family.

_____ 3. Ismene is, at first, unwilling to help Antigone bury Polyneices because Ismene
   a. thinks that Creon is right to forbid his burial.
   b. does not want to be punished for breaking the law.
   c. believes that the gods would oppose such behavior.
   d. believes that the dead can be neither harmed nor helped.

_____ 4. When Ismene shows reluctance to help Antigone bury Polyneices, Antigone
   responds with
   a. scorn.   c. understanding.
   b. pleading.   d. confused disbelief.

_____ 5. When Antigone goes ahead with her plan to bury Polyneices, she believes that
   a. she can avoid being caught.
   b. she may very well be put to death.
   c. Creon will spare her from punishment.
   d. the citizens of Thebes will protect her from Creon.

_____ 6. Creon's main concern at the beginning of the play has to do with
   a. acquiring the blessings of the gods.
   b. restoring political stability to the state.
   c. protecting Thebes from the Argive army.
   d. protecting his own and his family's safety.

_____ 7. Creon becomes extremely upset whenever he thinks he perceives a challenge to his
   a. wisdom.   c. morality.
   b. courage.   d. authority.

_____ 8. When Creon accuses Ismene of helping Antigone, Ismene claims that she
   a. is innocent.
   b. is partly guilty.
   c. is equally guilty.
   d. knew nothing of Antigone's plans.

Selection Test

Interpreting and Evaluating (32 points total; 8 points each)
Answer the following questions about conflict between the characters.

9. Who is the protagonist, and why do you think this?	**10.** Who is the antagonist, and why do you think this?

11. What is the central conflict between the two?

12. How does the conflict affect each character?

Evaluating and Connecting (20 points)
Use a separate sheet of paper to answer the following essay question.

13. In the conflict between Antigone and Creon, is either character *completely* in the right? Who do you think is *more* in the right? Support your opinions with reference to the first part of the play.

Name _____ Date _____ Class _____

Selection Test

Antigone, Part 2 (page 748)

Score

Recalling and Interpreting (49 points total; 7 points each)
Write the letter of the best answer.

_____ 1. Throughout his conversation with Creon, Haimon attempts to appeal to his
father's
    a. pride.   **c.** emotions.
    b. reason.   **d.** religious beliefs.

_____ 2. During his conversation with Haimon, Creon becomes more and more
    a. sad.   **c.** enraged.
    b. doubtful.   **d.** reasonable.

_____ 3. As Antigone prepares herself to be led away to the vault, she blames her situation on
    a. her stubbornness.
    b. the whims of the gods.
    c. the cowardice of the people of Thebes.
    d. the unholy actions of her father and mother.

_____ 4. After Teiresias has gone, Creon reacts to his warnings by showing
    a. bored unconcern.
    b. concern and doubt.
    c. fury and impatience.
    d. scornful amusement.

_____ 5. As the play progresses, what happens to the attitude of the Chorus?
    a. It begins to doubt the power of the gods.
    b. It becomes more sympathetic to Antigone.
    c. It becomes more firmly supportive of Creon.
    d. It loses interest in the conflict between Creon and Antigone.

_____ 6. At the end of the play, whom does Creon blame for the tragic events that have
unfolded?
    a. himself   **c.** Antigone
    b. Teiresias   **d.** Polyneices

_____ 7. Which of the following statements made by Creon proves to be one that he
should, himself, have taken to heart?
    a. "No traitor is going to be honored with the loyal man."
    b. "There's nothing in the world so demoralizing as money."
    c. "The inflexible heart breaks first, the toughest iron / Cracks first . . ."
    d. "The man who knows how to obey, and that man only, / Knows how to
give commands when the time comes."

Copyright © by The McGraw-Hill Companies, Inc.

Selection Test

Using Vocabulary (15 points total; 3 points each)
For each underlined word, write the letter of the word that means the OPPOSITE.

_____ 8.	defile	a.	fail
_____ 9.	prevail	b.	purify
_____ 10.	absolve	c.	accuse
_____ 11.	perverse	d.	modesty
_____ 12.	arrogance	e.	agreeable

Interpreting and Evaluating (18 points total; 6 points each)
Readers may have different thoughts about what caused Creon's downfall. For each of the three possible causes common to traditional tragedy, mark the bar graph to show how you would judge the importance of the cause. Then give reasons to support your opinions.

13. How important is tragic flaw?
    Why do you think this?

    not at all important   extremely important

14. How important are errors in judgment?
    Why do you think this?

    not at all important   extremely important

15. How important is fate?
    Why do you think this?

    not at all important   extremely important

Evaluating and Connecting (18 points)
Use a separate sheet of paper to answer the following essay question.

15. Do you consider any of the characters in this play heroic? If so, which ones, and why? If not, why not?

Selection Test

The Tragedy of Julius Caesar, Act 1 (page 777)

Recalling and Interpreting (72 points total; 9 points each)
Write the letter of the best answer. This exercise is continued on the next page.

_____ 1. When Murellus and Flavius see that the commoners intend to celebrate Caesar's triumph over Pompey, they respond with
    a. relief.   **c.** praise.
    b. anger.   **d.** amusement.

_____ 2. Antony's behavior demonstrates that his attitude toward Caesar is
    a. gently critical.
    b. enthusiastically loyal.
    c. cautious and distrustful.
    d. awestruck and worshipful.

_____ 3. When Cassius says, "The fault, dear Brutus, is not in our stars, / But in ourselves, that we are underlings," he is trying to tell Brutus that
    a. he should not try to change society.
    b. circumstances are controlled by fate.
    c. superstition is the cause of his problems.
    d. he has the power to change his own destiny.

_____ 4. The main political value that Brutus and Cassius share is
    a. pride in the wealth of the Roman empire.
    b. unquestioning loyalty to the Roman leader.
    c. respect for the Roman system of government.
    d. ambition to establish Roman rule all over the world.

_____ 5. Caesar's comment about Cassius's "lean and hungry look" expresses his
    a. concern for Cassius's welfare.
    b. pity for Cassius's social position.
    c. suspicion of Cassius's intentions.
    d. certainty that Cassius opposes him.

_____ 6. Casca and Cassius regard the disturbances in the weather and other unusual events as all of the following EXCEPT
    a. coincidences.
    b. supernatural omens.
    c. warnings to be taken seriously.
    d. evidence that their beliefs are correct.

_____ 7. The opposition to Caesar is mainly based on fear of his
    a. ambitions.   **c.** physical illness.
    b. popularity.   **d.** military strength.

Selection Test

_____ **8.** The conspirators want Brutus on their side mainly in order to

    a. gain financial assets.

    b. win the support of the military.

    c. establish Brutus as the new leader.

    d. make their campaign seem respectable.

Interpreting and Evaluating (8 points total; 4 points each)

Listeners are often affected by the rhythm of iambic pentameter. For each series of lines below, notice the stressed and unstressed syllables. Then describe what the rhythm of the language suggests to you, and briefly explain what may account for this effect.

> **FLAVIUS.** Go, go, good countrymen, and, for this fault,
> Assemble all the poor men of your sort;
> Draw them to Tiber banks and weep your tears
> Into the channel, till the lowest stream
> Do kiss the most exalted shores of all.

9. What does the rhythm of the language suggest to you?

Why?

> **BRUTUS.** Be not deceiv'd: if I have veil'd my look,
> I turn the trouble of my countenance
> Merely upon myself. Vexed I am
> Of late with passions of some difference,
> Conceptions only proper to myself,
> Which give some soil, perhaps, to my behaviors;

10. What does the rhythm of the language suggest to you?

Why?

Evaluating and Connecting (20 points)

Use a separate sheet of paper to answer ONE of the following essay questions.

11. Describe the difference between the way Cassius behaves when he is with Brutus and the way he behaves when he is away from him. Why might he behave differently while he is with Brutus?

12. In what sense is Brutus in conflict with himself?

Selection Test

Score

The Tragedy of Julius Caesar, Act 2 (page 800)

Recalling and Interpreting (72 points total; 8 points each)
Write the letter of the best answer. This exercise is continued on the next page.

_____ 1. At the beginning of act 2, what is Brutus's attitude toward killing Caesar?
    a. He is searching for a way to avoid this step.
    b. He is upset, but certain that it must be done.
    c. He is still trying to make up his mind about it.
    d. He is convinced that a "wait and see" approach is best.

_____ 2. Cassius worries that Caesar may not leave his home on this particular day because of
    a. illness.
    b. other plans.
    c. the strange events of the night.
    d. being warned about the ides of March.

_____ 3. Brutus urges the conspirators to spare Mark Antony, claiming that Antony
    a. is too widely beloved.
    b. is not a serious threat to them.
    c. lacks the courage to oppose them.
    d. has more loyalty to them than to Caesar.

_____ 4. Decius boasts of his ability to influence Caesar by
    a. flattering him.
    b. reasoning with him.
    c. appealing to his sense of humor.
    d. reminding him of his responsibilities.

_____ 5. Brutus's behavior makes Portia believe that her husband is
    a. ill.   **c.** troubled.
    b. angry.   **d.** disloyal to Caesar.

_____ 6. Caesar interprets the prophecy of the beast without a heart to mean that
    a. cruel, heartless men are plotting against him.
    b. he would be a heartless coward to stay at home.
    c. Calphurnia is heartless to beg him to stay at home.
    d. it would be heartless of him to ignore his wife's concerns.

_____ 7. Decius persuades Caesar to go to the Senate by using all of the following arguments EXCEPT that Caesar
    a. cannot fulfill his duties at home.
    b. has misinterpreted Calphurnia's dream.
    c. might lose his opportunity to be crowned king.
    d. might be mocked by the Senators if they suspected fear.

Selection Test

_____ 8. In his letter, Artemidorus warns Caesar of
a. men plotting against him.
b. opposition from the gods.
c. signs predicting his death.
d. an attack by a foreign enemy.

_____ 9. At the end of act 2, Portia's behavior demonstrates feelings of
a. pity for Caesar.   c. distrust of Brutus.
b. fear for her safety.   d. worry about Brutus.

Interpreting and Evaluating (12 points total; 6 points each)
Consider the use of asides in the following exchange of lines. Note why you think the characters speak the lines as asides and what the asides reveal about the characters.

> **CAESAR.** Be near me, that I may remember you.
> **TREBONIUS.** Caesar I will [*Aside.*] and so near will I be,
> That your best friends shall wish I had been further.
> **CAESAR.** Good friends, go in, and taste some wine with me,
> And we, like friends, will straightway go together.
> **BRUTUS.** [*Aside.*] That every like is not the same, O Caesar,
> The heart of Brutus yearns to think upon.

10. Why does Trebonius use an aside?	11. Why does Brutus use an aside?
What does his aside reveal about him?	What does his aside reveal about him?

Evaluating and Connecting (16 points)
Use a separate sheet of paper to answer the following essay question.

13. When does act 2, scene 1 take place? What kind of atmosphere does the setting help to create? How is this appropriate to the action of the scene?

Selection Test

The Tragedy of Julius Caesar, Act 3 (page 820)

Recalling and Interpreting (70 points total; 7 points each)
Write the letter of the best answer. This exercise is continued on the next page.

_____ 1. Artemidorus tries to get Caesar's attention in an effort to
      a. warn him.   **c.** distract him.
      b. praise him.   **d.** beg a favor of him.

_____ 2. At the beginning of this act, the mood of the conspirators could best be described as
      a. eagerly excited.   **c.** angry and aggressive.
      b. timid and reluctant.   **d.** anxious and suspicious.

_____ 3. In responding to the request for Publius Cimber's freedom, Caesar reveals feelings of
      a. doubt and insecurity.
      b. concern and sympathy.
      c. conceit and confidence.
      d. suspicion of the petitioners's motives.

_____ 4. When Caesar remarks, *"Et tu, Brute?"* he is expressing his
      a. fear of Brutus's strength.
      b. willingness to forgive Brutus.
      c. realization that Brutus never loved him.
      d. surprise that Brutus would turn against him.

_____ 5. Immediately after Caesar is killed, the Roman people respond with
      a. silent disbelief.   **c.** fear and panic.
      b. angry rebellion.   **d.** joyous celebration.

_____ 6. Cassius does not want Antony to speak at Caesar's funeral because he has fears regarding all of the following EXCEPT that
      a. no one knows what will happen.
      b. Antony may not speak well of Caesar.
      c. Brutus may be swayed by Antony's words.
      d. Antony may turn the people against the conspirators.

_____ 7. As Brutus speaks to the crowd, his listeners respond with
      a. disbelief.   **c.** grudging acceptance.
      b. adoring support.   **d.** demands for a full explanation.

_____ 8. Antony's funeral speech convinces the Roman people that the conspirators are
      a. foolish.   **c.** traitorous.
      b. honorable.   **d.** well-meaning but misguided.

Selection Test

_____ 9. Antony refers to the wound that Brutus gave Caesar as "the most unkindest cut of all" because
   a. Caesar loved Brutus.
   b. Brutus was unnecessarily cruel.
   c. Brutus stabbed Caesar in the heart.
   d. this was the wound that actually killed Caesar.

_____ 10. The angry mob attacks Cinna the poet because he
   a. questions their right to riot.
   b. declares that he hated Caesar.
   c. begs for mercy for the conspirators.
   d. has the same name as one of the conspirators.

Interpreting and Evaluating (15 points total; 5 points each)

Think about how Antony speaks in the presence of the conspirators and when he is alone with Caesar's body. Then answer the questions in the boxes.

11. How does Antony speak in the presence of the conspirators?	12. How does Antony speak when he is alone with Caesar's body?

13. What do you think accounts for the differences?

Evaluating and Connecting (15 points)

Use a separate sheet of paper to answer ONE of the following essay questions.

14. What might account for Brutus's use of prose versus Antony's use of verse in their addresses to the crowd?

15. In Antony's funeral oration, why do you think he repeatedly refers to Brutus as "an honorable man"?

Selection and Theme Assessment

Selection Test

The Tragedy of Julius Caesar, Act 4 (page 842)

Recalling and Interpreting (70 points total; 7 points each)
Write the letter of the best answer. This exercise is continued on the next page.

_____ 1. Antony sends for Caesar's will in order to determine whether
    a. the will is genuine.
    b. Caesar left money for him personally.
    c. he can use some of the money for military purposes.
    d. he can decrease the amount of money for the people.

_____ 2. Antony regards Lepidus as
    a. a lazy tag-along.
    b. an equal partner.
    c. an undeserving underling.
    d. an unreliable threat to his power.

_____ 3. When Brutus refers to Cassius as "a hot friend cooling," he means that Cassius
    a. is no longer angry with him.
    b. is coming around to his point of view.
    c. has lost his sense of drive and purpose.
    d. feels less friendship for him than he once did.

_____ 4. When Lucius Pella is punished for taking bribes, Cassius is angry for each of the following reasons EXCEPT that
    a. the punishment is too harsh.
    b. he believes Lucius was innocent.
    c. his request for leniency was ignored.
    d. Brutus is rigid in his application of the law.

_____ 5. In his argument with Cassius, Brutus accuses Cassius of
    a. greed.   **c.** weakness.
    b. ambition.   **d.** disloyalty.

_____ 6. Cassius claims superiority over Brutus in
    a. honesty.   **c.** experience.
    b. courage.   **d.** moral worthiness.

_____ 7. Brutus claims superiority over Cassius in
    a. honesty.   **c.** experience.
    b. courage.   **d.** practicality.

_____ 8. Brutus begins to get over his anger with Cassius when he sees that Cassius is
    a. just as angry as he is.
    b. innocent of all Brutus's charges.
    c. hurt and dismayed by their conflict.
    d. regretful about the assassination of Caesar.

Selection Test

_____ 9. Brutus wants to march to Philippi because he
   a. believes that the time is right.
   b. regards it as a matter of honor.
   c. wants to make a surprise attack.
   d. wants to get the battle over with.

_____ 10. The appearance of Caesar's ghost foreshadows the idea that
   a. Brutus will become the ruler of Rome.
   b. Brutus will suffer a mental breakdown.
   c. revenge will be taken for Caesar's murder.
   d. the ideals of the Roman republic cannot be destroyed.

Interpreting and Evaluating (16 points total; 8 points each)
Re-read Brutus's justification for following the plan he has proposed and then answer the questions about his words.

> **BRUTUS.** There is a tide in the affairs of men,
> Which, taken at the flood, leads on to fortune;
> Omitted, all the voyage of their life
> Is bound in shallows and in miseries.
> On such a sea are we now afloat,
> And we must take the current when it serves,
> Or lose our ventures.

11. According to Brutus, what happens if you *take* the tide at the flood stage?

    And if you *miss* the tide at flood stage?

12. In simple terms, what is Brutus saying?

Evaluating and Connecting (14 points total)
Use a separate sheet of paper to answer the following essay question.

13. Why do you think Cassius finally goes along with Brutus's plan to march to Philippi?

Selection Test

The Tragedy of Julius Caesar, Act 5 (page 858)

Recalling and Interpreting (64 points total; 8 points each)
Write the letter of the best answer. This exercise is continued on the next page.

_____ 1. The opposing generals meet and talk with one another in order to
    a. establish the rules of battle.
    b. insult and challenge one another.
    c. make one last attempt to achieve peace.
    d. determine the other side's willingness to fight.

_____ 2. Cassius regards the sight of ravens, crows, and kites as a
    a. coincidence.
    b. symbol of power.
    c. sign of defeat and death.
    d. representation of the enemy.

_____ 3. Brutus confesses that he would rather commit suicide than
    a. be returned to Rome in defeat.
    b. die at the hands of his enemies.
    c. have to admit that he was wrong.
    d. face Antony and Octavius in battle.

_____ 4. Cassius and Brutus bid each other farewell because they
    a. intend to end their alliance.
    b. know that they are about to die.
    c. secretly plan to commit suicide.
    d. believe that it's possible they will be killed.

_____ 5. Cassius regards Brutus's decision to attack Octavius's troops early as a
    a. tactical error.
    b. foolish whim.
    c. clever strategy.
    d. courageous move.

_____ 6. Cassius decides to commit suicide when he
    a. is lied to by Pindarus.
    b. misinterprets what Pindarus sees.
    c. correctly interprets what Pindarus sees.
    d. realizes that he about to be captured by the enemy.

_____ 7. Upon finding Cassius's body, Titinius commits suicide in order to
    a. prove his courage.
    b. demonstrate his loyalty to Cassius.
    c. avoid being blamed for Cassius's death.
    d. distract the enemy and give Brutus a chance to escape.

Selection Test   *(continued)*

_____ 8. As Brutus dies, he calls on Caesar to
   a. forgive him.
   b. take pleasure in his death.
   c. recognize him as a worthy Roman.
   d. consider the assassination revenged.

Interpreting and Evaluating (16 points total; 8 points each)
This play's title refers only to Julius Caesar. Does this make sense to you? Think about the characters and events of the play, and then answer the questions in the boxes below.

The Tragedy of Julius Caesar

9. Why might this title be considered? appropriate	10. Why might this title be considered inappropriate?

Evaluating and Connecting (20 points)
Use a separate sheet of paper to answer the following essay question.

11. One of Brutus's most striking characteristics is his idealism. Although this trait is admirable, it can also be seen as a tragic flaw. How does Brutus's idealism, throughout the play, help to lead to his downfall?

Selection and Theme Assessment

Selection Test

The Ring of General Macías (page 878)
and Marked (page 897)

Recalling and Interpreting (49 points total; 7 points each)
Write the letter of the best answer.

_____ 1. Raquel's statements about what she would wait for if her husband, Domingo, died
suggest that she believes
  a. little would change.
  b. she would lose her mind.
  c. she would never adjust to the loss.
  d. she would find comfort in daily routines.

_____ 2. In talking with Marica, Raquel indicates that the trait she finds most important in Domingo is his
  a. wealth.   c. intelligence.
  b. courage.   d. love for her.

_____ 3. Raquel's first reactions to Andrés and Cleto are
  a. fearful.   c. scornful.
  b. pitying.   d. respectful.

_____ 4. In dealing with the Federal captain, Raquel uses all of the following EXCEPT
  a. cleverness.   c. her social position.
  b. her beauty.   d. her husband's reputation.

_____ 5. Cleto is surprised to discover that Raquel is unusually
  a. brave.   c. proud.
  b. clever.   d. beautiful.

_____ 6. Raquel realizes that she has the power to affect all of the following EXCEPT
  a. the upcoming battle.
  b. her husband's survival.
  c. her husband's reputation.
  d. the final result of the war.

_____ 7. In "Marked," the speaker suggests that one should behave with
  a. caution.   c. confidence.
  b. kindness.   d. responsibility.

Using Vocabulary (15 points total; 3 points each)
Write the letter of the best answer. This exercise is continued on the next page.

_____ 8. A person who behaves ostentatiously is often referred to as a
  a. bully.   b. coward.   c. show-off.

_____ 9. A repressed laugh often comes out as a
  a. howl.   b. groan.   c. snicker.

_____ 10. One would be most likely to use the word *notorious* to refer to a famous
  a. actor.   b. criminal.   c. military leader.

_____ **11.** A word that means the opposite of *impertinent* is
   a. *polite*.   **b.** *fragile*.   **c.** *courageous*.

_____ **12.** A person who behaves regally seems to be quite
   a. shy.   **b.** witty.   **c.** self-confident.

Interpreting and Evaluating (18 points total; 6 points each)
Answer the questions below about the irony in the following lines from the play.

> **ANDRÉS.** You'll have to hurry that letter. The district is clear now.
>
> **RAQUEL.** I'll be through in just a moment. You might as well finish the wine while you're waiting.
>
> **ANDRÉS.** Thank you. A most excellent idea.
>
> **RAQUEL.** Why don't you give some to—Cleto?
>
> **ANDRÉS.** This is too fine a wine to waste on that boy.
>
> **RAQUEL.** He'll probably never have another chance to taste such wine.
>
> **ANDRÉS.** Very well. Pour yourself a glass, Cleto.
>
> **CLETO.** Thank you. [*He pours it*.] Your health, my captain.

13. How do these lines illustrate dramatic irony?

14. What verbal irony exists in these lines?

15. How do these lines add to situational irony in the play?

Evaluating and Connecting (18 points)
Use a separate sheet of paper to answer the following essay question.

16. What does Raquel gain by killing Andrés and Cleto? What does she lose?

Selection Test

from Le Morte d'Arthur (page 914)

Recalling and Interpreting (48 points total; 12 points each)
Write the letter of the best answer.

_____ 1. King Uther enters into an agreement with Merlin because of Uther's desire for
   a. safety.   c. a child.
   b. power.   d. Lady Igraine.

_____ 2. When Arthur is told the truth about his royal birth, he responds with
   a. fear.   c. delight.
   b. anger.   d. confusion.

_____ 3. Sir Launcelot goes off in search of adventure, looking for opportunities to
   a. learn new skills.   c. prove his fighting skills.
   b. discover new lands.   d. rid the kingdom of danger.

_____ 4. In this story, Sir Launcelot could be described as all of the following EXCEPT
   a. honest.   c. violent.
   b. modest.   d. dependable.

Using Vocabulary (10 points total; 2 points each)
For each underlined word, write the letter of the word that means the OPPOSITE.

_____ 5. accost   a. calm

_____ 6. ignoble   b. avoid

_____ 7. abashed   c. proud

_____ 8. prowess   d. honorable

_____ 9. tumultuous   e. incompetence

Interpreting and Evaluating (20 points total; 10 points each)
Read Sir Tarquine's comment below. Then note TWO things it reveals about his personality or values.

| "You are the most powerful knight I have fought yet, but I fear you may be the one whom in the whole world I most hate. If you are not, for the love of you I will release all my prisoners and swear eternal friendship." | 10. |
| | 11. |

Evaluating and Connecting (22 points)
Use a separate sheet of paper to answer the following essay question.

12. What would you say are Sir Launcelot's most impressive qualities and talents? How are they revealed? Do they make him heroic? Explain your opinions.

Selection Test

from **Sundiata** (page 934)

Recalling and Interpreting (45 points total; 15 points each)
Write the letter of the best answer.

_____ 1. Sundiata first becomes an object of admiration because of his
        a. loyalty.   **c.** wisdom.
        b. bravery.   **d.** strength.

_____ 2. Sundiata expects Balla Fasséké to help to inspire the soldiers and to
        a. be his advisor.   **c.** guarantee his lasting fame.
        b. protect his life.   **d.** justify his claim to the throne.

_____ 3. The various kings and chiefs aligned with Sundiata impress the army with
demonstrations of their
        a. loyalty.   **c.** cleverness.
        b. bravery.   **d.** physical ability.

Using Vocabulary (15 points total; 5 points each)
Write the letter of the best answer.

_____ 4. You could perpetuate a lie about someone by
        a. ignoring it.   **b.** repeating it.   **c.** challenging it.

_____ 5. The most important quality in a confidante is that he or she be
        a. clever.   **b.** self-assured.   **c.** trustworthy.

_____ 6. A word that means the opposite of *scrupulous* is
        a. *weak*.   **b.** *careless*.   **c.** *unfortunate*.

Interpreting and Evaluating (20 points total; 10 points each)
**What cultural values of ancient Mali do you see in this selection? In the boxes, note
two such values and how they are revealed.**

Values	How they are revealed
7.	
8.	

Evaluating and Connecting (20 points)
Use a separate sheet of paper to answer the following essay question.

9. Given the description of a tall tale, do you think this selection qualifies? Explain.

Selection and Theme Assessment

Open-Book Selection Test

The Passing of Arthur (page 944)

Recalling and Interpreting (64 points total; 8 points each)
Write the letter of the best answer. This exercise is continued on the next page.

_____ 1. Sir Bedivere twice disobeys King Arthur's orders to throw Excalibur into the lake because Bedivere
      a. wants to use himself.
      b. fears being accused of stealing it.
      c. knows it is worth a great deal of money.
      d. believes it could help Arthur's fame continue.

_____ 2. King Arthur believes that he may return someday to rule again, because
      a. Merlin has predicted this.
      b. the three queens promise this.
      c. he thinks of himself as immortal.
      d. he has always escaped danger in the past.

_____ 3. King Arthur persuades Sir Bedivere to throw Excalibur into the lake by
      a. repeatedly insisting that Bedivere follow his orders.
      b. describing the dangers of its coming into the wrong hands.
      c. explaining that this would make a mysterious barge appear.
      d. explaining that this was required of him when he received it.

_____ 4. What quality of Excalibur most impresses Sir Bedivere?
      a. its weight
      b. its beauty
      c. its sharpness
      d. its magical power

_____ 5. King Arthur's reaction to the sight of the barge suggests that
      a. it frightens him.
      b. it depresses him.
      c. he had expected it.
      d. he cannot believe his eyes.

_____ 6. The three queens receive King Arthur with
      a. joy.   **c.** relief.
      b. anger.   **d.** sadness.

_____ 7. When Sir Bedivere asks King Arthur what he should do, Arthur asks him to
      a. avenge him.
      b. pray for his soul.
      c. continue his work.
      d. tell the story of Camelot.

Open-Book Selection Test
(continued)

_____ 8. When the barge departs, Sir Bedivere climbs as high as he can in order to
      a. throw himself to his death.
      b. find a place to build a shrine.
      c. watch the barge as long as possible.
      d. get as far as possible from the place of tombs.

Interpreting and Evaluating (21 points total; 7 points each)
In the boxes below, describe the important elements of this narrative poem.

9. Describe the conflict.	10. Describe the resolution.

11. What do you think the climax of this story is? Why?

Evaluating and Connecting (15 points)
Use a separate sheet of paper to answer the following essay question.

12. What qualities and traits in King Arthur are revealed by this excerpt from *Idylls of the King,* and how are they revealed?

Selection and Theme Assessment

Selection Test

Arthur Becomes King (page 961)

Recalling and Interpreting (56 points total; 8 points each)
Write the letter of the best answer.

_____ 1. How do the people at the Forest Sauvage react to the news of King Uther's death?
     a. sadly   **c.** fearfully
     b. joyfully   **d.** with disbelief

_____ 2. In the parts of this excerpt set at the Forest Sauvage, the tone is mainly
     a. objective.   **c.** light-hearted.
     b. suspenseful.   **d.** formal and solemn.

_____ 3. Sir Ector agrees to go to London in the belief that the travelers can
     a. find out what is going on.
     b. have an entertaining adventure.
     c. make friends with political leaders.
     d. compete to become the next king of England.

_____ 4. Wart is offended and upset when Kay offers to pay him a shilling because
     a. this is such a small amount.
     b. this is too much for a simple errand.
     c. doing so suggests that Kay feels superior.
     d. doing so suggests that the errand will be difficult for Wart.

_____ 5. Wart forgives Kay for his treatment of him when he realizes that
     a. he will have a chance, later, to get even.
     b. he is not really Kay's biological brother.
     c. Kay is a knight, and he is just Kay's squire.
     d. Kay is simply suffering from a case of nerves.

_____ 6. Even though the sword in the stone appears to be valuable, Wart decides to borrow it because he
     a. cannot bear to disappoint Kay.
     b. believes the sword is his, by right.
     c. wants the shilling Kay has offered.
     d. fears punishment if he returns without a sword.

_____ 7. The excerpt suggests that Kay eventually tells the truth about how he came by the sword because he
     a. fears his father's anger.
     b. is, at heart, an honest person.
     c. wants Wart to treat him well.
     d. realizes that no one will believe him.

Selection Test

Using Vocabulary (10 points total; 2 points each)
Write the letter of the best answer.

_____ 8. An activity that is almost always done petulantly is
    a. sulking.   **b.** bragging.   **c.** gossiping.

_____ 9. When people throng, they are likely to feel
    a. fearful.   **b.** jostled.   **c.** soothed.

_____ 10. One would expect to find a sumptuous lifestyle in a
    a. mansion.   **b.** log cabin.   **c.** refugee camp.

_____ 11. A person would be likely to behave ruefully if he or she felt
    a. lonely.   **b.** excited.   **c.** ashamed.

_____ 12. A word that means the opposite of *vulgar* is
    a. *lucky*.   **b.** *silent*.   **c.** *tasteful*.

Interpreting and Evaluating (18 points total; 9 points each)
Consider how Wart's feelings about the sword change over the course of the excerpt. Then answer the questions in the boxes.

13. How does Wart feel about the sword the first time he removes it?	14. How does he feel about the sword at the end of the excerpt?
Why does he feel this way?	Why does he feel this way?

Evaluating and Connecting (16 points)
Use a separate sheet of paper to answer the following essay question.

15. What do you think the story suggests is the source of the power that allows Wart to remove the sword from the stone when no one else can? Think about the magical sights, sounds, and creatures in the churchyard and how you interpret these things.

     Selection and Theme Assessment

Selection Test

Where the Girl Rescued Her Brother (page 982)

Recalling and Interpreting (40 points total; 8 points each)
Write the letter of the best answer.

_____ 1. In order to belong to the Society of Quilters, a Cheyenne woman has to have
    a. great artistic skill.
    b. strength of character.
    c. a reputation as a warrior.
    d. the right family background.

_____ 2. The story suggests that the grizzly bear retreated from the women because it
    a. mistook them for men.
    b. was unwilling to harm anyone.
    c. had been weakened by an injury.
    d. recognized their determination and courage.

_____ 3. Crazy Horse's cry, "It is a good day to die," suggests that
    a. all of Crook's soldiers will die.
    b. he intends to fight to the death.
    c. he sees the battle as a suicide mission.
    d. sorrow has taken away his will to live.

_____ 4. The story suggests that Buffalo Calf Road Woman's action during the battle is
motivated mainly by her
    a. love for her brother.
    b. belief in magical protection.
    c. hatred of the "spider people."
    d. desire to demonstrate courage.

_____ 5. The story suggests that what the fighting men find most remarkable about the
rescue of Comes-in-Sight is that it is
    a. so sudden.
    b. so skillful.
    c. accomplished by a woman.
    d. accomplished by a Cheyenne.

Using Vocabulary (12 points total; 4 points each)
Write the letter of the best answer. This exercise is continued on the next page.

_____ 6. In order to vault, one must always use the muscles of the
    a. arms.   **b.** legs.   **c.** shoulders.

_____ 7. A person who makes a strategic decision is attempting to be
    a. helpful.   **b.** practical.   **c.** courageous.

Selection Test

_____ 8. To confront an enemy is to
        a. meet the enemy.
        b. defeat the enemy.
        c. bewilder the enemy.

Interpreting and Evaluating (36 points total; 12 points each)
**Like most legends, this one reveals a good deal about the values of the culture from
which it comes. In each box on the left, identify a cultural value that the legend
reveals. In each box on the right, explain how the legend reveals that cultural value.**

Cultural Value	How does the legend reveal this value?
9.	
10.	
11.	

Evaluating and Connecting (12 points)
Use a separate sheet of paper to answer the following essay question.

12. What moment in this legend did you find most suspenseful? What made that moment so
suspenseful?

Selection Test

Let's Sweat! (page 1002)

Recalling and Interpreting (45 points total; 15 points each)
Write the letter of the best answer.

_____ 1. When Giovanni asks who is playing in the World Series, the men laugh at her because
     a. they had already told her the answer.
     b. she could tell if she just looked at the TV.
     c. anyone who followed baseball at all would know.
     d. knowing which teams are involved is not the important issue.

_____ 2. Steve Krieder's comment about "a failure of our educational system" is meant to suggest that, even though he is a professional football player, he
     a. thinks fans overdo their devotion.
     b. never received much of an education.
     c. cares about education, just as other people do.
     d. cares more about the fans than they do about him.

_____ 3. Giovanni suggests that bowling is her favorite sport to watch on TV because
     a. it involves so few statistics.
     b. it is a completely nonviolent sport.
     c. she likes individual, rather than team, sports.
     d. it's easy to see the ball and understand the game.

Interpreting and Evaluating (30 points total; 15 points each)
In the boxes, note TWO things that can be inferred about Giovanni from this personal essay and provide details that support these inferences.

Giovanni is the type of person who is . . .	I can tell this because . . .
4.	
5.	

Evaluating and Connecting (25 points)
Use a separate sheet of paper to answer the following essay question.

6. What seems to be the main thing that Giovanni gets from athletics? Explain.

Open-Book Selection Test

From A Cat's Garden of Verses (page 1009)

Score

Recalling and Interpreting (56 points total; 14 points each)
Write the letter of the best answer.

_____ 1. Stevenson's cat could be described as all of the following EXCEPT
      a. hungry.   **c.** bloodthirsty.
      b. sentimental.   **d.** bitter or vengeful.

_____ 2. In which poem does the speaker express a fond wish?
      a. The Rain   **c.** Whole Duty of Cats
      b. Mealtime   **d.** Catty Thoughts

_____ 3. In which poem does the speaker declare a "rule" for cats?
      a. The Rain   **c.** Whole Duty of Cats
      b. Mealtime   **d.** Catty Thoughts

_____ 4. All of the poems contain alliteration in the last line EXCEPT
      a. The Rain.   **c.** Whole Duty of Cats.
      b. Mealtime.   **d.** Catty Thoughts.

Interpreting and Evaluating (24 points total; 8 points each)
In the boxes, compare the chief elements of "The Rain" with those of the poem it parodies (which is printed in the "Literary Elements" section on page 1011.)

5. *The Poem:* Stevenson's "Rain"		6. *The Parody:* Beard's "The Rain"
	Tone	
	Imagery	
	Theme or Idea Communicated	

Evaluating and Connecting (20 points)
Use a separate sheet of paper to answer the following essay question.

7. In a paragraph, explain how the poet created humor in "Whole Duty of Cats."

Selection Test

Appetizer (page 1015)

Recalling and Interpreting (45 points total; 9 points each)
Write the letter of the best answer.

_____ 1. How does the bear react to being provided with fish?
  a. She begins to fish for herself.
  b. She becomes suspicious of the narrator.
  c. She becomes dangerously eager for more.
  d. She threatens the narrator in order to keep the fish coming.

_____ 2. Which of these sayings seems to guide the bear's actions?
  a. Waste not, want not.
  b. A penny saved is a penny earned.
  c. A bird in the hand is worth two in the bush.
  d. Don't kill the goose that lays the golden eggs.

_____ 3. "I walk a few paces down the stream, hoping the bear will remember an
  appointment or become distracted and I can sneak away."
  In this passage, what literary technique does the author use to create humor?
  a. simile   c. alliteration
  b. personification d. exaggeration

_____ 4. "I have told myself for many years that I really do love nature, love being among
  the animals, am restored by wilderness adventure. Considering that right now I
  would like nothing better than to be nestled by my wife in front of a blazing fire,
  this seems to be a sentiment in need of some revision."
  In this passage, what does the author use to create humor?
  a. punning   c. understatement
  b. exaggeration   d. extended comparison

_____ 5. "His whole bearing—pardon the expression—tells me my intrusion into this bear
  world is a personal affront to his honor."
  In this passage, the author uses all of the following to create humor EXCEPT
  a. punning.   c. personification.
  b. word choice.   d. extended comparison.

Using Vocabulary (15 points total; 3 points each)
Write the letter of the best answer. This exercise is continued on the next page.

_____ 6. You respond to someone raptly if he or she
  a. angers you.   b. amuses you.   c. fascinates you.

_____ 7. If you are guilty of an impropriety, you have shown
  a. cruelty.   b. bad manners.   c. disregard for the law.

_____ 8. An example of a profound emotion is
  a. rage.   b. affection.   c. irritation.

Selection Test

_____ 9. One feels bereft as the result of
       a. a loss.   **b.** a threat.   **c.** an insult.

_____ 10. A person who does what is most expedient can be described as
       a. lazy.   **b.** selfish.   **c.** efficient.

Interpreting and Evaluating (20 points total; 5 points each)
In the top three boxes, describe the plot complications that are part of the rising action of this story. In the fourth box, describe the climax, or the moment of greatest suspense.

RISING ACTION	11. Plot complication
	12. Plot complication
	13. Plot complication

CLIMAX	14.

Evaluating and Connecting (20 points)
Use a separate sheet of paper to answer the following essay question.

15. List THREE words or phrases you would use to describe the narrator based on what happens in the story. Explain how you can tell that these descriptions are true of him.

Selection Test

from An American Childhood (page 1029)

Recalling and Interpreting (54 points total; 9 points each)
Write the letter of the best answer.

_____ 1. Mother often repeats the phrase, "Terwilliger bunts one," because she
     a. likes the sound.
     b. is a baseball fan.
     c. thinks it has a hidden meaning.
     d. wants to ridicule the announcer.

_____ 2. Mother repeats the names of things that
     a. sound unusual.
     b. sound French or Latin.
     c. others usually mispronounce.
     d. remind her of French or Latin.

_____ 3. When other people beat Mother to the punch line, she is
     a. annoyed.   c. embarrassed.
     b. delighted.   d. disappointed.

_____ 4. Mother has a tendency to do odd things when she is feeling
     a. sleepy.   c. bored.
     b. confused.   d. insecure.

_____ 5. In Mother's vocabulary, an "intelligent" utensil is one that
     a. is complicated.
     b. works all by itself.
     c. has more than one use.
     d. does well what it is supposed to do.

_____ 6. Mother thinks people should do all of the following EXCEPT
     a. tolerate cruelty.
     b. have unpopular opinions.
     c. stand up for what they believe.
     d. behave in an unconventional manner.

Using Vocabulary (10 points total; 2 points each)
Write the letter of the best answer. This exercise is continued on the next page.

_____ 7. A person is likely to speak tremulously if he or she is
     a. bored.   b. amused.   c. emotionally moved.

_____ 8. Responsible parents tell their children to eschew
     a. homework.   b. illegal drugs.   c. loyal friends.

_____ 9. A stolid person usually appears to be quite
     a. shy.   b. calm.   c. nervous.

Selection Test *(continued)*

_____ **10.** A word that means the opposite of *advocate* is
   a. *oppose.*   **b.** *persist.*   **c.** *complete.*

_____ **11.** Ostracism tends to make a person feel like
   a. a hero.   **b.** a weakling.   **c.** an outsider.

Interpreting and Evaluating (16 points)

12. In the passage below, underline each example of hyperbole. Then, on the right, explain what the passage reveals about the kind of person the author's mother was and what was important to her.

"Look," she said. "Whoever designed this corkscrew never used one. Why would anyone sell it without trying it out?" So she invented a better one. She showed me a drawing of it. The spirit of American enterprise never faded in Mother. If capitalizing and tooling up had been as interesting as theorizing and thinking up, she would have fired up a new factory every week, and chaired several hundred corporations.

Evaluating and Connecting (20 points)
Use a separate sheet of paper to answer the following essay question.

13. Imagine that the author's mother were your mother. What TWO things do you think you would like best about having her for a mother, and what TWO things do you think you would like least? Explain.

Selection Test

Score

What Is and Ain't Grammatical (page 1038)

Recalling and Interpreting (48 points total; 12 points each)
Write the letter of the best answer.

_____ 1. Which of the following sentences would Dave Barry say might prevent an applicant from getting a job as a firefighter?
     a. "The smell of anything burning makes me feel, like, super icky."
     b. "All I want is to wear them waterproof coats and boots so's I look cool."
     c. "Hope nobody'll have a duck fit if I refuse to climb a ladder, being as how heights are scary!"
     d. "I can't find a place on the application where I can write my fourteen life-saving awards down."

_____ 2. In defining an infinitive as "the word 'to' and whatever comes right behind it," Barry is pretending that
     a. he doesn't know what an infinitive is.
     b. no one can actually understand infinitives.
     c. there are no real rules about using infinitives.
     d. there are far too many rules about using infinitives.

_____ 3. Which of the following might Barry accept as a third rule of American grammar?
     a. Nouns are modified by adjectives.
     b. It is always better to use *whom* than *who*.
     c. "Is not" or "are not" is always better than "ain't."
     d. Verbs should agree with their subjects in number.

_____ 4. "Remember Elliot? He sounded extremely British, and as a result he got to be Attorney General, Secretary of State, Chief Justice of the Supreme Court and Vice President *at the same time*."
Which of the following literary techniques does Barry use to create humor in this passage?
     a. idioms   c. hyperbole
     b. metaphor   d. alliteration

Using Vocabulary (12 points total; 4 points each)
Write the letter of the best answer. This exercise is continued on the next page.

_____ 5. A prospective college student is one who is
     a. attending the college.
     b. applying to the college.
     c. risking flunking out of the college.

_____ 6. If you find an essay to be enlightening, it
     a. amuses you.   b. confuses you.   c. teaches you something.

_____ 7. A person who drones usually makes his or her listeners feel
     a. guilty.   b. bored.   c. entertained.

Selection Test

Interpreting and Evaluating (20 points total; 10 points each)

Each quotation on the left contains an allusion. In the boxes on the right, explain what is wrong with those allusions—that is, what Barry deliberately misunderstands about the situations he alludes to that makes the allusions humorous.

Allusion	Deliberate Misunderstanding
8. "Take the poet Geoffrey Chaucer, who couldn't even spell his first name right."	
9. "When the colonists came to America, they rebelled against British grammar."	
10. "[W]hen they wrote the Declaration of Independence, they deliberately misspelled many words."	

Evaluating and Connecting (20 points)

Use a separate sheet of paper to answer the following essay question.

11. What people, practices, situations and/or institutions is Barry ridiculing in this essay, and what point do you think he is making about them?

Name _____ Date _____ Class _____

Selection Test

The Car We Had to Push (page 1044)

Recalling and Interpreting (48 points total; 8 points each)
Write the letter of the best answer.

_____ 1. The narrator suggests that, as a boy, he responded to the Get-Ready man with
    a. fear.   **c.** pity.
    b. interest.   **d.** mocking amusement.

_____ 2. The Get-Ready man's shouted warnings during *King Lear* are particularly amusing for all of the following reasons EXCEPT that they occur
    a. when the stage and theater are dark.
    b. during one of the play's most light-hearted scenes.
    c. while one of the play's characters is also behaving quite oddly.
    d. while the mood of the characters is similar to the mood of the man.

_____ 3. The narrator suggests that he would like to relive the "exploding car" experience because
    a. the joke worked so well.
    b. the joke could be better arranged.
    c. he has begun to forget the details.
    d. not enough people witnessed the event.

_____ 4. In saying that his mother couldn't tell car parts from pantry utensils, the narrator suggests that she
    a. knew nothing about cars.
    b. knew nothing about cooking.
    c. had particularly bad eyesight.
    d. rarely examined anything closely.

_____ 5. The mother's warnings to her sons to be sure not to drive the car around without gasoline are nonsensical because
    a. gasoline is not a dangerous substance.
    b. a car can't be driven without gasoline.
    c. neither of the boys would ever take such a risk.
    d. driving a car without gasoline is not dangerous.

_____ 6. What does the narrator seem to find particularly amusing about Uncle Zenas's death?
    a. the cause of his death
    b. the results of his death
    c. the age he was when he died
    d. the family's response to his death

Using Vocabulary (15 points total; 3 points each)
For each underlined word, write the letter of the word that means the opposite.

_____ 7. lucid   **a.** neat

_____ 8. contend   **b.** faint

_____ 9. unkempt   **c.** cause

_____ 10. resonant   **d.** deny

_____ 11. repercussion   **e.** confused

Interpreting and Evaluating (21 points total; 7 points each)
For each passage, note something that is revealed about the character described. Then circle *DIRECT* or *INDIRECT* to show which characterization technique is used to reveal this particular piece of information.

Characterization technique(s) used

My father used to get sick at his stomach pushing the car, and very often was unable to go to work. He had never liked the machine, even when it was good, sharing my ignorance and suspicion of all automobiles of twenty years ago and longer.	**12.** What is revealed about the father? *INDIRECT DIRECT*
. . . my brother Roy got together a great many articles from the kitchen, placed them in a square of canvas, and swung this under the car with a string attached to it so that, at a twitch, the canvas would give way and the steel and tin things would clatter to the street. This was a little scheme of Roy's to frighten father . . .	**13.** What is revealed about Roy? *INDIRECT DIRECT*
[My mother] had an idea that the Victrola might blow up. . . . She could only suppose that it was propelled by some newfangled and untested apparatus which was likely to let go at any minute, making us all the victims and martyrs of the wild-eyed Edison's dangerous experiments.	**14.** What is revealed about the mother? *INDIRECT DIRECT*

Evaluating and Connecting (16 points)
Use a separate sheet of paper to answer the following question.

15. What characteristics do you think a person would need to be able to live happily in the family described in this story? Explain.

Selection Test

How I Changed the War and Won the Game (page 1054)

Recalling and Interpreting (48 points total; 8 points each)
Write the letter of the best answer.

_____ 1. The narrator reads newspapers to Doña Luisa and her friends because
     a. they cannot read.
     b. they cannot read English.
     c. she needs to practice her reading.
     d. she likes to keep the older women company.

_____ 2. Before beginning to read aloud, the narrator usually scans the paper to see which stories
     a. the women can understand.
     b. she is able to summarize best.
     c. will be least upsetting to the women.
     d. will be most interesting to the women.

_____ 3. The women's main reaction to news about battles is
     a. anger at the enemy troops.
     b. concern for their loved ones.
     c. doubt that the stories can be true.
     d. dismay over the military leadership.

_____ 4. The narrator provides inaccurate news one day because she
     a. is tired.
     b. misunderstands the story.
     c. wants to amuse the women.
     d. is irritated at being interrupted.

_____ 5. The ladies react to the narrator's made-up story with
     a. disbelief.   **c.** fear and horror.
     b. amusement.   **d.** anger at the narrator.

_____ 6. In discussing this writer's use of diction, one would describe her
     a. grammatical accuracy.
     b. construction of the plot.
     c. selection and use of words.
     d. use of particular sentence structures.

Using Vocabulary (12 points total; 4 points each)
Write the letter of the best answer. This exercise is continued on the next page.

_____ 7. If someone coerces you to do something, you are likely to feel
     a. proud.   **b.** resentful.   **c.** embarrassed.

_____ 8. Which of the following is the most likely destination for a pilgrimage?
     a. a store   **b.** a shrine   **c.** a local park

Selection Test

_____ **9.** To do something "on a whim" is to give in to

      a. fear.   **b.** anger.   **c.** an impulse.

Interpreting and Evaluating (24 points total; 8 points each)
In the boxes, answer the questions about this selection's main conflict.

10. The selection's main conflict is between . . .
and

11. The conflict exists because . . .	12. It is resolved by . . .

Evaluating and Connecting (16 points)
Use a separate sheet of paper to answer the following essay question.

13. Looking back as an adult, how does the narrator seem to feel about the way she handled the situation she describes in the selection? How can you tell?

Selection Test

A Marriage Proposal (page 1061)

Recalling and Interpreting (42 points total; 6 points each)
Write the letter of the best answer.

_____ 1. When Chubukov first greets Lomov, his attitude toward his neighbor is
    a. hostile.   **c.** friendly.
    b. careful.   **d.** suspicious.

_____ 2. The question of the Oxen Meadows comes up because
    a. Lomov has just come from there.
    b. the two neighbors always argue about them.
    c. Natalia has ordered her workers to mow them.
    d. while preparing to propose, Lomov mentions the two families' lands.

_____ 3. When Lomov offers the meadows to Natalia she responds by
    a. feeling angry and insulted.
    b. temporarily calming down.
    c. insisting on paying for them.
    d. realizing that he cares for her.

_____ 4. Natalia wants Lomov to come back so that
    a. he will propose and she can accept.
    b. he will propose and she can reject him.
    c. they can find another topic to argue about.
    d. they can continue the argument about the meadows.

_____ 5. From Lomov's dialogue, a reader can tell all of the following EXCEPT that he
    a. is easily excited.
    b. is a loving person.
    c. lacks self-confidence.
    d. thinks a great deal about himself.

_____ 6. The one common factor in all of the things Natalia and Lomov argue about is that
they are
    a. about land.
    b. questions of ethics.
    c. old family disputes.
    d. basically unimportant.

_____ 7. At the end of the play, Chubukov insists that Natalia and Lomov get married in a
hurry because Chubukov
    a. wants the meadows.
    b. wants Lomov as a son-in-law.
    c. is so frustrated by the conflicts.
    d. fears that, otherwise, Natalia may never marry.

Selection Test (continued)

Using Vocabulary (12 points total; 4 points each)
Write the letter of the best answer.

_____ 8. A hypochondriac is someone whose health is greatly influenced by his or her

      a. diet.   **b.** heredity.   **c.** imagination.

_____ 9. A pompous person is likely to be described as being

      a. lazy.   **b.** stuck-up.   **c.** argumentative.

_____ 10. A word that means the opposite of *affable* is

      a. *sensitive*.   **b.** *practical*.   **c.** *unfriendly*.

Interpreting and Evaluating (28 points total; 7 points each)
Elements of typical farce are listed on the left. In the boxes, describe these elements as they specifically appear in "A Marriage Proposal."

11. Surprises
12. Exaggeration
13. Physical Action
14. Improbable Events

Evaluating and Connecting (18 points)
Use a separate sheet of paper to answer the following essay question.

15. Identify TWO things that Chekhov pokes fun at in this farce and, in a paragraph or two, explain how he goes about doing so.

Selection and Theme Assessment

Open-Book Theme Test

Theme 1: Transitions

Part A. (40 points total; 20 points each) Use a separate sheet of paper to answer TWO of the following essay questions.

1. Many people in these stories undergo important transitions. Choose any TWO of these people. Write a paragraph or two in which you compare the causes and effects of the transitions that those people experience.

2. Many people in these stories find it necessary either to declare their independence or to defend it. Choose any TWO of these people. Why is independence so important to them? How do they try to claim or defend it? What results from their efforts?

3. Some of these stories involve conflicts that greatly affect parent-child relationships. In some cases, the conflict is between a parent and child. In other cases, the conflict is not between a parent and child but affects a parent-child relationship. Choose TWO examples of conflicts that affect relationships between a parent and child, and explain how they do so.

Part B. (20 points) Many people in these stories prize certain possessions. These possessions may or may not be objects.
- Circle the letter of ONE person.
- Answer the questions in the boxes for the person you have chosen.

a. Maggie in "Everyday Use"
b. Jonathan in "Civil Peace"
c. Jing-mei in "Two Kinds"
d. Luis in "Catch the Moon"

e. Luis's father in "Catch the Moon"
f. Mr. Davies in "A Child, a Dog, the Night"
g. Little Juan in "A Child, a Dog, the Night"
h. Mr. Carpenter in "With All Flags Flying"

What is the prized possession?

⇓

Why does the person prize it?

Name _____ Date _____ Class _____

Open-Book Theme Test
(continued)

Part C. (20 points) In "By the Waters of Babylon," John twice says, "It is better to lose one's life than one's spirit."
- Circle the letter of ONE person. *Do not choose a person from a selection you wrote about in Part B.*
- Indicate whether the person you chose would agree with John's statement or not.
- In the large box, give TWO reasons that support your answer.

a. Chee in "Chee's Daughter"
b. Old Man Fat in "Chee's Daughter"
c. Jonathan in "Civil Peace"
d. Jing-mei in "Two Kinds"

e. Jing-mei's mother in "Two Kinds"
f. Jerry in "Through the Tunnel"
g. the young man in "The Vision Quest"
h. Mr. Carpenter in "With All Flags Flying"

This person would ☐ agree. ☐ disagree.

How can you tell this?

Part D. (20 points total; 10 points each) Think about the symbols in these stories.
- Above each set of boxes, write the letter of ONE symbol. *Do not choose a symbol from a selection that you wrote about in Part B or C.*
- In the boxes, answer the questions about each symbol.

a. Grandma's quilts in "Everyday Use"
b. the VW hubcap in "Catch the Moon"
c. the piano in "Two Kinds"

d. the tunnel in "Through the Tunnel"
e. the picnickers in "What I Have Been Doing Lately"
f. the river in "What I Have Been Doing Lately"

4. Symbol: _____

What do you think it stands for in the story?

Why do you think this?

5. Symbol: _____

What do you think it stands for in the story?

Why do you think this?

Selection and Theme Assessments

Open-Book Theme Test

Theme 2: Making Choices

Part A. (40 points total; 20 points each) Use a separate sheet of paper to answer TWO of the following essay questions.

1. Of all the important choices made in these selections, which one do you think was the best? That is, which choice was the most intelligent or admirable? Which one do you think was the worst, most foolish, or most shameful? Explain.

2. Which TWO characters in these selections do you think undergo the greatest changes? How do they change, and why?

3. Choose TWO characters who make decisions that you would not have made if you were in their place. What decisions would you have made instead, and why?

Part B. (20 points) In many of these selections, the characters seek something important to them.
- Circle the letter of ONE character.
- Then answer the questions in the boxes for the character you have chosen.

a. the young man in "The White Heron"
b. the narrator of "The Boar Hunt"
c. the son in "Delicious Death"
d. Mr. White in "The Monkey's Paw"

e. Mrs. White in "The Monkey's Paw"
f. Carlos's mother in "Tuesday Siesta"
g. Tom in "Contents of the Dead Man's Pocket"
h. Juan in "The Censors"

What does the
character seek?

Why is it
so important
to the character?

What does the
character knowingly
risk or sacrifice
to get it?

Does the character
find what he
or she seeks?
Why or why not?

Open-Book Theme Test

Part C. (20 points) Think about the decisions the characters in these selections make. What do those decisions reveal about their priorities or what is most important to them?

- Circle the letter of ONE character. *Do not choose the same character you wrote about in Part B.*
- In the box on the left, describe an important decision he or she makes.
- In the box on the right, note what this decision reveals about the character's priorities or what he or she values most.

a. Sylvia in "The White Heron"	**f.** Tom in "Contents of the Dead Man's Pocket"
b. the narrator of "The Boar Hunt"	**g.** Juan in "The Censors"
c. the mother in "Delicious Death"	**h.** Lise in "The Ring"
d. Mr. White in "The Monkey's Paw"	**i.** the thief in "The Ring"
e. Carlos's mother in "Tuesday Siesta"	

Decision	Priorities

Part D. (20 points) In many of these selections, the action takes an unexpected turn.
Choose ONE selection. *Do not choose a selection you wrote about in Part B or Part C.*
Answer the questions in the boxes.

a. "The White Heron"	**c.** "The Monkey's Paw"	**e.** "The Censors"
b. "The Boar Hunt"	**d.** "Contents of the Dead Man's Pocket"	**f.** "The Ring"

What unexpected event occurs?	⇒	Who is surprised?
		⇓
		Why is the event surprising?

Open-Book Theme Test

Theme 3: Twists

Part A. (40 points total; 20 points each) Use a separate sheet of paper to answer TWO of the following essay questions.

1. In a paragraph or two, compare how any TWO characters from different stories in this theme are affected by dramatic twists in their lives or perceptions.

2. Bad things happen to some of the characters in this theme. Choose TWO such characters from different stories. Then, in a paragraph or two, discuss the bad things that happen to them, how their lives are affected, and whether you think they deserve what happens to them.

3. Some of the characters in these stories go out of their way to help others. Choose TWO of these characters and explain why their actions are unusually kind and what motivates them to take those actions.

Part B. (20 points) Think about how the plot twists in some of the stories change the reader's perception or understanding.
- Circle the letter of ONE story.
- In the box at the top, describe the plot twist.
- In the boxes at the bottom, answer the questions.

a. "The Happy Man's Shirt"   c. "An Astrologer's Day"   e. "The False Gems"
b. "The Californian's Tale"   d. "The Interlopers"

The Plot Twist

BEFORE the plot twist	AFTER the plot twist
What false perception or idea has the reader been encouraged to believe?	What truth or new understanding has been revealed to the reader?

Part C. (20 points) Think about the lessons or morals that these stories contain.
- Circle the letter of ONE story. *Do not choose a person you wrote about in Part B.*
- In the boxes below, answer the questions about one lesson or moral from that story.

Open-Book Theme Test
(continued)

a. "The Happy Man's Shirt"
b. "The Californian's Tale"
c. "The Interlopers"

d. "As It Is with Strangers"
e. "The False Gems"
f. "Mrs. James"

What is a lesson or moral of this story?	How is it communicated to the reader?
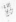	

Part D. (20 points) Think about what the symbols in these stories stand for.

- Circle the letter of ONE symbol. *Do not choose a symbol from a story that you wrote about in Part B or C.*
- In the boxes, answer the questions about that symbol.

a. the shirt in "The Happy Man's Shirt"
b. the letter in "The Californian's Tale"
c. the wine-flask in "The Interlopers"

d. the fried chicken in "As It Is with Strangers"
e. the gems in "The False Gems"
f. the hat bought by the client in "The Saleswoman"

What does this stand for in the story?

How can you tell?

Open-Book Theme Test

Score

Theme 4: Challenges and Consequences

Part A. (50 points total; 25 points each) Use a separate sheet of paper to answer TWO of the following essay questions.

1. It is a fact of life that bad things happen to good people. Choose any TWO "good" characters from this theme to whom bad things happen. What bad things happen to them and why? Do you see anything positive in these experiences? Explain.

2. With some of the stories in this theme, the reader's first impression of a character is very different from his or her final impression. Choose TWO characters for whom you found this to be true for you as a reader, and explain why your impression of them changed.

3. As you may know, an epitaph is something that is written in memory of one who has died. Choose any character in this theme who dies. In a paragraph or two, tell what THREE words or phrases you would use in an epitaph for this person, and why.

Part B. (15 points) Some characters in these stories stand out from others in some remarkable way.
- Circle the letter of ONE character.
- In the boxes, answer the questions for the character you have chosen.

---

a. Azucena in "And of Clay Are We Created"

b. the "sitting parent" in "Winter Night"

c. Noé in "Waltz of the Fat Man"

d. the figure who appears at midnight in "The Masque of the Red Death"

What is most remarkable about this character? In other words, what is the one thing about him or her that stands out most of all?

How is he or she affected by this remarkable quality, ability, experience, or situation?	How are others affected by it?

Open-Book Theme Test
(continued)

Part C. (15 points) Think about the meaning of these lines from a poem by Alfred, Lord Tennyson: "'Tis better to have loved and lost / Than never to have loved at all."
- Circle the letter of ONE character. *Do not choose a character you wrote about in Part B.*
- Answer the questions in the spaces.

    a. Ayah in "Lullaby"   **c.** the "sitting parent" in "Winter Night"

    b. Rolf in "And of Clay Are We Created"   **d.** Noé in "Waltz of the Fat Man"

Would the character agree with the sentiments expressed by Tennyson? ☐ Yes ☐ No
Why do you think this is so?

Part D. (20 points total; 10 points each) In many of the stories in this theme, a character's state of mind changes dramatically over the course of the story.
- For each set of boxes, circle the letter of ONE character. *Do not choose a character you wrote about in Part B or Part C.*
- In the "Before" and "After" boxes, describe the character's state of mind when he or she is introduced and then after a significant change takes place.
- In each large box, explain what accounts for the change.

4. **a.** Eckels in "A Sound of Thunder"   **c.** Rolf in "And of Clay Are We Created"

    b. Ayah in "Lullaby"   **d.** Azucena in "And of Clay Are We Created"

Before	After
Reason for the Change	

5. **a.** Felicia in "Winter Night"   **c.** Prince Prospero in "The Masque of the Red Death"

    b. Noé in "Waltz of the Fat Man"   **d.** Da-duh in "To Da-duh, in Memoriam"

Before	After
Reason for the Change	

Selection and Theme Assessments

Open-Book Theme Test

Score

Theme 5: Remembering

Part A. (40 points total; 20 points each) Use a separate sheet of paper to answer TWO of the following essay questions.

1. Choose any TWO writers from this theme and, in a paragraph or two, explain how events they wrote about seem to have affected their lives and why they might have chosen to write about those events years later.

2. Choose any TWO people from the selections in this theme who learn important lessons about life. In a paragraph or two, explain what those lessons are and how the people you chose learn them.

3. Choose any TWO people in these selections who make important decisions. What are the decisions? What do they reveal about what is most important to these people? Support your ideas with reference to the selections and your own ideas about life.

Part B. (20 points) Many of the people in this theme have strong reactions to other people, events, or things.
- Circle the letter of ONE person.
- Answer the questions In the first two boxes.
- In the third box, shade the bar graph to show how reasonable you think the person's reaction is, and explain why you think that.

a. Steinbeck, author of *Travels with Charley*

b. Thomas as a child in "A Child's Christmas in Wales"

c. Mathabane as a child in *Kaffir Boy*

d. Mathabane's mother in *Kaffir Boy*

e. Mathabane's father in *Kaffir Boy*

f. Mrs. Wakatsuki in *Farewell to Manzanar*

g. Premila in "By Any Other Name"

h. Aunt Tee's employers in "Living Well. Living Good."

i. Gomez as a child in "A Swimming Lesson"

To whom or what does the person react strongly?
What is his or her reaction?

How do you judge that reaction? Why?	(-) not at all reasonable		(+) very reasonable

Open-Book Theme Test
(continued)

Part C. (20 points) Think about the challenges that are central to the selections in this theme. Circle the letter of ONE selection. *Do not choose a selection you wrote about in Part B.*

- In the first box below, describe the central challenge of that selection.
- Fill in the bar graph to show how difficult you think that challenge is.
- In the next box, explain why you rated that challenge as you did.

a. *Travels with Charley*
b. *Kaffir Boy*
c. *Farewell to Manzanar*

d. "By Any Other Name"
e. "Living Well. Living Good."
f. "A Swimming Lesson"

Central Challenge		Reasons for Your Rating
	very difficult	
	very easy	

Part D. (20 points) In many of the selections in this theme, unexpected things happen. Choose ONE selection containing an event that was surprising to you. *Do not choose a selection you wrote about in Part B or Part C.*
Answer the questions in the boxes.

a. *Travels with Charley*
b. "A Child's Christmas in Wales"
c. *Kaffir Boy*
d. *Farewell to Manzanar*
e. "By Any Other Name"
f. "Living Well. Living Good."

What unexpected event occurs?

Why is the event surprising?

Selection and Theme Assessments

Open-Book Theme Test

Theme 6: Quests and Encounters

Part A. (40 points total; 20 points each) Use a separate sheet of paper to answer TWO of the following essay questions.

1. Which "quest" in this theme do you regard as the most difficult? Why?

2. Which "encounter" in this theme do you regard as the most fascinating? Why?

3. Imagine that you were interviewing the author of any one these selections. What TWO questions would you most want to ask the author that he or she doesn't address in the selection? Why would you want to ask these particular questions?

Part B. (20 points) Think about what is learned in these selections from observing.
- Circle the letter of ONE author.
- In the boxes, answer the questions about what the author you have chosen observes and learns in the selection.

a. Drakulić, the author of "Pizza in Warsaw, Torte in Prague"

b. King, the author of "I've Seen the Promised Land"

c. Stevens, the author of "Exploring Antarctic Ice"

d. Eiseley, the author of "The Angry Winter"

e. Thomas, the author of "The Tucson Zoo"

What is observed?

_____

_____

_____

_____

_____

What is learned from this observation?

_____

_____

_____

_____

_____

_____

Open-Book Theme Test

Part C. (20 points total) Many of the authors in this theme have strong feelings about particular places.

- Circle the letter of ONE author. *Do not choose an author from a selection you wrote about in Part B.*
- Answer the questions in the boxes for the author you have chosen.

a. Drakulić, the author of "Pizza in Warsaw, Torte in Prague"

b. King, the author of "I've Seen the Promised Land"

c. Stevens, the author of "Exploring Antarctic Ice"

d. Ehrlich, the author of *A Match to the Heart*

e. Eiseley, the author of "The Angry Winter"

f. Thomas, the author of "The Tucson Zoo"

About what place does the author write?
What words would you use to describe
the place the author mentions?

What strong feelings does the author
have in or about this place?

Why does he or she have
these strong feelings
about this place?

Part D. (20 points) Think about the strong feelings expressed in these selections.

On the line at the top, write the title of ONE selection. *Do not choose a selection you wrote about in Part B or Part C.*

- In the small boxes, note who expresses a strong emotion, what that emotion is, and to whom or what that emotion is directed.
- Answer the question in the large box.

Selection: _____

Person	feels	Strong Emotion	toward	Person, Animal, or Thing

Why does the person feel this particular way, and why is his or her reaction so strong?

Name _____ Date _____ Class _____

Open-Book Theme Test

Score

Theme 7: Loves and Losses

Part A. (40 points total; 20 points each) **Use a separate sheet of paper to answer TWO of the following essay questions.**

1. Choose TWO poems from this theme that focus on loss. In a paragraph or two, discuss what you can tell about what is lost in each poem, how it is lost, and how people in the poems are affected by these losses.

2. Many of the poems in this theme express love. Which TWO of these expressions do you admire most? Why? Support your choices with reference to the poems and your own views and experiences of life.

3. Many of these poems contain important lessons about life. Choose TWO poems in which lessons are offered. In a paragraph or two, tell what the lessons are and how they are conveyed.

Part B. (20 points) **Think about the effectiveness of the figurative comparisons in these poems.**
- **On the line, write the title of a poem containing an example of figurative comparison.**
- **In the top box, write down that example.**
- **In the middle box, note the two things that are compared.**
- **In the bottom box, jot down TWO ideas that the comparison communicates to the reader.**

Poem: _____

This simile or metaphor . . .	
compares . . .	*and*
and communicates the ideas and feelings that . . .	

Copyright © by The McGraw-Hill Companies, Inc.

Selection and Theme Assessments

Course 5, Theme 7 **183**

Open-Book Theme Test

Part C. (20 points) **Some of the speakers in these poems are strongly affected by elements of nature.**
- **Circle the letter of ONE poem. *Do not choose a poem you wrote about in Part B.***
- **In the top box, describe one element of nature that strongly affects the speaker of that poem.**
- **Then answer the questions in the other boxes.**

 a. "First Lesson"
 b. "Horses Graze"
 c. "A Blessing"

Element of Nature

How does the speaker react to it?
What is it about this thing that so strongly affects the speaker?

Part D. (20 points) **Many of these poems express admiration for a beloved person or animal.**
- **Circle the letter of ONE poem. *Do not choose a poem you wrote about in Part B or Part C.***
- **In the box on the left, identify the beloved person or animal.**
- **Then answer the question in the box on the right.**

 a. "Shall I Compare Thee to a Summer's Day?"
 b. "The Glory of the Day Was in Her Face"
 c. "Those Winter Sundays"
 d. "Horses Graze"
 e. "A Blessing"

What does the speaker love and/or admire about this person or animal?

Beloved Person or Animal

Copyright © by The McGraw-Hill Companies, Inc.

Open-Book Theme Test

Score

Theme 8: Issues of Identity

Part A. (40 points total; 20 points each) **Use a separate sheet of paper to answer TWO of the following essay questions.**

1. Choose any TWO people in these poems whom you find particularly interesting and, in a paragraph, explain what you find interesting about them.

2. Many of these poems feature people who have been strongly influenced by something or someone from the past. Choose any TWO of these people and, in two paragraphs, explain who or what from the past influences them, how they are influenced, and why they are influenced in these ways.

3. Choose any TWO of these poems and, in two paragraphs, discuss the main things honored or celebrated in them and why the speakers honor or celebrate these things.

Part B. (20 points) **Many of the people in this theme have strong reactions to other people, events, or things.**

- **On the two lines below, write the name of ONE person in this theme and the title of the poem in which he or she appears.**
- **Then answer the questions in the first two boxes below.**
- **In the third box, shade the bar graph to show how reasonable you think the person's reaction is, and explain why you think that.**

Person: _____

Poem: _____

To whom or what does the person react strongly?
What is his or her reaction?

How do you judge that reaction? Why?	not at all reasonable very reasonable

Name _____ Date _____ Class _____

Open-Book Theme Test   (continued)

Part C. (10 points) **Think about how imagery is used in these poems to communicate meaning.**
- **On the line below, write the title of ONE poem with strong images. *Do not choose a poem you wrote about in Part B.***
- **In the boxes below, identify the main subject of the poem, the image in the poem that you find most suggestive or effective, and the main idea or theme that the image helps to communicate.**

Poem: _____

Subject	Main Idea or Theme
Image	

Part D. (30 points total; 15 points each) **Some people in this theme embrace life while others fear it.**
- **For each pair of lines below, write the name of a person in this theme and the title of the poem in which she or he appears. *Do not choose people from a poem you wrote about in Part B or Part C.***
- **Make a mark in the small box next to the statement that accurately describes each person.**
- **In the area at the bottom of each box, explain your choices.**

Poem: _____

Person: _____
☐ This person EMBRACES life.
☐ This person FEARS life.
☐ What makes you think this is so?

Poem: _____

Person: _____
☐ This person EMBRACES life.
☐ This person FEARS life.
☐ What makes you think this is so?

Selection and Theme Assessments

Open-Book Theme Test

Theme 9: Observations and Expressions

Part A. (50 points total; 20 points each) **Use a separate sheet of paper to answer TWO of the following essay questions.**

1. Choose any TWO poems from this theme in which the speakers express strong feelings. Then, in a paragraph, explain what the speakers feel, and why.

2. To which TWO poems in this theme did you have the strongest emotional responses? (Your responses may have been either positive or negative.) In what ways did these poems affect you, and why do you think they affected you so strongly?

3. In "For Poets," "A Motto From Poets: Leave Stone," and "Constantly risking absurdity," the focus is on the responsibilities and/or role of the poet. Choose any TWO images from these poems that you find effective in communicating ideas about poetry and/or poets. Then, in a paragraph, quote or summarize these images and explain what they suggest to you.

Part B. (20 points) **Think about what is learned in these poems from observing.**
- **On the line at the top, write the title of one poem from this theme.**
- **In the boxes, answer the questions about what the speaker observes.**

The speaker of: _____

A.	What is observed?

B.	What is learned from this observation?

Open-Book Theme Test

Part C. (30 points total; 15 points each) **Think about the effectiveness of the figurative language (similes, metaphors, and personification) in these poems.**

- **For each set of boxes, write the title of a poem containing an interesting example of figurative language.**
- **In the top box, write down that simile, metaphor, or example of personification.**
- **In the middle box, note the two things that the figurative language compares.**
- **In the bottom box, note the ideas that it communicates to the reader.**

Poem: _____

This figurative language . . .

Compares . . .   and

and communicates the ideas that . . .

Poem: _____

This figurative language . . .

Compares . . .   and

and communicates the ideas that . . .

Open-Book Theme Test

Theme 10: Loyalty and Betrayal

Part A. (40 points total; 20 points each) **Use a separate sheet of paper to answer TWO of the following essay questions.**

1. Identify one character in this theme who is loyal to a cause (as opposed to a person). What is that cause, and how does the character demonstrate this loyalty? Then identify one character who could be seen as being guilty of a betrayal. Who or what is betrayed, and what is the act of betrayal?

2. Assume that you are the greatest actor in the world. Which character from any drama in this theme would you want to play, and why? Choose any role of either gender. (After all, in Shakespeare's time, men played all the roles—both male and female.)

3. The speaker of "Marked" advises writing, if necessary, in blood. Choose one character or group of characters from any of these dramas who follows this advice. Explain your interpretation of the metaphor "writing in blood" in terms of the actions of the character(s) you chose.

Part B. (20 points total; 10 points each) **Which characters could be considered tragic heroes?**

- **Choose TWO characters *from two different plays*.**
- **On the line above each set of boxes, identify one character.**
- **In the boxes, jot down your answers to the questions.**

Character: _____

What good qualities does this character possess?	
What is his or her tragic flaw?	
What forces (human or otherwise) or circumstances lead to his or her downfall?	

Character: _____

What good qualities does this character possess?	
What is his or her tragic flaw?	
What forces (human or otherwise) or circumstances lead to his or her downfall?	

Name _____ Date _____ Class _____

Open-Book Theme Test   *(continued)*

Part C. (20 points) **Consider the ways that "supporting" characters (as well as characters who never even appear on stage) contribute to *Antigone* and "The Ring of
General Macías."**

- **Circle the letter of ONE character.**
- **Answer the questions about that character.**

Antigone   **a.** Ismene   "The Ring of   **d.** Marica

           b. Eurydice   General Macías"   **e.** Cleto

           c. Teiresias   **f.** General Macías

How does the character help to advance the plot?
How does he or she add to your understanding of one or more major characters?
How does he or she add to your understanding of the play as a whole?

Part D. (20 points) **While Antigone and Brutus struggle with internal conflicts, their
"partners" (Haimon and Portia, respectively) try to understand what is going on. In
the boxes, identify**

- **one main character and his or her partner.**
- **the main character's conflict and how the partner tries to help.**
- **how you assess the relationship.**

Character	Partner	Is this a "good," successful relationship? Explain.
_____	_____	
Internal Conflict	Efforts to Help	

Copyright © by The McGraw-Hill Companies, Inc.

190 Course 5, Theme 10   Selection and Theme Assessments

Open-Book Theme Test

Theme 11: Heroism

Part A. (40 points total; 20 points each) **Use a separate sheet of paper to answer TWO of the following essay questions.**

1. Which one of the heroic characters in this theme do you find most admirable? Which one of these heroic characters do you find least admirable? Support your opinions with reference to the selection(s).

2. Choose TWO legends that communicate insights into human nature that you find interesting. Then, in a paragraph or two, explain what those insights are and how they are communicated in the selections.

3. Choose any TWO characters in these selections who experience dramatic changes in their fortunes or situations in life. In a paragraph or two, describe these dramatic changes and discuss who and/or what is most responsible for them.

Part B. (15 points) **Think about how the heroes in these legends are surprisingly ordinary in many ways.**
- **Circle the letter of ONE character.**
- **In the box on the left, list ways in which that character is ordinary.**
- **In the box on the right, list ways in which that character is extraordinary.**

a. King Uther in *Le Morte d'Arthur*
b. Sir Launcelot in *Le Morte d'Arthur*
c. Sundiata in *Sundiata*
d. King Arthur in "The Passing of Arthur"

e. Sir Bedivere in "The Passing of Arthur"
f. Wart in "Arthur Becomes King"
g. Buffalo Calf Road Woman in "Where the Girl Rescued Her Brother"

How the character is ordinary.	How the character is extraordinary.

Part C. (15 points) **Think about what motivates the characters' actions in these legends.**
- **On the lines, write the names of ONE character and the selection in which he or she appears. *Do not choose a character from a selection you wrote about in Part B.***

Open-Book Theme Test

- **In the box on the left, note what you think is the most important action taken by the character in that selection.**
- **In the box on the right, note what you think motivates that action.**

Character: _____

Selection: _____

MOTIVATIONS

ACTION

Part D. (30 points total; 15 points each) **Think about the cultural values these legends reveal.**

- **For each set of boxes, write the title of ONE selection. *Do not choose a selection you wrote about in Part B or Part C.***
- **In the boxes, note a cultural value revealed in the legend and how that value is revealed.**

Selection: _____

This cultural value . . .

is revealed by . . .

Selection: _____

This cultural value . . .

is revealed by . . .

Open-Book Theme Test

Theme 12: Comic Perspectives

Part A. (40 points total; 20 points each) **Use a separate sheet of paper to answer TWO of the following essay questions.**

1. Which of these selections hits your funny bone the hardest? Which seems least funny to you? Explain your choices.

2. If you knew you would be stuck in an elevator all day with someone from these selections and you could choose that person, who would you choose? Which person (from these selections) would you least like to share that experience with? Explain your choices.

3. Many of the situations, characters, and events in these selections are so absurd as to be unbelievable. Which selection, in your opinion, has the most ridiculous elements? Use details from the selection to support your choice.

Part B. (20 points) **Think about the struggles that are won and lost in these selections.**
- **Circle the letter of ONE person.**
- **Then, in the boxes, answer the questions.**

a. the narrator of "Appetizer"

b. the mother in *An American Childhood*

c. the grandfather in "The Car . . ."

d. the narrator of "How I Changed . . ."

e. Lomov in "A Marriage Proposal"

f. Natalia in "A Marriage Proposal"

What is the main
struggle this person faces?

Why or why not?

Does he or she win this struggle?

☐ yes   ☐ no

Name _____ Date _____ Class _____

Open-Book Theme Test   *(continued)*

Part C. (20 points) **Think about how the people in these selections are affected by realizations.**

- **Circle the letter of ONE person.** *Do not choose a person you wrote about in Part B.*
- **In the top box, note something important that the person comes to realize.**
- **In the bottom box, describe the effects of this realization on the person who makes it and on anyone else it affects.**

a. the author of "Let's Sweat!"

b. the narrator of "Appetizer"

c. the mother in *An American Childhood*

d. the grandfather in "The Car . . ."

e. the narrator of "How I Changed . . ."

f. Natalia in "A Marriage Proposal"

Realization
Effects

Part D. (20 points total; 10 points each) **Think about how humor is used in these selections to poke fun at people and things.**

- **On the line at the top of each set of boxes, write the title of a selection.** *Do not choose a selection you wrote about in Part B or Part C.*
- **In the box on the left, note one thing the selection pokes fun at.**
- **In the box on the right, explain how the selection accomplishes this.**

Selection: _____

This selection pokes fun at . . .	and it accomplishes this by . . .

Selection: _____

This selection pokes fun at . . .	and it accomplishes this by . . .

Answers

Everyday Use
Selection Test (page 1)

Recalling and Interpreting
(49 points total; 7 points each)

1. c
2. b
3. a
4. a
5. c
6. a
7. d

Using Vocabulary
(15 points total; 3 points each)

8. c
9. a
10. b
11. b
12. c

Interpreting and Evaluating
(21 points total; 7 points each)
Accept all reasonable responses. Possible answers could include

13. Mama only: Mama's, to do with as she will; something Maggie deserves; useful, warm
14. Dee only: to be used only decoratively; hers, if she wants them; safe only in her care; impressive to others
15. Mama and Dee: beautiful, representations of the past, valuable, meaningful symbols of family heritage and family ties, skillfully made, made with love

Evaluating and Connecting (15 points)
16. Answers will vary. Possible answers could include
   - Mama and Maggie would be depicted in a less positive manner. Dee has a good deal less respect for them and their lives than Mama does.
   - The story would be more political and less personal. Politics seem to be more important to Dee, and her interest in her heritage seems to be politically rather than emotionally based.
   - Dee would be depicted in a more positive manner. She doesn't see herself as being selfish like Mama does.
   - The story would have a more angry feeling to it, because Dee doesn't get what she wants while Mama does.

Chee's Daughter
Selection Test (page 3)

Recalling and Interpreting
(50 points total; 10 points each)

1. c
2. d
3. a
4. b
5. a

Using Vocabulary
(15 points total; 3 points each)

6. a
7. a
8. b
9. c
10. c

Interpreting and Evaluating
(18 points total; 9 points each)
Answers will vary. Possible answers could include

11. Mother's parents
   - her mother died
   - Navajo children belong to mother's clan
   - selfishness of Old Man Fat and his wife
   - authorities and both families would prevent Chee from taking her back
12. Father
   - new highway cutoff severely hurt local tourist business that Old Man Fat and his wife depended on
   - became financial burden on Old Man Fat and his wife
   - Chee regained faith in the land
   - land provided what Chee needed to convince Old Man Fat and his wife to give her up
   - Chee used his understanding of Old Man Fat and his wife to get what he wanted

Evaluating and Connecting (17 points)
13. Answers will vary. A model answer:
   - The theme is "Trust in the land."
   - This theme is communicated through the misfortune that falls on Old Man Fat and his wife when they turn their backs on the land. It is also communicated through Chee's experiences. When Chee turns his back on the land, he remains separated from the Little One. When he turns to the land for help, the Little One is returned to him.

Answers

Civil Peace
Selection Test (page 5)

Recalling and Interpreting
(54 points total; 9 points each)

1. d   4. b
2. b   5. c
3. a   6. b

Using Vocabulary
(15 points total; 3 points each)

7. a
8. b
9. b
10. a
11. c

Interpreting and Evaluating
(16 points total; 8 points each)
Answers will vary. Possible answers could include

12. • Suggested: little law and order in Jonathan's city
   By: no one tries to stop the thieves; thieves are bold enough to offer to call for help
   • Suggested: thieves are soldiers
   By: complete lack of concern about being seen or stopped; taunting way they offer to call "soja"

13. • Suggested: Jonathan knows he can't bargain with the thieves
   By: straightforward approach
   • Suggested: Jonathan willing to give up his money for safety
   By: telling the truth about how much money he has
   • Suggested: Jonathan angered by thieves' assumptions about his wealth
   By: offer he makes

Evaluating and Connecting (15 points)
14. Answers will vary. Possible answers could include
   • Jonathan has survived the horrors of a civil war, including the loss of a child.
   • Many of the things that happened during the war and since then haven't made sense to Jonathan.
   • Jonathan wants to feel that there is some sort of purpose or logic to the things that happen in life.
   • It comforts Jonathan to believe that, even though life doesn't make a great deal of sense to him, it does make sense to God.

Two Kinds
Selection Test (page 7)

Recalling and Interpreting
(49 points total; 7 points each)

1. a   5. c
2. b   6. b
3. a   7. c
4. d

Using Vocabulary
(15 points total; 3 points each)

8. c   11. c
9. a   12. a
10. a

Interpreting and Evaluating
(18 points total; 6 points each)
Answers will vary, depending upon the conflict students choose. Answers could include points similar to the following:

13. External, between Jing-mei and her mother
14. The conflict exists because of
   • each character's differing expectations of Jing-mei. The mother seems to expect too much; Jing-mei seems to expect too little.
   • each character's stubbornness.
   • a lack of honest and open communication between the two.

15. No
   It isn't resolved because
   • Jing-mei never fulfills her mother's expectations of her.
   • neither character tries very hard to accept and understand the other.
   • Jing-mei's mother dies without either of them having changed their minds about Jing-mei's genius.

Evaluating and Connecting (18 points)
16. Answers will vary. A model answer:
   • Jing-mei wants her mother to accept her for herself. She realizes she has failed and feels embarrassed. If her mother would accept her despite the talent-show failure, she would feel free to be herself and to be loved for who she is.
   • Her mother wants Jing-mei to try her best and to be the best she can be. She tells Jing-mei many times that she can succeed if she tries. Her mother is willing to sacrifice to help Jing-mei, if only Jing-mei will cooperate and not lose hope; she relents

when Jing-mei makes it clear that she would rather risk humiliation than apply herself.

Catch the Moon
Selection Test (page 9)

Recalling and Interpreting
(48 points total; 8 points each)

1. a
2. d
3. a
4. c
5. d
6. a

Using Vocabulary
(15 points total; 3 points each)

7. b
8. c
9. a
10. b
11. a

Interpreting and Evaluating
(15 points total; 5 points each)
Answers will vary. Possible answers could include

12. • Senses: sight, touch, hearing
    • Feelings or ideas: sarcasm; irony; exaggeration; very large pile; junkyard full of smashed, wrecked cars; Luis's father is proud of junkyard; Luis doesn't want it.
13. • Senses: sight, touch
    • Feelings or ideas: affection; sympathy; guilt; Luis's father is in pain; Luis knows it's his fault; Luis feels bad about his carelessness
14. • Senses: sight, touch
    • Feelings or ideas: suffering; triumph; Luis has worked hard; Luis has hurt himself; Luis's hard work is rewarded; hubcap is just right; Luis can provide what no one else can; Luis can use hubcap to further his relationship with Naomi.

Evaluating and Connecting (22 points)
15. Answers will vary. A model answer:
    At the beginning of the story, Luis is arrogant, bitter, self-destructive, uncooperative, negative, disrespectful, and in need of a major attitude adjustment. By the end, Luis's attitude has become more humble, caring, cooperative, and optimistic. Luis buried the grief he felt when his mother died. He spent several years acting out instead of confronting the bad feelings. His feelings for Naomi and the memories that she dredges up help him to confront his grief for the first time. This, in turn, allows him to begin caring again about himself and other people.

Through the Tunnel
Selection Test (page 11)

Recalling and Interpreting
(45 points total; 9 points each)

1. c
2. a
3. a
4. c
5. b

Using Vocabulary
(15 points total; 3 points each)

6. b
7. a
8. c
9. c
10. a

Interpreting and Evaluating
(16 points total; 4 points each)
Answers will vary. Model answers:

11. Mark: near the end of the plot line (near the end of the story)
12. Climax: Jerry's swimming through the tunnel
13. Why: Jerry's main goal, major turning point, moment of highest interest and greatest danger
14. Effect: resolves Jerry's external conflicts with own body and the tunnel and his internal conflict with fear

Evaluating and Connecting
(24 points total; 12 points each)
15. Answers will vary. Students could say that Jerry
    • has proven something vitally important to himself by mastering his fears and swimming through the tunnel.
    • accomplished what he set out to do; he feels no need to repeat his feat.
    • is now more comfortable with himself and feels mature enough to risk the "babyishness" of playing on his mother's safe beach.
    • having known the dangers of the rocky bay, can now return to the safety of his mother's beach without feeling ashamed or restless.
16. Answers will vary. Possible answers could include
    It is reasonable because
    • he knows that it can be done; he has seen other boys do it.
    • he has carefully trained for the ordeal.
    • it is something that he needs to do to feel independent and successful.

Answers

It is foolish because
- he is completely alone, so will die if he fails.
- the other boys who did it were older and more experienced.
- there is nothing to be gained from the ordeal except the knowledge that he has succeeded at something extremely dangerous.
- risking one's life just to prove something is like risking one's life on a dare.
- his mother trusted him to be responsible, but he behaved totally irresponsibly.

The Vision Quest

Selection Test (page 13)

Recalling and Interpreting

(56 points total; 8 points each)

1. a   5. b
2. d   6. d
3. c   7. c
4. d

Using Vocabulary

(12 points total; 3 points each)

8. b   10. a
9. a   11. b

Interpreting and Evaluating

(18 points total; 6 points each)

Answers will vary. Possible answers could include

12. What: belief that spirits live in nature
    How: spirit causes boulder to attack young man
13. What: importance of humility
    How: young man's lack of it angers spirit
14. What: respect for elders
    How: young man is foolish, his uncle is wise

Evaluating and Connecting (14 points)

15. Answers will vary. Possible answers could include
    The main message is that
    - knowledge results from humility, wisdom, and patience, not as a reward for suffering, courage, or determination.
    - the spirits reward only the humble with the gift of a vision.
    - acknowledging one's limitations is the only way to rise above them.
    The message is communicated by

- the events of the story. Nothing the young man does succeeds in helping him to achieve his goal.
- the uncle as he speaks to the young man at the end of the legend.

By the Waters of Babylon

Selection Test (page 15)

Recalling and Interpreting

(56 points total; 7 points each)

1. a   5. c
2. b   6. a
3. d   7. b
4. c   8. c

Using Vocabulary

(9 points total; 3 points each)

9. b   11. c
10. c

Interpreting and Evaluating

(21 points total; 7 points each)

12. Answers will vary but should reflect students' understanding that
    - John's main goal is to gain knowledge or to satisfy his curiosity.
    - this goal requires him to explore the Place of the Gods.
13. Reasons will vary but could refer to points similar to the following:
    - The gods have sent John the strong dreams that drive him to achieve this goal.
    - John is deeply religious and hopes to be a priest. To do so, he must follow the gods' bidding.
    - John believes that "it is better to lose one's life than one's spirit." He must pursue his goal or lose his spirit.
14. Answers will vary but could refer to points similar to the following:
    - John has gained knowledge and maturity.
    - John has become a priest and will one day become the high priest.
    - The future of John's people is now very different than it had been.
    - John's people will gain access to the books and objects that will help them to advance their society technologically.

Answers

- John has goals for his people that will set them on a course not unlike that of the civilization that was destroyed.

Evaluating and Connecting (14 points)

15. Answers will vary widely, depending upon the moral students identify and their own life experiences. A model answer:

   The moral of the story is that too much knowledge gained too quickly is a bad thing. People need time to prepare for changes and to deal with the problems that accompany progress. This moral is reasonable. In the story, "wisdom" did not bring the peace John assumed it must lead to, but the exact opposite. Support also lies in our society's struggles with ethical, moral, and social problems that exist because our technology has advanced so quickly. Test-tube babies, cloning, nuclear weaponry, and many other technological advances have raised important ethical questions that we cannot answer, but these unanswered questions do not stop us from using this technology.

What I Have Been Doing Lately

Selection Test (page 17)

Recalling and Interpreting
(48 points total; 8 points each)

1. c   4. d
2. c   5. a
3. d   6. b

Using Vocabulary
(12 points total; 4 points each)

7. b   9. b
8. c

Interpreting and Evaluating
(16 points total; 8 points each)
Answers will vary. Model answers:

10. Detail: the drizzle or dust falling on the narrator's tongue
    Senses: touch; taste; possibly also sight

11. Detail: stone striking the narrator's forehead
    Senses: touch; possibly also sight and hearing

Evaluating and Connecting (24 points)

12. Answers will vary widely. Possible answers could include
    The narrator seems to both hope for and fear adventure or the unknown, because

- she finds that what she has left behind has become different and unfamiliar.
- she deliberately jumps into a deep hole and then finds the experience sad and frightening.
- she approaches fascinating people only to find that they are not fascinating at all.
- she wanders, at first, with no pain or exhaustion and then becomes very tired and sad about being far from home.

The narrator seems to fear being alone, because
- she seems lonely throughout most of her adventures.
- she talks about missing all the people she has loved.
- her adventures begin when she answers a doorbell.
- she wants desperately to find someone who loves her waiting at home.

The narrator seems to fear that she and her mother do not really know each other, because
- a woman she thinks is her mother turns out not to be her.
- she talks about pretending to be a dutiful daughter.

The narrator seems to fear her own impulses, because
- she jumps into a deep hole that turns out to be an unpleasant experience.
- she throws stones at a monkey who then retaliates and hurts her.
- she crosses a large body of water to be with a fascinating group of people who turn out not to be at all what she thought they were.

With All Flags Flying

Selection Test (page 19)

Recalling and Interpreting
(49 points total; 7 points each)

1. b   5. c
2. a   6. c
3. d   7. a
4. b

Using Vocabulary
(15 points total; 3 points each)

8. a   11. c
9. a   12. a
10. b

Answers

Interpreting and Evaluating
(18 points total; 9 points each)

13. Answers will vary. Answers must identify Mr. Carpenter as a main character. Explanatory notes could make such points as the following:
    - Without him, there could be no story.
    - His decision to enter the old folks' home is central to the plot and provides the main conflict.
    - The story is mainly about him.
    - Many of his thoughts and feelings are revealed.
    Answers may identify Clara as a main or minor character. Explanatory notes supporting the view of her as a major character could make such points as the following:
    - She is the main obstacle to Mr. Carpenter's goals.
    - Mr. Carpenter interacts with her throughout most of the story.
    - She is used to illustrate the feelings of all of Mr. Carpenter's children.
    Explanatory notes supporting the view of Clara as a minor character could make such points as the following:
    - Very little is revealed about her outside of her interactions with Mr. Carpenter.
    - She complicates the story but isn't central to it.

14. Answers will vary. Answers must identify Mr. Carpenter as a round character. Explanatory notes could make such points as the following:
    - He reveals varied, contradictory traits.
    - His personality is complex.
    - He loves his family but is willing to break their hearts to avoid burdening them.
    Answers may identify Clara as a round or flat character. Explanatory notes supporting the view of her as round could make such points as the following:
    - She respects her father but demonstrates no respect for his decision.
    - She changes in the story from a happy, confident woman to a sad, helpless one.
    - She is kind and well-meaning but almost as stubborn as her father.
    Explanatory notes supporting the view of her as flat could make such points as the following:
    - She exhibits few personality traits.
    - Since little is revealed about her, she can't be considered a fully developed character.

Evaluating and Connecting (18 points)

15. Answers will vary. Students who believe the move is best for everyone might note that:
    - Mr. Carpenter would never have been happy in the care of any of his children.
    - He needs independence more than anything else; his move is the only way to get it.
    - He is right that, at least eventually, he would have burdened family members by living with them.
    - Although he seems heartless, his decision is motivated by love of his children.
    - This decision saves Mr. Carpenter from having to depend on love, kindness, and the use of other people's spare time to meet his needs.
    - The family can still spend time with him, and he can remain involved in their lives; this involvement will be voluntary rather than forced.
    Students who believe that the move is not best for everyone might note that:
    - Mr. Carpenter's decision is based on assumptions, not on facts.
    - He and his family would disagree strongly about what constitutes a burden.
    - He is concerned only with his own personal needs, fears, and desires, not his children's.
    - The decision is not the best for his family, because they are made miserable by it.
    - The decision is not the best for Mr. Carpenter, because he will be less independent, less respected, lonelier, and have fewer of his needs met in an institution.
    - At the time the story takes place, Mr. Carpenter is helpful, not burdensome; he could at least have delayed his entry into a home until he needed nursing care.

A Child, a Dog, the Night
Selection Test (page 21)

Recalling and Interpreting
(49 points total; 7 points each)

1. d
2. c
3. d
4. b
5. a
6. c
7. b

Answers

Using Vocabulary
(15 points total; 3 points each)

8. c   **11.** a
9. b   **12.** c
10. a

Interpreting and Evaluating
(21 points total; 7 points each)
Answers will vary. Possible answers could include
13.
- How does Mr. Davies feel about Black?
- Does Black miss him as much as he misses Black?
- What makes his father change his mind?
- What makes Mr. Davies give up Black?

14.
- What do the boy and dog do all day?
- What is the real reason Mr. Davies values Black?
- How does Black react to being separated from the boy?

15.
- Why does Black miss the boy so much?
- What did Black do while he was gone?
- How is the boy reacting to Black's absence?

Evaluating and Connecting (15 points)
16. Answers will vary. Students could say that
- the setting is a mining town in which the neighborhoods and social lives of the workers are totally separate and completely different from those of the owners.
- Mr. Labra, who is poor, works for Mr. Davies, who is wealthy. On the surface, the two seem to have little in common. In fact, one could blame the low wages that Mr. Davies pays the miners for Mr. Labra's poverty.
- Black and Little Juan seem to be able to communicate without words.
- despite their differences, Mr. Labra and Mr. Davies arrive at the same conclusion about Black and Little Juan at about the same time.
- it is unheard of in this mining town for rich men to sympathize with poor men and to give up things of great value to them.

A White Heron
Selection Test (page 23)

Recalling and Interpreting
(48 points total; 8 points each)

1. b   **4.** a
2. d   **5.** a
3. c   **6.** b

Using Vocabulary
(15 points total; 3 points each)

7. b   **10.** c
8. a   **11.** b
9. c

Interpreting and Evaluating
(21 points total; 7 points each)
Answers will vary. Model answers:
12. Conflict between: desire to please young man *and* loyalty to forest
Resolved by: decision not to reveal location of heron's nest
13. Gains could include two of the following: peace of mind, preservation of the heron, safeguarding her innocence, continuation of kinship with nature
14. Losses could include two of the following: ability to impress young man, possibility of deeper friendship, continued contact with outside world, ten dollars and what it could buy

Evaluating and Connecting (16 points)
15. Answers will vary. A model answer:
   The general place—a peaceful and isolated forest—is most important, because the central conflict in the story requires Sylvia to have a deep feeling of security in her new home and a sense of kinship with nature. Only in an isolated, natural setting could the young man have the effect he has, and only there would Sylvia be challenged in the way she is.
   The fact that the forest is in New England is less important, as are the specifics of the grandmother's house and the time that the story takes place. Probably any isolated, natural place where Sylvia had become content would work well for the story, because the specific kind of tree she climbs and the specific kind of bird she protects could vary without substantially affecting the story. It might make very little difference at all to have the story set in modern times, except that there are fewer isolated places today.

Answers

The Boar Hunt
Selection Test (page 25)

Recalling and Interpreting
(49 points total; 7 points each)

1. b   5. d
2. d   6. b
3. c   7. a
4. c

Using Vocabulary
(15 points total; 3 points each)

8. b   11. a
9. c   12. c
10. b

Interpreting and Evaluating
(16 points total; 8 points each)
Answers will vary. Model answers:

13. • excited, because enjoys hunting, challenges, and being with his friends
    • anxious, because when it gets dark, sleeping outside in the jungle begins to seem dangerous
14. • ashamed, because has decided that killing for pleasure is wrong
    • revolted, because his companions were eaten alive by the boars

Evaluating and Connecting (20 points)
15. Answers will vary. Possible answers could include
    • The use of first-person makes the reader identify with the main character.
    • If the story had a third-person narrator, the reader might not become as emotionally involved in the story.
    • The first-person narration makes the story more suspenseful because the narrator is one of the people whose life is endangered.
    • The narrator is deeply changed by the events of the story. The changes that he goes through make the story's lesson or theme effective.
    • An outside narrator would have to relate the character's thoughts and feelings. It is more direct and effective for the narrator to be the one who has these thoughts and feelings.

Delicious Death
Open-Book Selection Test (page 27)

Recalling and Interpreting
(60 points total; 10 points each)

1. a   4. c
2. b   5. c
3. b   6. b

Interpreting and Evaluating
(16 points total; 8 points each)
Answers will vary. Possible answers could include

7. pride, because
    • has killed quail by himself
    • associates hunting with maturity and manliness
    • they're result of his first hunting trip
   guilt, because
    • has never killed anything before
    • mother thanks the quail
   confusion, because
    • has never killed anything before
    • is influenced by his mother
    • gets mixed messages from mother
8. gratitude, because
    • believes quail have souls, or living spirits
    • believes quail made great sacrifice for her and son
   satisfaction, because
    • quail taste delicious
    • dinner with son is pleasant
   mixed happiness and sadness, because
    • sees quail as symbol of her son's childhood
    • sees hunting and killing as symbol of son's leaving childhood behind

Evaluating and Connecting (24 points)
9. Answers will vary. Students could say that the mother believed hunting was
       dangerous (lines 6, 11, and 12).
       permissible only if what was killed was eaten (line 13).
       a spiritual activity (lines 25–33 and 46–48).
       a kind of murder (lines 49 and 50).
   As to her son's hunting, students could say that the mother
       didn't want him to go (line 6).
       was afraid for him and his friends (lines 6, 11, 12, and 15–18).

Answers

gave in because he "stood up to" her (line 7).

saw it as a sign of his growing up (lines 7, 31–33, and 40–42).

supported him by
- buying bullets (lines 10 and 11).
- encouraging him to have a responsible attitude toward hunting (line 13).
- praying for him both before and after the hunt (lines 15–18 and 25–33).
- preparing the dinner with extra care (lines 20–22).

Finally, students could say that the mother used the occasion to make her son see

the legitimate purpose of hunting (line 13) over her son's illegitimate arguments (lines 7–9).

that animals have "souls" (line 48).

that adulthood carries responsibilities (lines 49–50).

The Monkey's Paw
Selection Test (page 29)

Recalling and Interpreting
(56 points total; 8 points each)
1. b
2. c
3. b
4. a
5. d
6. d
7. a

Using Vocabulary
(15 points total; 3 points each)
8. a
9. c
10. a
11. b
12. b

Interpreting and Evaluating
(14 points total; 7 points each)
13–14. Answers will vary. Possible answers could include
when Mr. White makes the first wish, because
- magic is intriguing
- reader expects wish to be fulfilled
- Morris's behavior has suggested the paw's power
- paw moves, suggesting wish will be fulfilled
- wish isn't immediately fulfilled, so reader wonders what will happen
when the nicely dressed stranger arrives, because
- no one knows who he is or what he wants
- seems his appearance is tied to wish
- his behavior suggests something isn't right

when Mrs. White tries to open the door near end of story, because
- it isn't certain what's on other side
- reader doesn't know if she'll get it open before husband stops her
- reader expects her to be confronted by son
- reader is anxious about son's arrival

Evaluating and Connecting (15 points)
15. Answers will vary. Most students will feel that the Whites did not deserve what happened to them because
- they had done nothing bad.
- no family member had exhibited greed, selfishness, cruelty, or any other serious character flaw in their interest in the monkey's paw.
- Mr. White had followed Morris's warning to wish only for something practical.
- even if it is bad to try to get something for nothing, no family member deserved to be punished so harshly and horribly for wishing for a moderate sum of money.
- Morris had not given the family any specific examples of horrible consequences resulting from wishing on the paw.
- Morris should have warned the family that one could not control how the wish was granted.
- Mr. White made a simple wish that he didn't expect to have granted; almost anyone would believe this to be harmless.

Students who feel that the family deserved what happened to them could say that
- Morris clearly thought that they would regret using the paw, and he was in a position to know; the Whites should have heeded him.
- no one should get involved with magic; it is too dangerous.
- trying to get something for nothing often has bad consequences.

Tuesday Siesta
Selection Test (page 31)

Recalling and Interpreting
(60 points total; 10 points each)
1. a
2. b
3. a
4. c
5. a
6. c

Answers

Using Vocabulary
(15 points total; 3 points each)

7. a
8. c
9. b
10. a
11. c

Interpreting and Evaluating
(7 points total)

12. Answers will vary. Possible answers could include
    objective, because author doesn't use opinion words, just straightforward description
    negative, because author makes town seem unattractive and uncomfortable
    sympathetic, because author makes town seem sad and life there seems difficult

Evaluating and Connecting (18 points)

13. Answers will vary. Possible answers could include
    The mother feels the need to visit her son's grave because
    • she loved him.
    • she thought he was a good man.
    • he died far from home.
    • she was not with him when he died.
    • she realizes how alone he was.
    • she needs a chance to say goodbye.
    The mother wants to show the town that Carlos had a family who loved him because
    • he died alone and unknown.
    • he was a complete stranger to the town; no one even knew his name.
    • she believes he was more and better than just "a thief."
    The mother is feeling
    • calm because she is doing what she thinks is right and necessary.
    • proud because she has natural dignity and because she was proud of who her son was.
    • anxious to present herself and her daughter well, perhaps to affect Carlos's reputation in the town, perhaps just because she has great pride.
    • sad because she loved her son and he is dead.

Contents of the Dead Man's Pocket
Selection Test (page 33)

Recalling and Interpreting
(49 points total; 7 points each)

1. b   5. c
2. c   6. d
3. d   7. b
4. a

Using Vocabulary
(10 points total; 2 points each)

8. b   11. c
9. e   12. a
10. d

Interpreting and Evaluating
(27 points total; 9 points each)
Answers will vary. Possible answers could include

13. months of work, all his research, dedication, professional advancement, ambition, success
14. meaningless effort, a wasted life, wrong choices, failure to live life, shortchanging himself, shortchanging his wife
15. he's glad to be alive; his priorities are different; he realizes how crazy it was to go after it before; retrieving it was all in vain; risking his life to retrieve it was all in vain; broken window, which saved him, has now cost him the paper, which nearly killed him

Evaluating and Connecting (14 points)

16. Answers will vary. Possible answers could include:
    The author probably chose third-person narration, limited to Tom, because this narration works well in that
    • it builds and maintains suspense.
    • it allows the reader to know what Tom is thinking and what his reasons are for doing what he does, without the drawbacks that first-person would have.
    • the story itself is limited to Tom. He is the one whose experience is described, who changes, who makes discoveries about life and priorities.
    First-person would not have worked well because
    • a narrator who functions in a story must survive to narrate it.

Answers

- knowing the narrator will survive would greatly reduce the suspense.
- keeping some distance from Tom allows him to be observed with objectivity.

Third-person omniscient would have worked almost as well, but would be a somewhat pointless approach because

- the only other character is Clare, who appears only briefly.
- Clare's thoughts and feelings are clear from her behavior and from the few things she says; it is not necessary to the story to reveal them more completely.
- what Clare is thinking or doing while she is away from the apartment is irrelevant to the story.
- what other people—on the street or in nearby buildings, for example—are thinking or doing are unimportant and would reduce the sense of Tom's isolation and desperation.

Third-person limited, but limited to someone other than Tom, would not have worked because an observer of the events could not have

- known why Tom did what he did.
- witnessed the events in the detail required to build and maintain suspense.

The Censors
Selection Test (page 35)

Recalling and Interpreting
(45 points total; 9 points each)

1. d
2. b
3. c
4. a
5. d

Using Vocabulary
(15 points total; 3 points each)

6. a
7. c
8. b
9. c
10. b

Interpreting and Evaluating
(24 points total; 8 points each)
Answers will vary. Possible answers could include

11. • when he turns in a fellow employee for arranging a strike
    • when he censors his own letter

12. • romantic
    • happy
    • principled; moral
    • independent; thinks for himself
    • not committed to his job
    • doesn't believe most letters contain anti-government messages
    • values freedom
    • enjoys life
    • values Mariana's happiness and safety
    • values his own life and safety

13. • doesn't enjoy life; unhappy
    • becomes more and more immersed in his job
    • begins believing in censorship
    • finds anti-government messages where they don't really exist
    • paranoid
    • values work-related promotions and achievements
    • values his job over himself and Mariana
    • captive; controlled by the authorities
    • immoral
    • no longer thinks for himself

Evaluating and Connecting (16 points)

14. Answers will vary. Possible answers could include
    Bureaucracy
    • Juan starts out a reasonable person but is changed into an ignorant robot by his experiences in the bureau.
    • Juan is eventually robbed of his humanity by the censorship bureaucracy.
    Censorship
    • Juan and the other censors believe that completely harmless messages are intended to destroy or overthrow the government.
    Totalitarianism, anti-democracy
    • The government in this story takes censorship to an extreme level of absurdity.

The Ring
Selection Test (page 37)

Recalling and Interpreting
(48 points total; 8 points each)

1. d
2. a
3. d
4. c
5. b
6. c

Answers

Using Vocabulary

(15 points total; 3 points each)

7. a	**10.** a
8. c	**11.** b
9. a	

Interpreting and Evaluating

(21 points total; 7 points each)

Answers will vary. Possible answers could include

12. immature, inexperienced, unrealistic, naïve, overly protected, possibly spoiled, playful, happy, optimistic

13. caring, loving, (overly) protective of Lise, responsible, traditional, proud, immature, inexperienced, unrealistic, naïve

14. desperate, dangerous, possibly lonely, thoughtful, wild, untamed, patient, controlled, mature for his age, experienced

Evaluating and Connecting (16 points)

Answers will vary. Possible answers could include:

15. Students could say that Lise gains
    - maturity.
    - experience with sorrow, sin, and/or evil.
    - more realistic views and expectations of Sigismund and their marriage.
    - an understanding of, and true compassion for, those less fortunate than herself.

    Students could say that Lise loses
    - her innocence.
    - the complete faith she had in Sigismund and his ability to protect her.
    - her unrealistic expectations.
    - her total self-absorption.

16. Students could say that Lise doesn't tell Sigismund because
    - she sees him in a more realistic light and resents him for his failure to shield her from reality.
    - she doesn't think he would understand.
    - she feels as if she has made a sacred pact with the thief.
    - what happened in the glen is too personal to share.
    - she feels compassion for the thief and doesn't want to endanger him.
    - her immaturity and self-absorption prevent her from understanding that the thief continues to pose a danger to others despite his decision to let her go.
    - she had felt a thrill in the thief's presence that she

did not want to tell her husband about.
    - she couldn't admit that she had done something so foolish.

    In addition, students could say that Lise does the right thing because
    - she has entered into a sacred, unspoken pact with the thief.
    - the thief did not harm her; it would be wrong of her to harm him.
    - Sigismund would never understand what happened.
    - there are some realizations that are better kept to oneself.

    Students could say that Lise did the wrong thing because
    - the thief is a murderer who poses a danger to all who come into contact with him.
    - his gesture with the knife was a threat to kill Lise; he will not hesitate to kill someone.
    - she cannot build a trusting relationship with Sigismund if she keeps secrets.

The Happy Man's Shirt

Selection Test (page 39)

Recalling and Interpreting

(42 points total; 7 points each)

1. d	**4.** a
2. c	**5.** b
3. a	**6.** d

Using Vocabulary

(15 points total; 3 points each)

7. b	**10.** b
8. a	**11.** a
9. b	

Interpreting and Evaluating

(18 points total; 9 points each)

Answers will vary. Model answers:

12. king discovers happy man who is a peasant and wears no shirt

    happiness has nothing to do with wealth, power, or status in society because
    - happy man has less money and lower position and status than any other character but is the only happy character

Answers

- fact that he's shirtless shows that happiness isn't something you can get from or give to another

13. happy man has shirt; it's taken back to prince; prince puts it on and lives happily ever after
happiness is an illusion because
   - prince doesn't realize that nothing has really changed but his shirt
   - his belief that the shirt brings happiness does, in fact, make him happy

Evaluating and Connecting (25 points)

14. Answers will vary. Possible answers could include
   - The main differences are that the happy man is happy and content while the other two men are not, and that he has considerably less status, power, and wealth than they do.
   - The young man symbolizes happiness and contentment.
   - The other two men symbolize power, social status, and wealth.
   - The differences between the happy man and the other two men underscore the moral that happiness has nothing to do with one's situation or status in life.

A Californian'a Tale
Selection Test (page 41)

Recalling and Interpreting
(56 points total; 8 points each)

1. b
2. a
3. d
4. a
5. b
6. c
7. c

Using Vocabulary
(15 points total; 3 points each)

8. b
9. a
10. b
11. a
12. c

Interpreting and Evaluating (14 points)

13. Answers will vary. Possible answers could include

Henry's pride in and attention to the house
- at first, seems proud, responsible, tidy
- later, seems obsessive, overdone, sad
miners' weeping as the letter is read
- at first, seems overly emotional
- later, makes perfect sense, since they're being reminded of a dead friend
Henry's distress as afternoon passes and wife doesn't arrive
- at first, seems silly
- later, seen as result of memory of the tragedy
Saturday evening party
- at first, seems like a welcome-home celebration
- later, seen as way to help a friend survive unbearable time in his life
drink reserved for Henry
- at first, seems mysterious
- later, seen as way of making Henry sleep so he can make it through the night

Evaluating and Connecting (15 points)

14. Answers will vary. Students who feel that the story would have worked as well in a different style could say that the story succeeds because of its plot and surprise ending, which would be there regardless of what style the author chose.
Students who feel that the story would not have worked as well in a different style could say that
   - the use of simple language corresponds with the simple life the characters lead.
   - the use of realistic dialogue makes Henry and his friends authentic and likable.
   - the conversational style makes the story read like a true account instead of like a piece of fiction.

An Astrologer's Day
Selection Test (page 43)

Recalling and Interpreting
(63 points total; 9 points each)

1. d
2. c
3. d
4. a
5. b
6. c
7. a

Answers

Using Vocabulary
(15 points total; 3 points each)

8. b
9. a
10. c
11. b
12. c

Interpreting and Evaluating (10 points)

13. Answers will vary. Possible answers could include

town is poor
- "hissing gaslights"
- "naked flares stuck on poles"
- "old cycle lamps"

merchants find ways to make do
- "hissing gaslights"
- "naked flares stuck on poles"
- "old cycle lamps"

shop area is filled with smells, noises, and shadows
- "hissing gaslights"
- "flare which crackled and smoked"
- "criss-cross of light rays and moving shadows"

atmosphere is mysterious
- "flare which crackled and smoked"
- "hissing gaslights"
- "criss-cross of light rays and moving shadows"

Evaluating and Connecting (12 points)

14. Answers will vary. Students who like the astrologer could say that he
- is perceptive about human nature.
- is clever in how he gets clients and then gets information from them.
- shows great presence of mind in his dealings with Guru Nayak.
- has worried about blood on his hands ever since leaving his village.

Students who dislike the astrologer could say that he
- is a phony.
- not only lies to Guru Nayak but also resents being underpaid to do so.
- has misled his wife for years about his past.
- has a violent past, which he feels little guilt about. His only concern about past behavior involves being made to answer for it.

The Interlopers
Selection Test (page 45)

Recalling and Interpreting
(60 points total; 12 points each)

1. c
2. b
3. a
4. d
5. c

Using Vocabulary
(15 points total; 3 points each)

6. b
7. a
8. b
9. a
10. c

Interpreting and Evaluating (10 points)

11. Answers will vary. Possible answers could include

Ecclesiastes
- The feuding men created the situation that destroys them.
- Hate brings both men into the forest, where they'll die.
- If Ulrich hadn't been focused only on his hatred, might have heeded the deer's restlessness.

Franklin
- Neither man wants the land for its practical use.
- The anger that drives both men is historical in nature; neither has suffered at the hands of the other.
- As soon as they reconcile, both men realize how foolish their feud has been.

Fosdick
- The hatred makes men behave irrationally.
- The hate ultimately results in death for both men.
- The men have been so obsessed by hate that it has controlled and ruined their lives.

Evaluating and Connecting (15 points)

12. Answers will vary. Possible answers could include
- The men might have been able to defend their reconciliation against human interlopers, but the successful interlopers will be wolves.
- Because the men waited until they were trapped to reconcile, no one will be aware of their reconciliation.
- The historic conflict between the two families will undoubtedly continue.

Answers

- Now that family members have died, the feud will probably intensify.

As It Is with Strangers
Selection Test (page 47)

Recalling and Interpreting
(55 points total; 11 points each)

1. c
2. d
3. a
4. c
5. d

Using Vocabulary
(15 points total; 5 points each)

6. b
7. c
8. a

Interpreting and Evaluating (10 points)

9. Only quotation *a* contains understatement. Explanatory notes will vary. Possible answers could include
   Understated
   - importance to Tiffany of having a brother
   - unlikelihood of forgetting such an important thing
   Reasons
   - create humor
   - emphasize absurdity of idea that Tiffany could have forgotten being told she has a brother
   - characterize Tiffany as a good-natured smart aleck
   - show that Tiffany knows her mother hasn't been completely honest

Evaluating and Connecting (20 points)

10. Answers will vary. Students could say that
    - Tiffany doesn't feel particularly close to her mother at that time because: her mother has kept a large secret (Jack's existence) from her; her mother has not shared her feelings and regrets with Tiffany; Tiffany is aware of the distance between her mother and herself; the emotional distance between them makes Tiffany feel awkward.
    - Tiffany wants to let her mother have some privacy.
    - Tiffany thinks that her mother needs to grieve in order to feel better, and comforting her would interfere with that process.
    - Tiffany is only fifteen years old and feels overwhelmed by all that has happened.
    - Taking care of herself is about all that Tiffany can handle right then.

The False Gems
Selection Test (page 49)

Recalling and Interpreting
(45 points total; 9 points each)

1. d
2. b
3. b
4. a
5. d

Using Vocabulary
(15 points total; 3 points each)

6. b
7. c
8. c
9. b
10. a

Interpreting and Evaluating
(20 points total; 10 points each)
Choices will vary. Possible answers could include

11.
   - gems are real
   - wife received gifts from at least one person
   - wife not who she seemed to be
   - Lantin eager to impress others
   - Lantin loves or needs luxury

12.
   - how wife really felt about Lantin
   - why wife did what she did
   - whether gifts were from one man or many
   - how long deceit went on
   - whether wife was given jewels or money, she invested in jewels

Evaluating and Connecting (20 points)

13. Answers will vary. Students could say that the title might refer to
    - the first wife's modesty and virtue—"gems" that turned out to be false
    - Lantin's happiness and contentment—"gems" that turned out to be false
    - Lantin's wives, who turn out not to be what they appear. He prizes the first for her beauty, modesty, and devotion, but she accepts gifts in secret. He prizes the second (at least initially) for her virtue, but a violent temper is not a virtue.
    - wealth and luxury, which are prized and sought after but bring no true happiness. The only apparent improvement in Lantin's life is that he eats better when he's wealthy than when he's poor. Wealth does not cure his grief. Wealth does not bring him happiness with his second wife.

Answers

- pretenses. Lantin criticizes his first wife for wearing pretend jewelry, but he himself later pretends to greater wealth than he has.
- truth. Lantin was much happier while his first wife was deceiving him.
- reality. People cannot always tell what is real and what is not.
- anything that pretends to be what it is not
- anything that has a value other than what it is thought to have

The Saleswoman and Mrs James
Selection Test (page 51)

Recalling and Interpreting
(49 points total; 7 points each)
1. c
2. a
3. b
4. d
5. a
6. c
7. a

Using Vocabulary
(15 points total; 3 points each)
8. a
9. b
10. c
11. c
12. a

Interpreting and Evaluating
(16 points total; 8 points each)
Answers will vary. Possible answers could include
13.
- clever
- cruel
- domineering
- determined
- manipulative
- good at insulting someone while appearing to compliment her
- good with words
- a psychological bully
14.
- not delicately featured
- perhaps a bit overweight
- not youthful
- has sense of her own style
- resists being bullied

Evaluating and Connecting (20 points)
15. Answers will vary.

Identifying similarities, students could say that both women
- have jobs where they must serve other women.
- are determined.
- make fun of the women they serve.
- use words to their advantage, suggesting much more than they say.
- are witty.

Identifying differences, students could say that
- the saleswoman is insulting; Mildred simply refuses to be taken advantage of.
- the saleswoman has no clear reason to make fun of her customer; Mildred has good reason to look down on Mrs. James for her superior attitude.
- the saleswoman tries to manipulate others; Mildred simply tries to keep herself from being manipulated.
- the saleswoman is a snob; Mildred dislikes snobbery.
- the saleswoman is in retail sales; Mildred is a domestic worker.

A Sound of Thunder
Open-Book Selection Test (page 53)

Recalling and Interpreting
(48 points total; 8 points each)
1. d
2. c
3. b
4. a
5. b
6. a

Using Vocabulary
(15 points total; 3 points each)
7. a
8. b
9. c
10. b
11. c

Interpreting and Evaluating
(21 points total; 7 points each)
Notes will vary. Possible answers could include
12.
- unnaturalness of Machine
- Machine's ability to overpower nature
- incredible speed with which Machine operates
- Machine's ability to control time
13.
- power of men to change history
- fragility of history
- fragility of nature
- nature's dependence on men
- enormity of risk the men are taking
- enormity of the men's arrogance

Answers

14. • *Tyrannosaurus's* physical power
    • *Tyrannosaurus's* resemblance to machine
    • terror instilled by *Tyrannosaurus*
    • *Tyrannosaurus's* seeming invulnerability
    • *Tyrannosaurus's* superiority over the men
    • *Tyrannosaurus's* threat to the men

Evaluating and Connecting (16 points)

15. Answers will vary. Possible answers could include
    Will Eckels's fall from the Path affect the future?
    • His action could change all of time, although no one knows for certain.
    • The answer is yes, it will.
    • The change is foreshadowed by Travis's discussion of what could happen if someone were to step off the Path and the possible domino effect of killing even one seemingly unimportant thing from the past.
    How has Eckels's action changed history?
    • This action could be minor or significant.
    • The answer is the social climate of the U.S. is less supportive of democracy and more supportive of fascism.
    • This change is foreshadowed in the discussion that takes place before the trip about what things would have been like if Deutscher had been elected.

Lullaby
Selection Test (page 55)

Recalling and Interpreting
(49 points total; 7 points each)

1. a   5. d
2. d   6. b
3. c   7. b
4. d

Using Vocabulary
(8 points total; 2 points each)

8. a   10. b
9. b   11. c

Interpreting and Evaluating
(27 points total; 9 points each)

12–14. Notes will vary. Possible answers could include
Ayah and Chato learn of Jimmie's death
• Ayah feels alienated from the white world

• Chato is Ayah's link to the white world
• Ayah has no reason to admire the white world
• the white world is an intrusion on Ayah's world
• Ayah is a strong-spirited woman
• Ayah doesn't openly show her emotions
• Ayah is hit hard by son's death
• Ayah is more traditional than her husband
Chato breaks his leg
• Ayah's family is always one accident away from disaster
• Ayah's family is oppressed by Chato's employer
• discrimination is a fact of life for Ayah
Doctors come to take Danny and Ella away
• Ayah is baffled by the white world
• the white world is dangerous to Ayah
• the white world treats Ayah with little respect
• Ayah is deeply attached to her children
• Ayah depends heavily on Chato to protect her family from the white world
• Ayah is deeply affected by nature
Danny and Ella are taken away
• Ayah fears and dislikes white people
• Ayah's mistrust of white people is well-founded
• without children, Ayah has no hope or joy
• Ayah blames Chato for what happens to children
• Ayah never recovers from losing children
• Ayah never forgives Chato for loss of children
• after Ayah loses children, she has nothing left to lose
Chato is fired by the rancher
• Ayah wants Chato to suffer
• Ayah's mistrust of white people is well-founded
• Ayah never trusted whites the way Chato did
• Ayah is bitter
• Ayah has little or no reason to believe her life will improve
Danny and Ella visit Ayah
• government, in effect, stole Ayah's children
• Ayah's children never come back to live with her
• Ayah probably has no idea what happened to children
• Ayah's mistrust of white people is well-founded
• Ayah has nothing left to lose
• Ayah gave up hope long ago
• Ayah keeps feelings locked inside

Answers

Evaluating and Connecting (16 points)

15. Answers will vary. Students who believe that the story has a hero will most probably say that Ayah is the hero because
    - she is the main character.
    - she endures great tragedy.
    - her loyalty to Chato is strong.

    Students who say that the story has no hero could say that Ayah and Chato are the only possible heroes in the story, but
    - they lead empty, miserable lives.
    - they are not able to protect themselves from mistreatment by white people.
    - they no longer care deeply about anyone or anything, including themselves.
    - by the end of the story, Chato is an alcoholic suffering from memory loss and other problems typical of alcoholism.
    - at the end of the story, Ayah does nothing to prevent Chato's death.

    Students who believe that the story has a villain will most probably identify the U.S. government and/or white people in general because they
    - are responsible for the war in which Jimmie dies.
    - take the two younger children away from Ayah and Chato.
    - allow the mistreatment of Chato by his employer.

    Some students may say that Chato is a villain for the same reasons that Ayah blames him for the bad things that happen to them.

And of Clay Are We Created

Selection Test (page 57)

Recalling and Interpreting

(54 points total; 9 points each)

1. d
2. a
3. b
4. b
5. c
6. d

Using Vocabulary

(15 points total; 3 points each)

7. c
8. a
9. c
10. b
11. c

Interpreting and Evaluating

(15 points total; 5 points each)

Notes will vary. Possible answers could include

12. Words and phrases:
    - smiled
    - smile that crinkles his eyes
    - makes him look like a little boy
    - everything was fine
    - soon they would have her out
    - tensed
    - screamed
    - trapped
    - caught
    - collapsed
    - held by the bodies . . . clinging

    Slash mark:
    - between the sentences ending "have her out" and beginning "He signaled"
    - between the sentences ending "the girl screamed" and beginning "They tried again"

13. hopeful, encouraging, optimistic, suspenseful, tense
14. horrifying, shocking, depressing, heartbreaking, pessimistic, shocked

Evaluating and Connecting (16 points)

15. Answers will vary. Students could say that Rolf needs saving from
    - the burden of his past.
    - the guilt and sorrow he feels over his "abandonment" of his sister.
    - the sorrow, anger, and terror created in him by his father's abuse.
    - the horror and terror of his memories of the war and what was done to the concentration camp prisoners.
    - the wall that has closed him off from his feelings for so long.

    Students could say that Azucena saves Rolf by
    - being a role model.
    - being his soul mate.
    - touching him emotionally in a way that no one had ever been able to.
    - bringing him back in touch with his emotions.
    - showing him how to confront his worst nightmares with dignity.

Answers

Columbia's Mortal Agony
Selection Test (page 59)

Recalling and Interpreting
(55 points total; 11 points each)

1. a
2. d
3. b
4. c
5. a

Using Vocabulary
(15 points total; 3 points each)

6. b
7. c
8. c
9. b
10. a

Interpreting and Evaluating
(16 points total; 8 points each)

Notes will vary. Possible answers could include

11. objective, distant, restrained, logical, scientific
12. no emotions expressed; few, if any, emotional words used; no opinions given; many factual details having to do with speed, size, location, etc.

Evaluating and Connecting (14 points)

13. Answers will vary. Possible answers could include
    The author's attitude toward Omaira is objective, distant, restrained, and matter-of-fact. This attitude is appropriate because
    • a reporter is supposed to focus on the facts and the truth.
    • a reporter isn't supposed to get emotionally involved, because such involvement could negatively affect the presentation of facts.
    The author's attitude toward Omaira is objective, distant, restrained, matter-of-fact, and insensitive. This attitude is inappropriate because
    • what happens to Omaira is horrifying and heart-breaking.
    • the author uses Omaira's plight only to add interest to his story.
    • any victim, but especially a child, deserves more respect and sensitivity.

Winter Night
Selection Test (page 61)

Recalling and Interpreting
(50 points total; 10 points each)

1. b
2. c
3. d
4. d
5. c

Using Vocabulary
(15 points total; 3 points each)

6. a
7. b
8. a
9. c
10. c

Interpreting and Evaluating
(20 points total; 10 points each)

Notes will vary. Possible answers could include

11. A. yes
    • reader has important information about mothers and camps that Felicia doesn't
    • Felicia assumes the mothers are absent temporarily and for relatively harmless reasons; reader knows otherwise
    • reader suspects the girl in the camp cries little and is quiet due to hopelessness; Felicia would not suspect this
    B. yes
    • reader suspects that other girl came to a tragic end; Felicia would not suspect this
    • reader realizes woman is embracing other girl as well as Felicia; Felicia doesn't
    • reader realizes woman takes some comfort from holding Felicia; Felicia probably doesn't
12. A. no
    • woman means exactly what she says
    • woman doesn't tell Felicia the full truth, but leaving out details is not ironic
    A. yes
    • woman says "very quiet" but actually means "hopeless"
    • woman does not correct Felicia's misunderstanding about the mothers' absence
    B. yes
    • reader knows that woman means something different by "asleep" than Felicia realizes

Evaluating and Connecting (15 points)

13. Answers will vary. Students could say that the mother is startled because

Answers

- the scene isn't anything like the one that she usually finds when she returns late at night.
- it surprises her to find Felicia out of bed and sleeping in another woman's arms.
- her daughter is curled up in the arms of a complete stranger.
- the story suggests that there is no such intimacy between the mother and daughter.
- she is overcome with guilt and feelings of inadequacy as a mother.

Regarding whether the mother will want the woman to babysit Felicia again, students might say that the mother

- will want the woman to sit again because there is no evidence that the mother is cruel or abusive, only that she is selfish. Knowing that this sitter meets some of her daughter's emotional needs will make it easier for the mother to stay out late guilt-free.
- won't want the woman to sit again because the woman's concern for Felicia makes the mother feel guilty and bad about not staying home with Felicia. She won't want to feel this way every time she goes out.

Waltz of the Fat Man

Selection Test (page 63)

Recalling and Interpreting
(54 points total; 9 points each)

1. a   4. a
2. b   5. b
3. c   6. d

Using Vocabulary
(10 points total; 2 points each)

7. c   10. a
8. a   11. c
9. b

Interpreting and Evaluating
(24 points total; 6 points each)
Notes will vary. Possible answers could include
12. • companionship, community
    • love, intimacy
    • understanding

- happiness
- purpose, meaning, reason for living
13. no, because
    - they're disgusted by his appearance
    - they fear or are put off by his behavior
    - they're very different from him
    - they misunderstand him
    - his attitude toward women is immature, clueless, strange, and offensive
    - his behavior, especially toward women, is odd, offensive, desperate, and creepy
14. • no, because clocks are objects, objects don't have feelings
    - yes or somewhat, because he believes they're more than objects; he believes he has a special relationship with them; he believes it's possible to communicate with them; they're what get him through each day
15. yes, because
    - like him, they're "animals" who "dance"
    - they are attracted to him, need him, feel incomplete without him
    - their innermost natures or souls are similar to his
    - what makes him different from "normal" people is what makes him "normal" among circus people

Evaluating and Connecting (12 points)
16. Answers will vary. Students might say that the existence of the thin girl shows the extent of Noé's
    - loneliness.
    - weirdness.
    - desperation.
    - identity problems.
    - need to express himself.
    - tragic situation in life.
In addition, students might say that the thin girl makes them feel
    - more compassionate toward Noé, because the thin girl shows how desperate, sad, and lonely he is.
    - puzzled or put off by Noé, because the idea of Noé's having a thin girl inside of him with whom he dances all night outside of town is weird and mysterious.

Answers

The Masque of the Red Death
Selection Test (page 65)

Recalling and Interpreting
(54 points total; 9 points each)

1. b
2. d
3. b
4. d
5. c
6. a

Using Vocabulary
(10 points total; 2 points each)

7. a
8. b
9. b
10. a
11. a

Interpreting and Evaluating
(20 points total; 5 points each)
Answers will vary. Possible answers could include

12. • creepy, nightmarish
    • unreal
    • dangerous, threatening
    • tasteless
    • festive
13. • creepy, nightmarish
    • dangerous
    • immoral
    • exciting
    • unreal
14. • run from reality
    • are shallow and selfish
    • think themselves above it all
    • are easily bored with life
    • have strange values (throw parties during a plague)
    • have no taste or very bad taste
    • are immoral, have little humanity
15. • revolted, disgusted
    • uneasy, bothered, disturbed, horrified
    • angry
    • amazed, interested, fascinated

Evaluating and Connecting (16 points)
16. Answers will vary. Students who feel that the deaths of Prince Prospero and his guests are tragic might say that
    • the Red Death causes the guests to suffer. (The prince's death is instantaneous.)
    • no one has done anything that is actually wicked, and they do not deserve their fate.

• the prince and his guests thought they could escape the Red Death, but instead they become victims. Students who feel that these deaths are not tragic might say that they
• were asking to be struck down because they mocked Death.
• did nothing to ease the suffering of the other victims.
• felt little or nothing for the other victims.
• taunted Death by behaving as if they could control it.
• showed disrespect for the other victims by partying during the deadliest period of the plague.

To Da-duh, in Memoriam
Selection Test (page 67)

Recalling and Interpreting
(45 points total; 9 points each)

1. b
2. a
3. a
4. d
5. b

Using Vocabulary
(15 points total; 3 points each)

6. c
7. b
8. a
9. b
10. a

Interpreting and Evaluating
(24 points total; 6 points each)
Answers will vary. Possible answers could include

11. • narrator earns Da-duh's respect
    • narrator captures Da-duh's interest
    • narrator wins first of many confrontations with Da-duh
    • Da-duh captures narrator's interest
    • first connection is made between them
    • confrontational tone of the relationship is set
12. • Da-duh begins sharing herself and her culture with narrator
    • narrator begins sharing herself and her culture with Da-duh
    • close relationship between them begins to develop
    • Da-duh's trust in narrator increases
    • each person's knowledge of other's culture increases
13. • Da-duh's pride takes a beating
    • Da-duh's world view changes for worse

Answers

- Da-duh's world stops making sense to her
- Da-duh feels defeated
- Da-duh loses interest in the ground
- Da-duh loses hope and faith in her world
- narrator begins to feel what will be long-lasting guilt
14. • relationship between Da-duh and narrator ends
- Da-duh never gets to see Empire State Building
- narrator never gets to apologize or make up for what she did
- narrator is left with lasting sense of guilt and regret

Evaluating and Connecting (16 points)
15. Answers will vary. Students might say that the setting of the story is very important because
- the contrast between the setting and New York City is essential to the story's theme, plot, and characterization.
- one of the story's premises is that the characters are who they are because of where they live.
- the conflict between the two main characters is closely tied to where they live.
- descriptions of the setting help the reader to sympathize with the main character, for whom that setting is nearly everything.
- descriptions of the setting help the reader to understand more fully the nature of Da-duh's defeat in her confrontation with the narrator and all that she represents.

from Travels with Charley
Selection Test (page 69)

Recalling and Interpreting
(50 points total; 10 points each)

1. a   4. c
2. b   5. d
3. d

Using Vocabulary
(15 points total; 3 points each)

6. a   9. a
7. a   10. b
8. c

Interpreting and Evaluating (20 points)
11. Answers will vary. Possible answers could include
    Between:
    • training *and* ability to question

- mind *and* heart
- habit *and* rebellion against habit
- duty *and* freedom (or free will)
- desire to shoot coyotes *and* wish to let them live

Exists because:
- trained to shoot, but questions training as he watches coyotes
- can't think of good reason to do as he's been trained
- mind is filled with hard, fast rules, but heart tells him to question those rules
- he's a good, fair, smart man

Is resolved by:
- Steinbeck listening to his conscience and reason
- Steinbeck deciding against killing the coyotes

Evaluating and Connecting (15 points)
12. Answers will vary. Possible inferences could include
- Steinbeck has begun to sympathize with the coyote he is watching ("panting tongue," "leap and struggle," "torn heart").
- He views the rifle as harsh and cruel ("angry steel").
- Only someone who could not imagine the results could commit the act ("I would be long gone").
- Nature is harsh ("a naked, eyeless skull, a few picked bones . . .").
- Shooting the coyotes would destroy beauty ("a few rags of golden fur").
- The act would be brutal ("leap and struggle," "torn heart").
- He doesn't want to pull the trigger (all of the emotional language he has used).

A Child's Christmas in Wales
Selection Test (page 71)

Recalling and Interpreting
(54 points total; 9 points each)

1. c   4. d
2. b   5. a
3. d   6. a

Using Vocabulary
(10 points total; 2 points each)

7. c   10. c
8. b   11. b
9. a

Answers

Interpreting and Evaluating

(18 points total; 6 points each)

Answers will vary. Possible answers could include

12. Senses:
    - sight
    - touch

    Feelings and ideas:
    - snow is magical
    - surprise, delight
    - a cozy feeling of being home during a snowfall
    - snow covering everything
    - snow connects us to the past
    - postman covered in snow

13. Senses:
    - sight
    - taste
    - hearing

    Feelings and ideas:
    - bells heard all over town
    - town covered in snow
    - weather very cold and crisp
    - town is next to the sea
    - town has a fairy-tale setting

14. Senses:
    - sight
    - touch

    Feelings and ideas:
    - the aunts have nothing to do
    - fear
    - discomfort
    - uselessness
    - delicacy, fragility

Evaluating and Connecting (18 points)

15. Answers will vary. In discussing things they find appealing, students might include points similar to the following:
    - The boys have a lot of freedom. Few children today are allowed to roam all over town.
    - The boys play adventurous and imaginative games that require little planning and few toys. Enjoying life seems to come naturally to them.
    - Thomas's family seems very close, and the holiday is enjoyed with many relatives.
    - The boys have nothing to fear except "ghosts." They are not worried about drugs, violence, and so on.

- Customs seem important to Thomas's family and appear to bind the family together.
- It would be nice to live in a place where nature, such as the sea near Thomas's home, is a big part of one's life.

In discussing things that they don't find appealing, students could mention

- a lack of material advantages (computers, televisions, toys).
- unfamiliar foods.
- the seemingly sexist division of labor in the Thomas home (the uncles do nothing helpful on Christmas).
- the seeming unfairness of leaving some aunts out of activities that others are involved in.
- the crowded, bustling nature of the Thomas's holiday.

from Kaffir Boy
Selection Test (page 73)

Recalling and Interpreting

(42 points total; 7 points each)

1. b	4. c
2. b	5. c
3. a	6. d

Using Vocabulary

(15 points total; 3 points each)

7. a	10. a
8. c	11. b
9. b	

Interpreting and Evaluating

(28 points total; 14 points each)

Answers will vary. Possible answers could include

12. Mathabane's mother, because she believes
    - it offers the only hope for better life
    - it's needed for decent job
    - it gives power
    - it makes a person good
    - it gives a person pride
    - she wanted education but never had opportunity

    Mathabane's grandmother, because she
    - supports her daughter
    - believes the streets are dangerous
    - thinks children should be allowed to learn

    strange woman on the street, because she

Answers

- lost a child to gangs
- wishes she had made her son attend
- believes gang members die early and violently

principal, because
- he clearly sees value in education.

Mathabane himself, in the end, because he
- comes to understand his mother's view
- doesn't want to die on the street
- sympathizes with mother's situation
- values mother's efforts on his behalf
- is angry with father and wants to oppose him

13. Mathabane's father, because he
- thinks education is used by white people against black people
- thinks it only prepares black people for jobs they can't have
- doesn't want to spend money on school
- opposes his wife and her ideas
- is bitter about life and sees no hope
- has been influenced by tribal ideas
- doesn't see that his life might have been better if he'd been educated

boys in gang, because they
- believe school children are beaten
- believe students have no freedom
- would prefer to run around on the streets
- see no possible benefits of school

Mathabane himself, at first, because he
- is influenced by gang's feelings
- doesn't want to lose his freedom
- has never had benefits explained to him before
- is afraid of what might happen there

government, because
- educated population could threaten its power
- uneducated population is easier to control

Evaluating and Connecting (15 points)

14. Answers will vary. Students could say that the monologue
persuades Mathabane to attend school.
- It lets him see that school offers opportunities.
- It makes him see that his father's life has been negatively affected by not attending school.
- It makes him see his father as a man in whose footsteps he does not want to follow.

deeply moves Mathabane's emotions.

- Many things she speaks of are terribly sad (his father's ignorance, her lack of opportunities).
- She is so full of hope for him and so determined to make any sacrifices necessary to ensure a better life for him.

sets Mathabane squarely on his mother's side against his father in the battle over the family's way of life.
- His mother's arguments convince him that what she wants is both just and reasonable and what his father wants for the family is neither.
- His mother's promise also ties him more closely to her, especially considering the trouble she has already had to get him into school against his father's wishes.

from Farewell to Manzanar
Selection Test (page 75)

Recalling and Interpreting
(56 points total; 8 points each)

1. a	5. b
2. d	6. d
3. b	7. c
4. c	

Using Vocabulary
(10 points total; 2 points each)

8. c	11. c
9. a	12. b
10. b	

Interpreting and Evaluating
(20 points total; 10 points each)
Answers will vary. Possible answers could include

13. easily frightened
- terrified of a child she thinks is Chinese
- afraid of tough schoolmates on Terminal Island

friendly
- tries to make friends with bus driver
- announces to crowd that her bus is full of Wakatsukis

cheerful, easygoing
- looks forward to bus ride
- is accepting of inconveniences of camp life
- finds several aspects of camp life appealing

close to her family
- enjoys sharing bed with mother
- gets along well with siblings

- seems quite proud of oldest brother

sympathetic
- can see things from others' point of view
- realizes how difficult things are for mother
- feels sorry about oldest sister's difficulties in camp
- feels lucky compared to families split up in different camps

14. insightful, intelligent, thoughtful
    - understands and can explain a lot about each family member's reaction to Manzanar

forgiving
    - shows little bitterness about what her family was put through during the war

has good memory
    - remembers many details from long-ago events

has sense of humor
    - finds humor in situation many would see as tragic

Evaluating and Connecting (14 points)

15. Answers will vary. Possible answers could include
    The children may have found the camp easier to bear because they
    - probably weren't as upset by a lack of cleanliness, hygiene, and privacy as adults were.
    - were more likely to see the new situation as an adventure.
    - were not as aware of what it meant to be interned.
    - probably worried less about the war's outcome, the future, and so on than did the adults.
    - had fewer responsibilities than the adults.

    The narrator may have found the camp easier to bear than others in her family because
    - she had been miserable at the last two places they lived.
    - she enjoyed living with all the members of her family, including those who would not have been living with her elsewhere, such as Woody.

    Woody may have found Manzanar easier to bear than the mother of the family because
    - Woody and his wife had more living space and privacy than she did.
    - he has a naturally cheerful attitude and a good sense of humor.
    - he is outgoing, which seems to help him feel less like a victim and more in control of whatever situation he is in.

By Any Other Name

Selection Test (page 77)

Recalling and Interpreting

(56 points total; 8 points each)

1. d	5. d
2. c	6. b
3. c	7. a
4. a	

Using Vocabulary

(10 points total; 2 points each)

8. c	11. c
9. b	12. c
10. a	

Interpreting and Evaluating

(20 points total; 10 points each)
Answers will vary. Possible answers could include

13. Associations:
    - embarrassment, discomfort
    - British children with attitudes of superiority
    - solemn, quiet Indian children
    - Indian children sitting at back of class
    - being distrusted and insulted
    - trying to adapt and fit in
    - headmistress and her superior attitude
    - teachers and their unfairness
    - changed names
    - boredom
    - eating sandwiches
    - competing at games
    - heat
    - feeling disconnected
    - strangeness
    - confusion

    Atmosphere:
    - unpleasant, uncomfortable
    - disturbing
    - serious
    - hot
    - heavy
    - unfriendly

14. Associations:
    - happiness, pleasure
    - taking siestas
    - security

- mother and other family
- ayah
- winning at games
- freedom
- beauty
- nature
- playing in the garden
- smelling the flowers
- eating curry and other traditional Indian foods

Atmosphere:
- pleasurable, pleasant
- joyous, happy
- warm, comforting, cozy
- secure
- peaceful

Evaluating and Connecting (14 points)

15. Answers will vary. Possible answers could include
    The author disagrees.
    - Calling the sisters by different names makes them feel confused, insulted, and out of place.
    - The headmistress's behavior shows her disrespect for them and the value of their real Indian names.
    - Santha thinks of herself differently, depending on what she is called. She goes so far as to disconnect the girl she is at school from the girl she really is.
    - The selection suggests that people put great value in being called by their correct, real names.
    The author agrees.
    - It is the headmistress who needs to appreciate the ideas suggested by Shakespeare.
    - The headmistress should realize how shallow her preference for English names is.
    - Changing the girls' names doesn't change how they are treated in the school.

Living Well. Living Good.

Selection Test (page 79)

Recalling and Interpreting

(48 points total; 8 points each)

1. a   4. b
2. c   5. a
3. d   6. b

Using Vocabulary

(10 points total; 2 points each)

7. a   10. a
8. b   11. b
9. c

Interpreting and Evaluating

(27 points total; 9 points each)
Answers will vary. Possible answers could include

12. - Negro, black, or African American
    - proud
    - working-class
    - fun-loving, social, friendly
    - happy, satisfied with their lives
    - ageless, aging well
    - sympathetic, kind-hearted
    - agreeable, easygoing, tolerant
    - don't believe the world owes them anything

13. - white
    - wealthy
    - upper-class
    - lonely, friendless, miserable
    - not aging well
    - pathetic

14. - Living well is more a matter of personality and character than it is of wealth or luck.
    - One can learn the art of living well.
    - People who approach life as an adventure have more chances for happiness.
    - "Life seems to love the liver of it."

Evaluating and Connecting (15 points)

15. Answers will vary. Students could say Angelou implies that the couple are the way they are because they
    - stopped entertaining, socializing, and enjoying the company of others.
    - stopped enjoying each other's company.
    - didn't love life enough.
    - weren't able to take pleasure in small things.
    - may have felt that the world owed them something.
    - allowed themselves to be trapped by their physical limitations.
    - didn't know how or where to look for the fun in life.
    - allowed money to imprison and inhibit them.

Answers

A Swimming Lesson
Selection Test (page 81)

Recalling and Interpreting
(45 points total; 9 points each)

1. d   4. c
2. a   5. c
3. d

Using Vocabulary
(15 points total; 3 points each)

6. a   9. c
7. b   10. b
8. b

Interpreting and Evaluating
(24 points total; 6 points each)
Answers will vary. Possible answers could include

11. • due to poisonous fish, few learned to swim
    • slaves were shipped across sea
    • sea separated slaves from homeland
    • slaves who jumped from ships drowned
12. • not easily frightened
    • knew how to swim a little
    • swam for joy of it
    • felt strong and capable
    • as granddaughter's role model, couldn't give in to fear
13. • didn't know how to swim
    • didn't trust her body
    • sea was huge
    • sea was wild
    • sea seemed mysterious
14. • learned to swim
    • learned to understand the sea
    • learned to trust her body
    • learned to take pride in strength

Evaluating and Connecting (16 points)
15. Answers will vary. Possible answers could include
    • How to swim
      • taught her how to conquer her fears
      • showed her how to take control of her life
    • To be proud of being an African American
      • enhanced her sense of self
    • To be confident and proud

• brought greater chance for success and happiness
• allowed her to live up to her potential
• Not to let what she could not do stand in the way of what she could do
  • opened up opportunities and possibilities
  • even activities she wasn't expert at could give joy

Pizza in Warsaw, Torte in Praque
Selection Test (page 83)

Recalling and Interpreting
(54 points total; 9 points each)

1. d   4. a
2. c   5. c
3. d   6. b

Using Vocabulary
(15 points total; 3 points each)

7. a   10. a
8. c   11. b
9. b

Interpreting and Evaluating
(16 points total; 4 points each)
Answers will vary. Possible answers could include

12. • in Warsaw, can't take getting a pizza for granted
    • in Warsaw, getting pizza is a luxury
13. • many foods we think common are unknown in Eastern Europe
    • in Eastern Europe, any new food worth trying
    • in Eastern Europe, a new food is "good" because of what it represents, not necessarily for its flavor
14. • can't take finding torte in Prague for granted
    • finding torte in Prague is so hard one usually doesn't even try
    • necessary in Prague to settle for less
15. • communism failed because didn't provide steady supply of necessities such as housing, milk, fruits, vegetables
    • Eastern Europeans didn't object to politics of communism as much as to shortages of basic goods

Evaluating and Connecting (15 points)
16. Answers will vary. Possible answers could include
    • People are much more alike than they are different. (Eastern Europeans under communism had the

Answers

same basic needs, wishes, and concerns that Americans today have. Problems may vary greatly, but people are much the same.)

- Living with the constant need to locate and obtain basic food products is so exhausting that it is a miracle anyone could accomplish anything else.
- Friendship and the pleasures of socializing can survive even the most trying conditions.
- A government does not necessarily reflect the desires or ideals of the people it governs.
- We take far too much for granted and have little idea how lucky we are.

I've Seen the Promised Land

Selection Test (page 85)

Recalling and Interpreting

(45 points total; 9 points each)

1. c
2. c
3. b
4. a
5. d

Using Vocabulary

(15 points total; 3 points each)

6. a
7. c
8. c
9. b
10. b

Interpreting and Evaluating

(20 points total; 10 points each)

11–12. Answers will vary. Students might note, about King's audience, that

- there are powerful people who will try to divide them.
- they must stick together.
- lack of unity will result in no change. They will always be treated like slaves.
- no one can set them free but themselves.
- they must take responsibility for their freedom.
- they are, in a sense, a "chosen people."
- they must be willing to give up what is familiar to venture into new territory.
- they must willingly follow a good leader.
- they have been treated with cruel injustice.

Evaluating and Connecting (20 points)

13. Answers will vary. Possible answers could include

- The "promised land" is the U.S. after the success of the Civil Rights movement.
- King feels that the U.S. Constitution "promises" this land to all Americans and that African Americans are on the verge of seeing that promise fulfilled.
- King might also describe this land as: free, in that it guarantees all Americans the same rights and freedoms; blessed, in that it reflects his religious beliefs; joyous, in that it is home to many people thrilled to experience true freedom for the first time in their lives; diverse, in that it is a land of many peoples and races.

Exploring Antartic Ice

Selection Test (page 87)

Recalling and Interpreting

(50 points total; 10 points each)

1. c
2. b
3. a
4. c
5. b

Using Vocabulary

(10 points total; 2 points each)

6. a
7. c
8. c
9. b
10. a

Interpreting and Evaluating

(24 points total; 8 points each)

Notes will vary. Possible answers:

11. Rating: very important
    Reasons:
    - many factual details
    - deals with science; science is about facts
    - informs reader about Antarctic and its exploration

12. Rating: not very important
    Reasons:
    - no strong stands on any issues
    - no effort to change anyone's mind about anything
    - seems to want to convince people of beauty, fascination, importance of Antarctic, but providing straight information is more important

13. Rating: somewhat important
    Reasons:
    - begins with suspenseful anecdote

Answers

- includes details that are more entertaining than informative (such as penguins watching)

Evaluating and Connecting (16 points)
14. Answers will vary. Students might say that the author's statement seems believable because
    - she should know, as a person who has been there and explored it.
    - the freezing temperatures and vegetation are not suited to human life.
    - there is no permanent solid mass on which people could build permanent structures, since the ice appears and disappears each year.
    - not even the *Nathaniel B. Palmer* can go everywhere the crew wants it to go as quickly as they need it to.

    Students who doubt the accuracy of this statement might point out that
    - we've been to the moon, after all.
    - no one believed that the ship that set out to venture deep into the Antarctic in 1986 would succeed (or even survive), but it did.
    - there are too many other things that people have said couldn't be done that have been accomplished.
    - the technology may one day exist to allow people to live in the Antarctic.
    - people have adapted to living under extremely harsh conditions in other parts of the world.

from **A Match to the Heart**
Selection Test (page 89)

Recalling and Interpreting
(48 points total; 8 points each)

1. b	4. c
2. d	5. b
3. b	6. a

Using Vocabulary
(10 points total; 2 points each)

7. b	10. c
8. a	11. c
9. b	

Interpreting and Evaluating
(24 points total; 8 points each)
12–14. Answers will vary. Possible answers could include
    - spiritual, religious; tries to follow Buddhist instructions about dying
    - loyal, responsible; own dangerous situation doesn't prevent her from worrying about dogs
    - creative, imaginative, observant; does good job of giving important details to communicate experience of being struck by lightning
    - good-humored, good-natured; jokes about poor medical care she receives when life is on the line
    - independent; lives on a ranch miles from nearest paved road
    - unemotional, unsentimental; matter-of-fact about husband's abandoning her in time of need

Evaluating and Connecting (18 points)
15. Answers will vary. Students might find it extraordinary
    - that the author manages to get herself back to her house, because a quarter of a mile is a very long way for a person in her condition to travel.
    - that the author lives so far from even the nearest paved road, because we don't think of most places in the U.S. as being that far removed from "civilization" anymore.
    - that no one at the first hospital even cleans the author's wounds, because everyone knows this is necessary to avoid infection.
    - that so many things go wrong at the first hospital, because we expect hospitals to be safe, well-equipped, and well-run.
    - that the doctor at the second hospital doesn't follow standard medical procedures and releases the author after a minimal exam, because we think of doctors as being more careful and more caring.
    - that medical care anywhere in the U.S. could be so poor, because we tend to think that we have a good health care system.
    - that the author's husband leaves her alone in her condition, because it must have been obvious that she needed care and attention.
    - that any one person can be treated so badly by so many people in so many different places.

Answers

The Angry Winter
Selection Test (page 91)

Recalling and Interpreting
(56 points total; 8 points each)

1. c
2. a
3. b
4. d

5. b
6. d
7. b

Using Vocabulary
(9 points total; 3 points each)

8. b
9. a

10. b

Interpreting and Evaluating
(20 points total; 10 points each)

Answers will vary. Possible answers could include

11. • scholar and mild-mannered dog
    • fossils; artifacts
    • civilization; scholarship
    • reason; logic
    • peacefulness; lack of conflict
    • dependability
    • companionship
    • snow, cold; blizzard
    • midnight; darkness
    • modern human
    • sense of satisfaction; happiness
    • owner/pet relationship

12. • early man and beast
    • wildness; insecurity; chaos
    • "every man for himself"
    • instinct; instinctual responses
    • strong desire to survive at any cost
    • anger; conflict; competition
    • danger
    • conflict between human and beast for food
    • strangers; enemies
    • snow; cold
    • shadows; darkness; midnight

Evaluating and Connecting (15 points)

13. Answers will vary. Possible answers could include
    • The narrator believes the experience shows that early humans and dogs were savage creatures driven by instinct; the experience has a lasting effect only in how it revealed to the narrator that,

although modern humans are sophisticated and civilized, and dogs are domesticated, some remnants of early savage instinct remain with both humans and dogs to this day.
    • The narrator believes the experience reveals how early instinct can influence both human and dog behavior; he indicates the experience won't have a deep, lasting effect for him or his dog. The dog has already forgotten the incident, and the narrator puts the bone away on a high shelf, noting that the shadows have vanished and saying that he and Wolf had best suppress those instincts.

The Tucson Zoo
Selection Test (page 93)

Recalling and Interpreting
(36 points total; 12 points each)

1. d
2. b

3. b

Using Vocabulary
(12 points total; 4 points each)

4. a
5. b

6. a

Interpreting and Evaluating
(30 points total; 15 points each)

Answers will vary. Possible answers could include

7. • they're adorable and marvelous
   • he's "coded" to react favorably to them
   • instinct makes him "hanker for friends"
   • his DNA code includes instinct for altruism

8. • they work together
   • he's "coded" to react favorably to them
   • he thinks they offer valuable lesson about human behavior
   • his DNA code includes instinct for altruism
   • he admires their altruism

Evaluating and Connecting (22 points)

9. Answers will vary. Students might say that Thomas reveals that he
   • has an active imagination. Most people wouldn't imagine that ants think on any conscious level.
   • is unconventional. Some people wouldn't think about ants in such human terms. They would think

Answers

of them as organisms or insects or something very different from people.
- doesn't worry too much about impressing others or about injuring his reputation in the scientific community.
- values altruism and group efforts. His questions reveal a desire to experience the reaching of a group goal.
- values the individual. He is especially interested in knowing how any single ant is affected by a group's success.

Eldorado
Selection Test (page 94)

Recalling and Interpreting
(45 points total; 15 points each)
1. c
2. b
3. d

Interpreting and Evaluating
(30 points total; 15 points each)
4–5. Answers will vary. Possible answers could include
- brave, courageous; set off on his own to find Eldorado
- determined, stubborn; grows old searching for Eldorado
- ignorant, naive; wastes life searching for something that doesn't exist
- romantic, idealistic; believes in existence of legendary place
- sad, unhappy, unfulfilled; shadow comes over his heart as time goes by
- pathetic, pitiful; when very old (probably dying), asks a spirit where Eldorado might be

Evaluating and Connecting (25 points)
6. Answers will vary. Possible answers could include
The only true reward is found in heaven.
- The pilgrim shadow tells the knight that he must ride "Down the Valley of the Shadow" to find Eldorado; the phrase suggests that Eldorado exists but not in this life.
- Eldorado can be found "Over the Mountains / Of the Moon," a vague reference that suggests that it is not where any mortal can find it.
People can waste their entire lives seeking something that doesn't exist.

- The knight spends his life searching for Eldorado.
- Only when he is old and weak, perhaps dying, does he find out that his life's effort has been pointless.
The search for wealth can destroy a life.
- The poem mentions no details of the knight's life, suggesting that nothing was important except his search.
- The knight never finds what he seeks.
- The knight, at the end, has nothing of value in his life.

One Perfect Rose and Shall I Compare Thee . . .
Selection Test (page 95)

Recalling and Interpreting
(56 points total; 7 points each)
1. b
2. d
3. b
4. a
5. b
6. a
7. a
8. c

Interpreting and Evaluating
(24 points total; 12 points each)
Notes will vary. Model answers:
9. Quatrain 1: beloved is gentler, lovelier, more eternal than day in summer
Quatrain 2: summer not perfect; sometimes too hot or cloudy; beauty doesn't last
Quatrain 3: speaker's poetry will make beloved (or her beauty) immortal
10. As long as people live and can read, this poem will keep idea of the beloved alive, making her immortal.

Evaluating and Connecting (20 points)
11. Answers will vary. Students could suggest that Parker may have wanted to poke fun at the speaker (or herself).
- She portrays the speaker (who may well be herself) as someone more interested in wealth and material goods than in true love, which is not a complimentary characterization.
- She portrays the speaker (who may well be herself) as shallow while portraying the man who sends her the rose as sincere and, at least in comparison to her, deep.

Answers

romantic love in general.

- She focuses on a token traditionally given by men to women in whom they are romantically interested, and she makes fun of the deep meaning this gesture supposedly has.
- She suggests that gestures of romantic love are easy to come by and, perhaps, less meaningful than they are thought to be.
- She contrasts the rose as a symbol of romantic love with what the speaker considers a really useful and desirable possession.

men whom the speaker (or she) has dated.

- The speaker is exasperated with the man who has sent her only one single rose.
- The speaker suggests that this is the type of man she always attracts.

Simile and Well. I Have Lost You; and I Lost You Fairly
Open-Book Selection Test (page 97)

Recalling and Interpreting
(56 points total; 8 points each)

1. c
2. c
3. b
4. c

5. d
6. a
7. c

Interpreting and Evaluating
(24 points total; 8 points each)
Answers will vary. Possible answers could include

8. Deer:
   - predators
   - hunters
   - natural enemies
   People:
   - emotional pain
   - saying or doing the wrong thing
   - causing hurt
   - the end of the relationship
9. Deer:
   - with caution
   - watch, look, listen
   - ready to flee danger
   People:
   - carefully
   - tentatively

- insecurely
- watch what they say and do

10. Deer:
    - yes; deer often survive if they are cautious
    - yes; being careful and watchful is natural to deer, keeps them alive
    People:
    - yes; obviously concerned and caring; this may allow them to get over problem
    - yes; people who respond to problems by taking extra care can work things out
    - no; once people start watching everything they say and do, love begins to die
    - no; they're too ready to run, which for them will be quitting
    - no; once people become this threatened by each other or their relationship, hope is gone

Evaluating and Connecting (20 points)
11. Answers will vary. Possible answers could include
    - Behave honestly; tell the truth.
    - Keep your dignity; behave with dignity.
    - Do not play games.
    - Do not try to manipulate the other person.
    - Do not try to hold someone who does not want to be held.
    - Understand what the other person wants.
    - Enjoy what you have while you have it.
    - Give up gracefully when you must.
    - Be yourself; remain true to yourself.
    - Be realistic about the other person's feelings.
    - If it doesn't work out, get over it (or at least try).
    - Don't think you're the only person who's ever been in love.
    - Don't ruin what has been good by trying to keep the relationship going when it isn't good any more.

The Glory of the Day Was in Her Face and Missing You
Open-Book Selection Test (page 99)

Recalling and Interpreting
(60 points total; 10 points each)

1. c
2. a
3. d

4. a
5. c
6. a

Answers

Interpreting and Evaluating
(20 points total; 10 points each)

7–8. Answers will vary. Possible answers could include

Example A:
Compares: beloved's voice *to* dove's voice
Conveys:
- loveliness of beloved's voice
- low, soft quality of beloved's voice
- calming effect of beloved's voice

Example B:
Compares: beloved's smile *to* light
Conveys:
- joyous effect of beloved's smile
- warmth and loveliness of beloved's smile

Example C:
Compares: speaker's state of mind, situation, or attitude *to* unsolvable math equation written on chalkboard
Conveys:
- speaker's confusion
- speaker's frustration, or feeling that demands being made can't be fulfilled
- speaker's feeling of helplessness

Example D:
Compares: speaker's state of mind, situation, or attitude *to* pair of useless or unused oars
Conveys:
- speaker's sense of going nowhere
- speaker inability to change situation
- sense of waste

Evaluating and Connecting (20 points)

9. Answers will vary. Students might say that both speakers expect the separations to be permanent because
   - in the world of the speaker of "The Glory of the Day . . . ," all seems to have come to an end. Everything is "one with all the dead" since the beloved is gone and there is nothing in the poem to suggest that this situation will ever change. Indeed, the beloved may be dead.
   - everything in the life of the speaker of "Missing You" has come to a standstill. Nothing makes sense, nothing works, and the speaker seems to see no relief in sight.

   Students might say that the speaker of "Missing You" is hopeful for the eventual return of the beloved because

- line 5 refers to buds that are waiting, not dead, and that are in suspended animation, meaning they may eventually blossom.
- Although the speaker is miserable at the moment, nothing clearly suggests that he or she believes this situation is permanent.

First Lesson and Those Winter Sundays
Open-Book Selection Test (page 101)

Recalling and Interpreting
(60 points total; 6 points each)

1. b   6. a
2. c   7. c
3. b   8. c
4. d   9. a
5. d   10. a

Interpreting and Evaluating
(24 points total; 6 points each)
Answers will vary. Possible answers could include

11. - nature restores the spirit; speaker tells daughter that when "fear cramps," she should "lie back" and let the sea hold her
    - survival requires ability to relax; speaker indicates that when life's struggles tire the daughter, she should "lie up, and survive"
    - faith is essential; speaker indicates that daughter needs faith to lie back and let the sea hold her
    - children have to fight their own battles in life; girl's parent won't always be there to protect her; at some point, she'll swim to her own "island"
    - fear is crippling; speaker says fear "cramps your heart"
    - one must know what in life is dependable; speaker tells daughter to lie back; what she has learned will hold her

12. - love can show itself in many ways; son doesn't realize until he's grown that father's actions were motivated by love
    - love can be silent and undemonstrative; father is these things but his behavior shows love
    - one can learn by example; son looks back at ways his father demonstrated love and responsibility
    - parent's love may not be appreciated in childhood;

Answers

son doesn't appreciate or understand father's love until he's grown

- basic domestic chores can be difficult and demanding; starting the morning fires required willingness to be up in the "blueblack cold"
- love is demanding; what the father does is hard; love's duties are "austere" and "lonely"

Evaluating and Connecting (16 points)

13. Answers will vary. Students might describe the father's love as

- quiet, silent.
- undemonstrative.
- cold, solemn.
- plain and simple, straightforward.
- unreturned, unreciprocated.
- misunderstood, unappreciated, taken for granted.
- sad, depressing.
- noble, heroic, self-sacrificing, unselfish.

Students might say that the speaker failed to appreciate and understand his father's love because

- children do not realize how difficult it is just to keep a home going.
- children tend not to be grateful for the basics—food, warmth, shelter—unless they must live without them.
- there was a lot of anger and tension in the home.
- the poem suggests that the father was not emotionally demonstrative.
- the father did not demand recognition of the sacrifices he made for his son.

Horses Graze and A Blessing

Open-Book Selection Test (page 103)

Recalling and Interpreting

(48 points total; 8 points each)

1. d
2. c
3. d
4. a
5. d
6. a

Interpreting and Evaluating

(28 points total; 14 points each)

Answers will vary. Possible answers could include

7. • their simplicity; repetition emphasizes ordinary things they do, such as eating

- lack of concern with petty concerns; describes their oblivion as "majestic" and says they're "nobly oblivious"
- gentleness; describes it as "wonderful"
- satisfaction with life; speaks positively of fact that they "do not wish that they were otherwise"
- way of life; speaks positively of how they lead their lives—eating, grazing, talking to friends, and so on
- appreciation of life, optimistic viewpoint; speaks positively of the way they "love the world"

8. • friendliness, kindness; appreciates that they come to meet him and make him feel wanted

- gratitude; speaker thrilled to be source of so much joy
- trusting nature; speaker glad to have one nuzzle him
- way they feel; describes delicate skin of pony's ear

Evaluating and Connecting (24 points)

9. Answers will vary. Possible answers could include

- follies (foolish and/or wicked actions) (lines 12 and 13)
- the complexity of economic activities, the study of economics, government, bureaucracy (lines 12–15)
- the constant hustle and bustle of modern life; the tendency to always be fighting to get ahead, to get somewhere where one is not (line 25–27)
- the inability to live in the present (lines 29–31)
- the inability to appreciate reality and the simple things in life (lines 36–40)

10. Answers will vary. Students might say that the speaker is feeling

- joyously one with nature.
- thrilled.
- part of something much larger than himself or herself.

Students might say that the speaker is feeling this way because of

- being so joyfully accepted by the ponies, who are creatures of nature.
- living so much in the moment.
- experiencing a sense of union with the pones.
- feeling a sudden, strong appreciation for the natural world.

Answers

Afro-American Fragment and Heaven
Open-Book Selection Test (page 105)

Recalling and Interpreting
(60 points total; 10 points each)
1. b   4. d
2. d   5. c
3. a   6. d

Interpreting and Evaluating
(24 points total; 6 points each)
Answers will vary. Possible answers could include
7. distant, foreign, strange
   • his roots are many generations removed from Africa
   • Africa is "So long, / So far away"
   • he knows little about Africa
   • he doesn't understand the "song"
   mysterious, fascinating
   • it calls to him in a way he can't understand
   • he can sense "bitter yearnings"
8. distant, foreign, strange
   • she's never been there, doesn't feel drawn to it
   • she thinks of it only as "blue flower" on a map
   mysterious: her son is drawn to it even though she isn't
9. flat: it's on "the pancake plains"
   difficult: air is thin
   lonely, grim, unpleasant
   • its features are broken fences, rattletrap cars
   • it is "mean and grubby"
   wild: there are shootouts and fistfights
10. magical, heaven-like
    • he is a "dreamer"
    • he feels drawn to his ancestral roots
    beautiful, lovely
    • he's imaginative
    • he associates China with the lovely mountains he sees in the distance

Evaluating and Connecting (16 points)
11. Answers will vary. Possible answers for "African-American Fragment":
    • The songs are anything that reminds the speaker of Africa or that speaks to him about his African roots.

• The songs could be actual songs or anything else that comes from, or has been influenced by, African culture.
• The songs are subconscious "messages" that are rooted in his genes.
Possible answers for "Heaven":
Singing seems to symbolize a person's attachment to a place.
   • For the speaker's son, China is only "an octave away," suggesting that the separation is only one of physical distance.
   • For the speaker, the separation is greater. The fact that she "can't sing that far" suggests that she can't actually feel China, that it isn't part of her soul as it is part of her son's.
Singing is imagining or dreaming.
   • The speaker's son ("a dreamer") has no trouble imagining China. For him, China is "only an octave away."
   • Having never seen China, the speaker cannot imagine it. She cannot "sing that far."

The Base Stealer and To Satch
Open-Book Selection Test (page 107)

Recalling and Interpreting
(48 points total; 12 points each)
1. d   3. b
2. d   4. a

Interpreting and Evaluating
(30 points total; 15 points each)
Answers will vary. Model answers follow.
5. Image: runner standing between bases with arms spread out, each hand pointing to a base
   Ideas and feelings:
   • runner's intense focus
   • careful balance of runner's body
   • runner's readiness to act
   • suspense
   • excitement
6. Image: pitcher turning around and saying to God, "How about that!"
   Ideas and feelings
   • pitcher's pride in his abilities

Answers

- pitcher's innocent, childlike nature
- pitcher's love of baseball
- joy

Evaluating and Connecting (22 points)

7. Answers will vary. Possible answers could include
   Both poems communicate the joy of playing baseball.
   - In "The Base Stealer," the pure joy of running bases is communicated through such phrases as "bouncing tiptoe," "kid skipping rope," "tingles," and "hovers like an ecstatic bird."
   - In "To Satch," the pure joy of the game is communicated through imagery; the pitcher pitches stars and then turns to God to share the happiness he gets from pitching strikes.
   Both poems communicate the idea that baseball is a game of skill.
   - In "The Base Stealer," the runner's skill is emphasized in phrases such as "Poised between going on and back, pulled / Both ways taut like a tightrope-walker," and "Delicate, delicate, delicate, delicate—now!"
   - "To Satch" is a tribute to Satch's pitching skills. Satch is portrayed as being larger-than-life and his skills as being good enough to impress or amaze even God.

Ex-Basketball Player and Miss Rosie

Open-Book Selection Test (page 109)

Recalling and Interpreting

(56 points total; 7 points each)

1. b
2. c
3. c
4. d
5. c
6. b
7. c
8. d

Interpreting and Evaluating

(30 points total; 10 points each)
Answers will vary. Possible answers could include

9. "Ex-Basketball Player":
   - sympathy
   - admiration
   - sadness
   - regret over wasted life

"Miss Rosie":
   - sympathy
   - sadness
   - concern

10. "Ex-Basketball Player":
   - "stands tall among the idiot pumps"
   - "He was good: in fact, the best"
   - "ball loved Flick"
   - "His hands were like wild birds."
   - "he just sells gas"
   - "His hands are fine and nervous on the lug wrench. / It makes no difference to the lug wrench, though."
   - "Grease-gray"
   - "just nods / Beyond her face toward the bright applauding tiers / Of Necco Wafers, Nibs, and Juju Beads"

"Miss Rosie":
   - "in your old man's shoes / with the little toe cut out"
   - "waiting for your mind / like next week's grocery"
   - "used to be the best looking / gal in Georgia"
   - "used to be called the Georgia Rose"
   - "I stand up / through your destruction"

11. "Ex-Basketball Player":
   - Flick was once a great athlete whose skills he greatly admired
   - Flick never achieved his potential
   - Flick isn't particularly happy
   - Flick's life is at a dead-end
   - Flick doesn't seem to have lived or grown since high school

"Miss Rosie":
   - Miss Rosie has come down in life
   - Miss Rosie has had a hard life
   - Miss Rosie is old and poor
   - Miss Rosie seems alone in the world and in great need of another's care

Evaluating and Connecting (14 points)

12. Answers will vary. Students might say that the speaker
   - is saying that she won't let what has happened to Miss Rosie happen to her.
   - challenges fate, defies it to do to her what it has done to Miss Rosie.
   - intends to do something to prevent a similar fate for others.

Answers

- is determined to take a more active role in her own life and in the lives of others.
- feels indignant, defiant, responsible, and empowered.

The Road Not Taken and We Are Many
Open-Book Selection Test (page 111)

Recalling and Interpreting
(64 points total; 8 points each)

1. a
2. b
3. b
4. d
5. c
6. d
7. b
8. a

Interpreting and Evaluating
(20 points total; 5 points each)
Answers will vary. Possible answers could include

9. • curiosity
   • bewilderment
   • frustration
   • dismay
10. • the speaker
    • the speaker's behavior
    • the human condition
11. • lists odd things about himself that he doesn't understand
    • does things he doesn't intend to
    • doesn't behave as he'd like to
    • envies "even the horses" in movies
    • would like to see if other people have same problem
12. • finds his behavior odd and confusing
    • embarrasses himself
    • thinks his "real" self is better than "other" selves
    • wants to be proud of himself
    • most people want to make sense to themselves

Evaluating and Connecting (16 points)
13. Answers will vary. Students could indicate that the speaker realizes that the choice is pretty much a final one; there probably won't be a chance to make the choice again because
    • time changes people and things; it is impossible to go back to exactly the way things once were.

- it is difficult to change direction once one has set a course in life.
    There are things that must be given up or got out from under.
    One choice leads to another and another ("way leads on to way").
- people change over time, may not want what they once wanted, and/or do not have the same opportunities that they once had.
- people often get trapped by the lives they have chosen or decisions they have made.

The Floral Apron and My Mother Pieced Quilts
Open-Book Selection Test (page 113)

Recalling and Interpreting
(56 points total; 8 points each)

1. c
2. b
3. c
4. a
5. d
6. d
7. b

Interpreting and Evaluating
(24 points total; 12 points each)
Answers will vary. Model answers follow:

8. Image: woman wearing floral apron, cleaning squid while children watch
   Description:
   • everyday
   • domestic
   • humorous
   Communicated:
   • woman is used to cleaning squid, doesn't think much about it
   • children, on the other hand, are grossed out
9. Image: woman arranging brightly colored fabric pieces
   Description:
   • lovely
   • surprising
   • colorful
   Communicated:
   • mother was artistic
   • importance of arrangement of pieces
   • mother's skill and care
   • speaker's respect for mother and pride in her talent

Answers

Evaluating and Connecting (20 points)

10. Answers will vary. Students might say that the apron is important to the speaker of "The Floral Apron" because
    - it was worn by her teacher, "an elder of the tribe," who taught her Chinese traditions and customs, "how to honor the village, the tribe."
    - to her, it has come to symbolize tradition, community, family, and respect for knowledge.

    For "My Mother Pieced Quilts," students could say that the quilts are important to the speaker because they
    - were made by her mother, whom she admired and loved.
    - reflect the family's past and tell family stories.
    - have protected and warmed the family in both body and spirit.
    - were skillfully, artistically, and lovingly made.

A Bus Along St. Clair: December and Freeway 280
Open-Book Selection Test (page 115)

Recalling and Interpreting
(48 points total; 12 points each)

1. b   3. b
2. a   4. c

Interpreting and Evaluating
(32 points total; 16 points each)
Answers will vary. Possible answers could include

5. Feeling:
    - positive
    - longing
    - saw it as a way out
    - wanted it
    - approving

    Reasons:
    - wanted to escape the neighborhood ("Once, I wanted out")
    - was unhappy with her life as it was ("wanted the rigid lanes / to take me to a place without sun, / without the smell of tomatoes burning")
    - saw it as route to freedom, more exciting life
    - wanted changes it would bring

6. Feeling:
    - negative
    - bitterness

    - resentment
    - sees it as destructive

    Reasons:
    - it's responsible for destruction of neighborhood ("The freeway conceals it / all beneath a raised scar.")
    - loss of neighborhood makes her feel like she's lost an important part of herself ("Maybe it's here / . . . where I'll find it, that part of me / mown under / like a corpse")
    - wants to recover part of herself that used to be less important to her

Evaluating and Connecting (20 points)
7. Answers will vary. Possible answers could include
    The speaker is
    - nature.
    - wilderness.
    - eternity; time.
    - something supernatural that prevails.

    The message is that
    - mankind can try to erase nature by building cities but will not succeed.
    - nature, or time, is more powerful than any human endeavor.
    - the wilderness exists under everything mankind builds, just waiting to reassert itself.
    - mankind is temporary, nature is eternal.
    - there are eternal powers that are stronger than mankind and more enduring than human effort.

Making a Fist and What We Believe
Open-Book Selection Test (page 117)

Recalling and Interpreting
(36 points total; 12 points each)

1. a   3. c
2. c

Interpreting and Evaluating
(40 points total; 20 points each)
Answers will vary. Possible answers could include

4. Symbolizes:
    - desire to live
    - possession of inner strength or fighting spirit

* life, survival
* struggle, conflict

Support:

* mother defines dying as "When you can no longer make a fist"
* through life, speaker continues making fist, suggesting he or she is fighter, actively fighting against death

5. Symbolize:

* spiritual beliefs of people in poem
* the culture in poem
* people in poem
* truth
* tradition

Support:

* horses are essential element of poem
* people make blankets for the horses
* horses listen to people's stories
* people believe they were once horses, will be again

Evaluating and Connecting (22 points)

6. Answers will vary. Students might say that the mother's response is

* wise. It has several levels of meaning and provides a lasting lesson about life.
* respectful and sympathetic. It treats the child's exaggerated fear of dying seriously.
* creative. It is an answer that is very clear, simple, and easy to understand.
* appropriate. It is an effective response to a child's fears of death.

Foreign Ways and Song for My Name

Open-Book Selection Test (page 119)

Recalling and Interpreting

(45 points total; 15 points each)

1. c   3. d
2. d

Interpreting and Evaluating (40 points total; 20 points each)
Answers will vary. Possible answers could include

4. Senses:

* sight
* hearing

Idea or feeling:

* speaker is Midwesterner
* speaker has graceful, easy way of running
* speaker has American accent
* compared to Chinese, speaker is noticeable, perhaps loud, dramatic, or flamboyant

5. Senses:

* sight
* hearing
* touch

Ideas or feeling:

* peacefulness
* mother's delicacy
* cleanlines

Evaluating and Connecting (15 points)

6. Answers will vary. Students might describe the tone as proud.

* The speaker suggests pride in her name, mentioning people and things to which it is connected and indicating pride in the ability to withstand hardship.
* The speaker knows her name will be with her forever and seems to like this idea.
* The speaker says her mother loves "such a name," and her mother is described in very positive terms.

solemn or serious.

* The speaker details hardships she associates with her name.
* The speaker's life as a person with "that name" seems bleak and difficult.

Night Clouds and Tiger Year

Open-Book Selection Test (page 121)

Recalling and Interpreting

(54 points total; 9 points each)

1. b   4. a
2. b   5. c
3. d   6. a

Interpreting and Evaluating

(24 points total; 8 points each)
Answers will vary. Possible answers could include

7. sight, possibly also touch and smell

Answers

8. **a** stars *and* flowers
   b. stars *and* people
   c. stars' "hands" *and* clouds
9. **a** what the stars look like
   b. stars just coming out
   c. moon is moving
   d. moon is very special

Evaluating and Connecting (22 points)
10. Answers will vary. Possible answers could include
    • Energetic. The clouds are very active; they "rush," "beat," "stand," "paw," "fly," and "strain."
    • Desperate: The clouds are driven by the need to avoid being killed by the sun.
    • Hardworking: The clouds "strain" their "utmost."
    • In a hurry: The clouds "rush" and "fly."
    • Frightened: The clouds beat upon the glass Heavens and paw at its doors.

For Poets and Reapers
Open-Book Selection Test (page 123)

Recalling and Interpreting
(56 points total; 7 points each)
1. b
2. d
3. a
4. a
5. b
6. c
7. d
8. c

Interpreting and Evaluating
(24 points total; 12 points each)
Answers will vary. Possible answers could include
9. Image: person emerging from hole on bright sunny day
   Feelings and ideas:
   • joy
   • love of life
   • appreciation of nature
   • poets need to expose themselves to life
   • poets shouldn't "hole themselves up"
   • experiencing nature is vital to poets
   Theme: Poets must be active and open to experience.
10. Image: bloody mower blade rotating through field
    Feelings and ideas:
    • disgust
    • shock

• life is cheap
• life goes on
• machines don't care
Theme: Life goes on despite the needs and hurts of the individual.

Evaluating and Connecting (20 points)
11. Answers will vary. Possible answers could include
    • The speaker urges poets to soar so high and sing so beautifully that they impress even those who do these things naturally, the birds.
    • The speaker is talking about the need for poets to expand their thoughts, their emotions, and their experiences of life.
    • This might be particularly important to poets because poetry is a very expressive genre. Those who have very limited experiences, emotions, and ideas have very little to share and express.

Three Haiku and Two Tanka
Open-Book Selection Test (page 125)

Recalling and Interpreting
(60 points total; 12 points each)
1. b
2. d
3. b
4. a
5. c

Interpreting and Evaluating (20 points)
Answers will vary. A model answer follows:
6. Image: branch with raindrops hanging from it
   Response:
   • sense of familiarity
   • pleasure
   • delight in description

Evaluating and Connecting (20 points)
7. Answers will vary. Possible answers:
   The poets' attitude is wistful. Several of the poems stress the idea that the beauty of nature and its pleasures are temporary.
   The attitude is appreciative. Each of the poems deals with nature, and several are quite detailed.
   The attitude is positive. Even the second haiku, which suggests a negative feeling, also suggests an associated positive feeling.

Spring is seen as bringing joy.

- The sad tone of the second haiku comes from the speaker's realization that the joy spring brings is temporary rather than from any negative reaction to spring itself.
- The first tanka expresses delight in a spring scene.
- The second tanka suggests the speaker's belief that life in a flowerless place would be almost unbearable.

A Motto from Poets: Leave Stone and Constantly risking absurdity

Open-Book Selection Test (page 127)

Recalling and Interpreting

(64 points total; 8 points each)

1. d
2. b
3. a
4. d
5. c
6. d
7. b
8. c

Interpreting and Evaluating

(20 points total; 5 points each)

9–12. Answers will vary. Possible answers could include

- to risk personal humiliation and failure; "constantly risking absurdity / and death"
- to entertain readers; "performs / above the heads / of his audience"
- to educate, inform, or bring fresh insights to readers; "performs / above the heads / of his audience"
- to bring personal insights into the work; "climbs on rime / to a high wire of his own making"
- to discover and communicate the truth; "and all without mistaking / any thing / for what it may not be"
- not to shy away from the hard truths of life; "For he's the super realist / who must perforce perceive / taut truth"
- to seek out beauty; "in his supposed advance / toward still higher perch / where Beauty stands and waits"
- to capture and communicate beauty; "a little charleychaplin man / who may or may not catch / her fair eternal form"

Evaluating and Connecting (16 points)

13. Answers will vary. Possible answers could include

- The motto that poets use fails to consider the fleeting nature of life, a poet's work, and fame or success.
- Writers, or poets, should recognize the fact that their work, like trees, will "die."
- Although growth, change, and fame are desirable, the durability of one's work is also of great value.
- Part of the value of poetry is simply the recording of the fact that one existed and felt.

let my spirit in time and Jazz Fantasia

Open-Book Selection Test (page 129)

Recalling and Interpreting

(56 points total; 7 points each)

1. b
2. d
3. b
4. c
5. a
6. d
7. a
8. b

Interpreting and Evaluating

(24 points total; 6 points each)

9–10. Answers will vary. Model answers:
music notes flying into space

- peaceful, mellow
- uplifting
- smooth, predictable rhythm

rivers flowing toward a sunrise

- cool and warm at the same time
- constant, flowing rhythm
- pleasurable, soothing

11–12. Answers will vary. Model answers:
racing car fleeing from motorcycle cop

- exciting, thrilling
- loud
- jarring, jolting
- unpredictable

Mississippi steamboat on a river at night

- mellow, peaceful
- somewhat sad and lonely
- soft and quiet

Answers

Evaluating and Connecting (20 points)

13. Answers will vary. Possible answers could include
    - Each speaker's attitude is one of appreciation, admiration, and enthusiasm.
    - The speaker of "let my spirit fly in time" holds this attitude because listening to jazz sets her spirit free, fills her with pleasure, and takes her on a pleasurable emotional journey.
    - The speaker of "Jazz Fantasia" holds this attitude because of the emotional effects of listening to jazz. The music has the power to inspire a wide range of emotional reactions. It seems that a single night's worth of jazz can provide a lifetime's worth of emotional experiences.

from Big River: The Adventures of Huckleberry Finn
Selection Test (page 131)

Recalling and Interpreting
(40 points total; 10 points each)
1. d
2. c
3. b
4. b

Interpreting and Evaluating
(40 points total; 10 points each)

5–6. Answers will vary. Possible answers could include
    - superstitiousness; at first, believes Huck is a ghost
    - practicality; knows how to live on his own in the wild
    - honesty; tells Huck he's run away
    - fairness, trustworthiness; runs away from owner only because she betrays him
    - intelligence; doesn't blindly trust owner, keeps an ear out when slave trader begins visiting
    - courage; plans to take considerable risks in search for freedom
    - appreciation, gratitude; expresses deep gratitude for Huck's offer of help

7–8. Answers will vary. Possible answers could include
    - cleverness; fakes death to escape father
    - straightforwardness; doesn't try to keep what he's done secret from Jim
    - curiosity; asks Jim lots of questions

- independent; doesn't care what others think of his decision to help Jim
- courage; plans to help Jim reach freedom at danger to himself
- wisdom; realizes Jim has better chance of escape with his help
- kindness, selflessness; plans to help Jim reach freedom at danger to himself

Evaluating and Connecting (20 points)

9. Answers will vary. Students might note some of the following advantages to Huck:
    - He won't be alone in the world.
    - He'll gain Jim's friendship and loyalty.
    - He'll have the general satisfaction that results from being the kind of person who helps friends in need rather than deserting them.
    - He'll have somewhere to go and something to do instead of just drifting aimlessly.
    - It sounds like it could lead to an enjoyable and exciting adventure.

Students might note the following disadvantages to Huck:
    - He has to give up some of his freedom.
    - He could be severely punished for helping a runaway slave.

Antigone, Part 1
Selection Test (page 133)

Recalling and Interpreting
(48 points total; 6 points each)
1. a
2. c
3. b
4. a
5. b
6. b
7. d
8. c

Interpreting and Evaluating
(32 points total; 8 points each)
Answers will vary. Possible answers could include
9. Protagonist: Antigone
   Support:
    - play named after her
    - she's main character
    - main conflict is between her and Creon
    - she's easiest to sympathize with

Answers

10. Antagonist: Creon
    Support:
    - he's important character but not main one
    - he's Antigone's main opposition
    - main conflict is between Antigone and him
11. Conflict:
    - between Creon and Antigone
    - involves loyalty to state versus loyalty to family
    - involves doing what one knows to be right versus following the law
    - involves duty to state versus duty to gods
12. Effects on Antigone:
    - she's alienated from Ismene
    - she's imprisoned and sentenced to death
    Effects on Creon:
    - his authority is threatened
    - his ability to rule is threatened
    - his family's happiness is upset

Evaluating and Connecting (20 points)

13. Answers will vary. Most students will argue that neither character is completely in the right because
    - both are fanatics.
    - neither considers compromise.
    - neither sympathizes in the least with the other, even though there are ample reasons for doing so.

    In addition, most students will probably argue that Antigone is more in the right, noting that
    - she is serving a greater purpose (duty to family and duty to the gods) than Creon is (the authority of the state).
    - her cause is more just than Creon's is. The consequences of her brother's not being buried are far greater than those that Creon fears would be the case if he were to allow the burial.
    - Antigone's actions would pose no real threat to a wise and strong leader.

    Students who argue that Creon is more in the right might note that
    - Polyneices's actions were treasonous.
    - as the leader of the state, Creon is in the right to outlaw the burial of a traitor.
    - as the leader of the state, it is Creon's duty to do what is best for the state as a whole as opposed to what is best for his family.

Antigone, Part 2
Selection Test (page 135)

Recalling and Interpreting
(49 points total; 7 points each)

1.	b	5.	b
2.	c	6.	a
3.	d	7.	c
4.	b		

Using Vocabulary
(15 points total; 3 points each)

8.	b	11.	e
9.	a	12.	d
10.	c		

Interpreting and Evaluating
(18 points total; 6 points each)
Answers will vary. Model answers:

13. Rating: very important
    Reasons:
    - Creon's pride keeps him from obeying gods, even when they show displeasure by refusing offerings
    - Creon's pride keep him from seeing that Antigone's actions are moral
    - Creon's pride starts chain of events leading to suicides of son and wife
14. Rating: somewhat important
    Reasons:
    - Creon's errors in judgment contribute to tragedy but aren't most important cause
    - Creon's errors in judgment make him see Antigone as threat to his power
    - Creon's errors in judgment result in his failing to understand Haimon's warning
    - Creon's errors in judgment make him unable to see way out of his predicament
15. Rating: very important
    Reasons:
    - fate has doomed Oedipus's family members
    - Creon can be seen as tool of fate

Evaluating and Connecting (18 points)
16. Answers will vary. Students might consider none of these characters heroic because
    - those who stand up for justice—Antigone and Haimon—kill themselves when the going gets tough.

Answers

- Creon can't be considered heroic because he is responsible for the tragedy.
- Ismene and Eurydice function mainly as victims; they do nothing that one could consider heroic.

Antigone heroic because
- she defies the laws of the state to uphold those of the gods, knowing full-well that the consequence is likely to be death.
- she never swerves from her higher purpose or regrets her actions.

Creon heroic because
- he, like all tragic heroes, is basically a good man who is tragically flawed.
- he, in the end, comes to regret his behavior and tries to do the right thing; tragically, it is too late.
- he comes to take full responsibility for the tragedy that befalls the family.

Haimon is heroic because
- he follows his conscience, defying his father and the laws of the state.
- shows courage in opposing his father.
- makes every effort to persuade his father to do what is right.
- is a good person who is basically caught in the middle of a tragic situation.

The Tragedy of Julius Caesar, Act 1

Selection Test (page 137)

Recalling and Interpreting

(72 points total; 9 points each)

1. b
2. b
3. d
4. c
5. c
6. a
7. a
8. d

Interpreting and Evaluating

(8 points total; 4 points each)
Answers will vary. Possible answers could include
9. Suggests:
   - heartbeat
   - regular drumbeat

- solemn march
- someone who is serious and concerned

Reasons:
- nearly perfect iambic pentameter
- use of short, simple words

10. Suggests:
    - stopping and starting
    - bursts of energy
    - someone who is uncertain
    - someone who has mixed feelings

Reasons:
- imperfect iambic pentameter
- irregular rhythm in third line
- interruption of the regular rhythm
- emphasis on first syllable of "merely," second syllable of "myself," and "vexed" break up regular rhythm
- one extra syllable in sixth line

Evaluating and Connecting (20 points)

11. Answers will vary. Possible answers could include
    In Brutus's presence, Cassius
    - flatters Brutus.
    - tries to encourage Brutus to talk.
    - declares great affection for Brutus.
    - carefully tests Brutus's response to his comments about Caesar.

    When he is away from Brutus, Cassius
    - expresses his certainty of being able to win Brutus.
    - boasts about his ability to influence Brutus.
    - makes his deep hatred of Caesar obvious.

    His behavior changes because
    - it is very important to win Brutus to his side.
    - he cannot risk offending Brutus.
    - he must be sure of Brutus before revealing too much to him.

12. Answers will vary. Possible answers:
    - Brutus respects the Roman system of government but hates Caesar's increasing power within it.
    - Brutus fears tyranny but also fears the responsibility of leadership.
    - Brutus cares for Caesar personally but hates the way he rules.
    - Brutus sees himself as Caesar's equal but recognizes Caesar's power.

Answers

The Tragedy of Julius Caesar, Act 2
Open-Book Selection Test (page 139)

Recalling and Interpreting
(72 points total; 9 points each)

1. b
2. c
3. b
4. a
5. c

6. b
7. a
8. a
9. d

Interpreting and Evaluating
(12 points total; 6 points each)
Answers will vary. Possible answers could include
10. Reasons:
   - secret thought that can't yet be revealed (except to audience)
   - Shakespeare wants audience aware of irony—Caesar wants Trebonius nearby, while Trebonius intends to help murder him
   Reveals:
   - intends to follow through with assassination
   - takes some pleasure in deceiving Caesar
11. Reasons:
   - personal thought that can't yet be revealed (except to audience)
   - Shakespeare wants audience in on Brutus's moral struggle
   Reveals:
   - conscience bothered by deceiving Caesar
   - has some qualms about assassination
   - has mixed feelings
   - is deep person who examines feelings, motives, etc.

Evaluating and Connecting (16 points)
12. Answers will vary. Possible answers could include Act 2, scene 1 takes place on the ides of March at night—specifically,
   - a night when the weather is stormy.
   - a night when there are earthquakes.
   - a night when people are having nightmares.
   - a night when comets are streaking across the sky.
   - a night when supernatural events are said to take place (the appearance of ghosts, visions of blood, etc.).
   - on a date Caesar has been warned about.

The setting contributes to an atmosphere that is
   - dark, shadowy.
   - eerie, spooky.
   - suspenseful.
This atmosphere is appropriate to a scene about
   - conspiracy.
   - dark secrets.
   - plans to commit murder.

The Tragedy of Julius Caesar, Act 3
Selection Test (page 141)

Recalling and Interpreting
(70 points total; 7 points each)

1. a
2. d
3. c
4. d
5. c

6. c
7. b
8. c
9. a
10. d

Interpreting and Evaluating
(15 points total; 5 points each)
Answers will vary. Possible answers could include
11. With conspirators:
   - tactfully
   - haltingly
   - cautiously
   - respectfully
12. With body:
   - boldly
   - angrily
   - explosively
13. Difference:
   With conspirators:
   - fears being killed
   - realizes danger of angering conspirators
   - needs to figure out what to do
   - must restrain himself in order to get revenge later
   With body:
   - is overcome by sight of body
   - doesn't need to restrain true feelings
   - releases emotion previously held in
   - is free to speak truthfully

Answers

Evaluating and Connecting (15 points)

14. Answers will vary. Possible answers could include
    - Brutus speaks in prose because his greatest concern is to explain, not to inspire.
    - Brutus wants to get his speech over with.
    - Brutus wants to lull the crowd, which he tries to do with logic.
    - Antony wants to challenge and inspire, which he can do more easily with verse.
    - Antony wants the words to ring in his listeners' ears, to be memorable.
    - Verse stirs emotions more easily than does prose.
    - Verse emphasizes Antony's passion and conviction.

15. Answers will vary. Students could say that Antony's repeated refererence
    - allows him to begin without alienating the crowd.
    - keeps his remarks from challenging Brutus's widespread reputation.
    - honors the letter (but not the spirit) of his agreement with Brutus about the nature of his address to the crowd.
    - points out the difference between Brutus's behavior and his reputation.
    - gradually allows this description to shift from supposedly sincere to clearly ironic.
    - makes the crowd see for itself just how ironic the description is.

The Tragedy of Julius Caesar, Act 4

Selection Test (page 143)

Recalling and Interpreting

(70 points total; 7 points each)

1. d	6. c
2. c	7. a
3. d	8. c
4. b	9. a
5. a	10. c

Interpreting and Evaluating

(16 points total; 8 points each)
Notes will vary. Possible answers:

11. Taking:
    - leads to fortune
    - success

Missing:
    - getting stuck in shallows and miseries
    - failure

12. • human activities—good fortune and bad fortune—come and go in waves
    - when you're ready, take advantage of moment or risk everything
    - time is right to march
    - they should take advantage of current strength to go on to victory
    - if they wait, they may lose chance and be defeated

Evaluating and Connecting (14 points)

13. Answers will vary. Possible answers could include
    - guilt over having argued with Brutus when he was grieving over Portia's death
    - the sense that Brutus is deeply committed to this plan
    - a desire to avoid further conflict with Brutus
    - a desire to repair his relationship with Brutus

The Tragedy of Julius Caesar, Act 5

Selection Test (page 145)

Recalling and Interpreting

(64 points total; 8 points each)

1. b	5. a
2. c	6. b
3. a	7. b
4. d	8. d

Interpreting and Evaluating

(16 points total; 8 points each)
Answers will vary. Possible answers could include

9. Appropriate:
    - action driven first by plot against Caesar, later by chaos following his death
    - without Caesar, no plot
    - Caesar's presence felt throughout, first as leader and later as ghost
    - Caesar is most famous of characters
    - Caesar is most significant historical figure

10. Inappropriate:
    - Caesar dies midway through play
    - play concentrates on motivations, actions, feelings of Cassius and Brutus

Answers

- Caesar portrayed as arrogant, pompous, unlikeable in every way
- sympathies are with murderers, not victim
- Brutus is hero of play
- tragedy is conspirators' downfall, not Caesar's death

Evaluating and Connecting (20 points)
11. Answers will vary. Students could note that Brutus's idealism
- causes him to become involved in the murder in the first place.
  Brutus is manipulated by Cassius's appeals to his idealism.
  Brutus fails to see Cassius's selfish and hateful motivations for what they are.
  Brutus assumes that Cassius is like him and is driven by the same concerns.
- makes him oppose the murder of Antony.
  If Antony had been killed with Caesar, the conspirators would have succeeded.
  Brutus should have recognized the type of person that Antony was.
- makes him allow Antony to give a funeral speech.
  It is Antony's clever manipulation of the crowd that creates widespread opposition to the conspirators.
  Brutus should have realized that Antony could, and would, do this.
- leads him to think that merely explaining to the crowd the conspirators' reasons for their action
- would be sufficient to create order and stability.
- creates conflict between Cassius and him. Brutus is shocked and infuriated by Cassius's greed, only because he was too idealistic to see this quality in Cassius much earlier.
- makes him the leader of the rebellion.
  Cassius and the other conspirators want the appearance of high ideals, so they make Brutus the leader.
  Brutus is a poor choice as the leader of a political rebellion.
  Cassius has more military experience and is a better strategist.

The Ring of General Macías and Marked
Selection Test (page 147)

Recalling and Interpreting
(49 points total; 7 points each)
1. c   5. a
2. b   6. d
3. c   7. c
4. b

Using Vocabulary
(15 points total; 3 points each)
8. c   11. a
9. c   12. c
10. b

Interpreting and Evaluating
(18 points total; 6 points each)
Answers will vary. Possible answers could include
13. • audience knows wine is poisoned, soldiers don't
- audience knows Raquel's letter won't be delivered to husband; soldiers expect to deliver it
- audience knows Raquel wants both soldiers poisoned; Andrés thinks she's being proper hostess
14. • when Raquel says "I'll be through in a moment," she really means she'll be "through" with soldiers, not with letter
- when Raquel says "He'll probably never have another chance to taste such wine," she really means it's his last chance to taste anything
- when Raquel says "such wine," she really means "poisoned," not "fine"
15. • soldiers expect to leave safely, not die
- audience expects Raquel to respond to social justice of rebels' cause; instead she kills them

Evaluating and Connecting (18 points)
16. Answers will vary. Possible "gains" include
- preservation of the family's honor.
- preservation of her husband's reputation.
- preservation of her own sense of honor in that she, at least, has not behaved traitorously to the Federal cause.
- avoidance of the pain of living with a man she can no longer respect.

Answers

Possible "losses" include
- her husband.
- her marriage.
- the chance of happiness, both present and future.
- the guilt she may suffer over killing men she has come (to some degree) to admire and respect.

from Le Morte d'Arthur
Selection Test (page 149)

Recalling and Interpreting
(48 points total; 12 points each)
1. d
2. d
3. c
4. b

Using Vocabulary
(10 points total; 2 points each)
5. b
6. d
7. c
8. e
9. a

Interpreting and Evaluating
(20 points total; 10 points each)
10–11. Answers will vary. Possible answers could include
- honorable, courteous
- powerful knight, good fighter
- wants justice or revenge; holds a grudge
- values pride, honor, nobility, bravery, justice
- loved brother; values family
- goes to extremes
- recognizes others' strengths

Evaluating and Connecting (22 points)
12. Answers will vary. Possible answers could include
- Sir Launcelot's most impressive qualities are
    courage.
    confidence.
    chastity.
    loyalty.
    physical attractiveness.
- His most impressive talent is skill at combat.
- He displays courage, confidence, and skill at combat in his encounters with other knights. He regularly challenges other knights, and meets their challenges, without a second thought, and he always wins.

- His chastity is demonstrated in
    his refusal to become the lover of any of the queens.
    his explaining to the young noblewoman his reasons for not taking a lover.
- His loyalty is demonstrated through
    his refusing to be untrue to Gwynevere.
    his following through on his promises to the young noblewoman and her father.
- These qualities and talents make him heroic because
    they are, by definition, heroic.
    they are rare and impressive.
    he uses them to defend the weak.
- These qualities and talents do not make him heroic because
    he has qualities besides these "impressive"ones, such as arrogance and brutality.
    he never does anything that does not come naturally to him; he never challenges himself.
    he is too interested in bloodshed.
    his deep love for Gwynevere hints at disloyalty to his king.

from Sundiata
Selection Test (page 150)

Recalling and Interpreting
(45 points total; 15 points each)
1. d
2. c
3. d

Using Vocabulary
(15 points total; 5 points each)
4. b
5. c
6. b

Interpreting and Evaluating
(20 points total; 10 points each)
7–8. Notes will vary. Possible answers:
violence:
- as boy, Sundiata ripped tree from ground in response to insult
- Sundiata's army preparing for great battle
- hundreds of animals slaughtered in sacrifice
- Fran Kamara described as able to "split ten skulls at a time"

Answers

- Fran Kamara violently splits tree, talks of doing same to enemies
- Kamandjan violently pierces mountain with sword

family love and loyalty:
- half-sister Nana Triban so loyal, she risks life to return to him
- Nana Triban expresses love and sympathy for Sundiata
- Sundiata concerned for sister and griot, relieved at their return

physical strength, horsemanship, warrior skills:
- physically strongest men are seen as most worthy of respect
- other warriors shout approval of deeds of Fran Kamara and Kamandjan
- Balla Fasséké extols Mali's "heroes"—warriors and their leaders

respect for tradition, the past:
- Balla Fasséké respected and valued as Mali's historian
- Balla Fasséké valued by Sundiata because he would perpetuate Sundiata's memory
- Sundiata depends on Balla Fasséké to inspire army by extolling Mali's heroes
- Balla Fasséké inspires army by extolling Mali's heroes

cleverness, self-reliance, resourcefulness:
- Nana Triban shows these qualities in escaping evil husband
- much of excerpt spent on Nana Triban's escape

magic, spirituality:
- Soumaoro feared as sorcerer/magician with great powers
- Sundiata recognizes importance of destroying Suomaoro's magic
- soothsayers advise Sundiata to sacrifice hundreds of animals

Evaluating and Connecting (20 points)

12. Answers will vary. Students who believe the selection qualifies as a tall tale could make points similar to the following:
    - It fulfills the requirements of a tall tale reasonably well.
    - The story is told quite seriously, describing wildly exaggerated deeds as if they were true.

- The characters are likeable (or, at least, not unlikeable).
- Some characters possess extraordinary traits that enable them to perform improbable feats.
- Seven-year-old Sundiata is said to have ripped a tree from the ground and to possess the strength of ten men.
- Fran Kamara's physical strength enables him to split a great mahogany tree in two with one stroke of his sword.
- Kamandjan's physical strength and horsemanship enable him to carve a wide tunnel through a great mountain, almost instantaneously, with his sword.

All of the other chiefs are said to have performed great feats as well.

Students who believe the selection does not qualify could make points similar to the following:
- It meets most of the requirements of a tall tale, but only barely.
- As it is only an excerpt, a fair judgment is very difficult.
- It is told all too seriously; most familiar American tall tales are much more humorous.
- The characters, as presented here, are not particularly likeable.
- Sundiata, the "hero" and main character, is said to have the strength of ten men, but he shows no extraordinary traits and performs no exaggerated deeds. In fact, he does very little at all.
- Only three people, counting seven-year-old Sundiata, are shown to possess extraordinary traits and perform improbable feats.

The Passing of Arthur
Open-Book Selection Test (page 151)

Recalling and Interpreting
(64 points total; 8 points each)

1. d	5. c
2. a	6. d
3. a	7. b
4. b	8. c

Interpreting and Evaluating
(21 points total; 7 points each)

Answers will vary. Possible answers could include

Answers

9. Bedivere's conflicts:
   * has to decide whether to obey Arthur's orders
   * wants to be obedient but can't bear to throw sword into lake
   * is scolded and lectured by Arthur
   Arthur's conflicts
   * is struggling with death
   * is struggling with weakness
   * argues with Bedivere
   * must overcome Bedivere's reluctance to obey
10. • Bedivere puts aside doubts, follows Arthur's order
    * three queens carry Arthur off to Avilion
    * whether Arthur wins conflict with death is not resolved
11. Bedivere's throwing sword into lake
    * is high point of story
    * resolves major conflict in story
    Arthur's sailing off on barge
    * until this moment, what will happen to Arthur is unknown
    * this is end of entire Arthur legend

Evaluating and Connecting (15 points)

12. Answers will vary. Possible answers could include
    * strength of purpose. Even though he is weak and dying, Arthur is determined to fulfill the requirements made of him.
    * courage. Arthur faces death with regrets only for the passing of an era.
    * love for his knights. Arthur is deeply saddened by the loss of the men he loved.
    * sense of authority.
    Arthur fully expects complete obedience from Sir Bedivere without any explanation at all for why he wants him to take what seems to be a pointless and wasteful action.
    He is deeply angered by Bedivere's disobedience.
    * honor. Arthur does not hesitate to fulfill the requirement made of him to throw his beloved sword into the lake.
    * piety.
    * Arthur wants Bedivere to pray for his soul, believing that great things can be accomplished through prayer.
    * He refers to the earth being "bound by gold chains about the feet of God."

Arthur Becomes King
Selection Test (page 153)

Recalling and Interpreting
(56 points total; 8 points each)

1.	a	5.	d
2.	c	6.	a
3.	b	7.	b
4.	c		

Using Vocabulary
(10 points total; 2 points each)

8.	a	11.	c
9.	b	12.	c
10.	a		

Interpreting and Evaluating
(18 points total; 9 points each)
Answers will vary. Possible answers could include
13. Initial feelings:
    * grateful
    * respectful
    * pleasantly surprised
    Reasons:
    * Kay needs a sword quickly
    * believes it's part of war memorial
    * doesn't realize meaning of pulling sword free
14. Later feelings:
    * bitter
    * regretful
    * annoyed
    * frightened
    Reasons:
    * realizes sword's significance
    * doesn't want to be king
    * is uncomfortable with how it makes Kay and Ector treat him
    * is happy with his life and doesn't want it to change so greatly

Evaluating and Connecting (16 points)
15. Answers will vary. Students could say that the source of the power is
    Merlyn, or his magic.
    * He is a magician (although his magic is barely mentioned in this excerpt).
    * It is only after Wart calls on Merlyn for help that he is able to release the sword.

the sword.

- It has been enchanted so that only the one right person can remove it. Wart possesses the right qualities, including goodness and innocence.
- As soon as Wart takes hold of it, he begins to notice strange and extraordinary things.

the animals, or nature as a whole.

- The animals appear in the churchyard specifically to support and encourage Wart with their love.
- The animals can speak to Wart.
- All sorts of natural enemies gather together peacefully to help a human.
- The light in the churchyard takes on an extraordinary brightness and clarity.

Wart.

- He senses magic in the churchyard, even if he isn't aware that he is creating it.
- He can understand the animals.
- His personal qualities, extraordinary education, and royal blood make him the right person to become king.

love.

- Wart is a loving son and pupil. Sir Ector and Merlyn obviously have a great love for him.
- Wart tries to get the sword for Kay's benefit, not his own.
- The animals are described as Wart's "lovers and helpers," and Wart feels his power grow on account of their love.

Where the Girl Rescued Her Brother

Selection Test (page 155)

Recalling and Interpreting

(40 points total; 8 points each)

1. b   4. a
2. d   5. c
3. b

Using Vocabulary

(12 points total; 4 points each)

6. b
7. b
8. a

Interpreting and Evaluating

(36 points total; 12 points each)

9–11. Answers will vary. Possible answers could include bravery:

- women defended families when men were away
- women and boys get their weapons to defend against grizzly; Quilter woman confronts it
- in battle, white soldiers outnumber Lakota and Cheyenne
- brother fights on, even outnumbered and after pony killed
- Buffalo Calf Road Woman rides into battle to save brother
- fighting pauses as everyone watches and cheers BCRW's brave action
- inspired by BCRW's bravery, Lakota and Cheyenne force whites to retreat

honesty, trustworthiness, high moral character:

- wives of important men had to have high morals
- whites break promises, so Cheyenne don't trust them

responsibility:

- wives of important men share their responsibilities
- Quilter woman saves people from grizzly
- warriors defend the people
- BCRW and other women show support for warriors by watching battles
- BCRW saves brother

honor, fairness:

- BCRW respected for being honorable
- BCRW follows husband and brother into battle because it's honorable thing to do
- Quilter woman talks to grizzly and gives it chance to retreat

craft, workmanship:

- women have Society of Quilters to make and decorate clothes, etc.
- warriors wear beautiful clothes into battle so enemies will respect them

physical strength, fighting abilities, horsemanship:

- story praises warriors for being fierce, talented fighters, good horsemen
- Crook respected as worthy opponent

respect for nature:

- Quilter woman speaks respectfully to grizzly, calls him "grandfather"

Answers

Evaluating and Connecting (12 points)

12. Answers will vary. Possible answers could include when Buffalo Calf Road Woman sees brother attacked, because
    - he is surrounded, outnumbered, horseless, and low on ammunition.
    - the reader knows that something must be done, or he will die.
    - the reader knows that she must do something about the situation, but what can it be and will it succeed?

    when Buffalo Calf Road Woman gallops into battle to rescue her brother, because
    - she has no weapons.
    - she must enter right into the battle.
    - she must get to him in time, he must get onto the horse, and they must escape from armed enemies.
    - the reader can imagine how improbable it is that she will succeed.

    any moment in which Buffalo Calf Road Woman is, or may become, threatened is suspenseful, because she is the main character in the legend and, thus, it is her actions and fate that the reader cares most about.

Let's Sweat!
Selection Test (page 157)

Recalling and Interpreting
(45 points total; 15 points each)
1. c
2. a
3. d

Interpreting and Evaluating
(30 points total; 15 points each)
4–5. Answers will vary. Possible answers could include
- fun-loving, fun to be around, entertaining; essay's tone is lighthearted and humorous
- insightful; realizes father calls her "honey" when she tries his patience
- proud, determined; learns all she can to make sure she's not embarrassed
- dislikes violence; hates violent TV shows
- modest, unassuming; makes fun of herself, admits using other people's ideas and comments

Evaluating and Connecting (25 points)

6. Answers will vary. Students might say that the main thing Giovanni gets from athletics is entertainment or amusement.
    - She uses televised athletic competitions to keep her company when she is on the road.
    - When she is sitting in a hotel room, she enjoys watching TV sports, snacking, and cheering loudly for her favorites.

    the preservation of her self-esteem and standing in the family.
    - She began to follow sports after embarrassing herself by revealing her ignorance of baseball in front of her father's friends.
    - She's competitive, as are the other members of her family.

From A Cat's Garden of Verses
Open-Book Selection Test (page 158)

Recalling and Interpreting
(56 points total; 14 points each)
1. b   3. c
2. a   4. d

Interpreting and Evaluating
(24 points total; 8 points each)
Answers will vary. Possible answers could include
5. • Tone:
     tender
     conversational
   • Imagery: gentle rain falling on land and sea, people and ships
   • Idea communicated:
     rain is falling peacefully
     rain affects everyone in similar way
6. • Tone:
     sarcastic
     mean-spirited, vengeful, or bitter
     darkly comic
   • Imagery:
     rain drenching people
     rain drowning dog
     dog dying of flu
   • Idea communicated:
     rain useful if it harms an enemy
     hatred of neighbor's dog

Answers

Evaluating and Connecting (20 points)

7. Answers will vary. Students might say that the poet created humor by
   - naming the poem, "Whole Duty of Cats." It is funny that

   pursuing and showing off mice is characterized as a "duty."

   dealing viciously with mice is portrayed as being a cat's *whole* duty, as if there were no greater calling on earth.
   - indicating in the first line that killing mice is a bad thing to do, and then going on to argue that it is bad only if it is done too quickly—before the mouse can be adequately tortured and shown off to other cats.
   - using the term "little head," as if the mouse were a treasured creature that the cat felt protectively toward.
   - using a two-syllable rhyme for the last two lines.
   - having Robert Louis Stevenson's cat be the speaker of the poem.

Appetizer
Selection Test (page 159)

Recalling and Interpreting
(45 points total; 9 points each)

1. c   4. c
2. d   5. d
3. b

Using Vocabulary
(15 points total; 3 points each)

6. c   9. a
7. b   10. c
8. a

Interpreting and Evaluating
(20 points total; 5 points each)

11–13. Answers will vary. Possible answers could include
   - narrator spies bear
   - narrator feeds first fish to bear
   - narrator catches and feeds several more fish to bear
   - bear belches
   - bear leans against narrator
   - narrator lands huge, smart fish
   - bear grabs fish, breaks fishing line
   - second bear appears
   - narrator removes waders and exits water
   - narrator begins waddling down path, plopping waders on ground and singing
   - second bear runs away
   - first bear follows narrator
   - narrator takes off running for truck
   - bear runs after narrator

14. Answers will vary. Possible answers could include
   - narrator runs toward truck
   - narrator throws himself into truck cab
   - narrator pulls into cannery parking lot with bear on truck hood
   - bear bounds off truck hood

Evaluating and Connecting (20 points)

15. Answers will vary. Answers could include such traits and support as the following:

   cool-headed:
   - doesn't panic when bears show up
   - figures out how to please the first bear while slowly working his way toward his truck
   - manages to tie on new lures, play fish, and so on, while feeling greatly threatened

   goofy: tries to sing a death song as Native Americans traditionally do, but all he can come up with is "Jingle Bells"

   nature lover:
   - ordinarily practices "catch-and-release" fishing
   - doesn't like having to kill the fish to keep the bear happy
   - would prefer to let salmon re-populate
   - normally feels refreshed by being in nature

   funny:
   - finds continually amusing ways to describe events
   - uses wide array of techniques to make the story funny

   honest:
   - doesn't portray himself as being particularly courageous or wise in this situation
   - includes many embarrassing details

   clever:
   - uses waders to confuse bears
   - gradually works his way toward the path
   - drives to a cannery

Answers

from An American Childhood
Selection Test (page 161)

Recalling and Interpreting
(54 points total; 9 points each)

1. a
2. a
3. b
4. c
5. d
6. a

Using Vocabulary
(10 points total; 2 points each)

7. c
8. b
9. b
10. a
11. c

Interpreting and Evaluating (16 points)

12. Answers will vary. Possible answers could include
    Hyperbole (underlined):
    - Whoever designed this corkscrew never used one.
    - The spirit of American enterprise never faded in Mother.
    - She would have fired up a new factory every week, and chaired several hundred corporations.

    Reveals:
    - curious
    - takes nothing for granted
    - perfectionist, demanding
    - appreciates quality
    - values intelligence
    - practical
    - energetic
    - intellectual

Evaluating and Connecting (20 points)

13. Answers will vary. What students might like best is that she
    - is fun-loving.
    - is loving and nurturing.
    - believes in her children and has high expectations of them.
    - is unpredictable, making everyday life an adventure.
    - is the type of mother other kids think is really cool.
    - is very intelligent and knows about a lot of interesting things.

What students might like least is that she
- seems so often to be unhappy and/or dissatisfied with things.
- seems quite selfish at times.
- doesn't always care about how others are affected by her actions.
- enjoys embarrassing other people, including her children.
- makes no attempt to refrain from annoying her loved ones and, in fact, seems sometimes to go out of her way to do so.
- is very demanding of others.

What Is and Ain't Grammatical
Selection Test (page 163)

Recalling and Interpreting
(48 points total; 12 points each)

1. d
2. a
3. b
4. c

Using Vocabulary
(12 points total; 4 points each)

5. b
6. c
7. b

Interpreting and Evaluating
(20 points total; 10 points each)
Answers will vary. Possible answers could include

8. • "Geoffrey" is correct, if uncommon, spelling
   • no "right" way for someone to spell his or her own name
   • implies name spelling devalues Chaucer's poetry or reputation
   • last name also looks misspelled, seems just as peculiar

9. • colonists rebelled for political, not grammatical, reasons
   • differences in British and American English aren't result of deliberate rebellion
   • silly idea that anyone would rebel against grammar

10. • spellings correct at that time
    • spellings change over time

Answers

- idea of accusing colonists, Jefferson, etc., of misspelling is silly
- raises silly question of why colonists, Jefferson, etc., would *deliberately* misspell

Evaluating and Connecting (20 points)

11. Answers will vary. Students could say that Barry is ridiculing
    - people who say things like "I cannot overestimate the importance of grammar." He points out that this can easily be overestimated.
    - Americans. He suggests that Americans
        tend to view all of history and culture in terms of modern American attitudes and standards.
        are careless toward language, grammar, and spelling.
        are overly impressed by people who are, or sound, British.
        can't cope with more than two rules of grammar.
    - people who think they know grammar rules that they don't actually understand.
        He acts as if splitting an infinitive is a terrible crime, but then acts as if he doesn't even know what an infinitive is.
        He quotes the split infinitive rule, probably knowing full well that this is an oft-repeated but misunderstood "rule."
        The first of his "only" two rules is one that many people seem to follow while trying to sound educated (always using *I* instead of *me*).
    - stilted, overly formal, or "business" English. He makes fun of the use of *finalize* and *undersigned*.
    - everything and everyone he can fit into his column. In an all-out effort to be funny, and under the guise of promoting good grammar, he takes jabs at
        people who abuse the language.
        people who fuss too much about people who abuse the language.
        job interviews.
        ignorance in general.
        airlines.
        historical people and events.
        himself.

The Car We Had to Push
Selection Test (page 165)

Recalling and Interpreting
(48 points total; 8 points each)

1. c	4. a
2. b	5. b
3. a	6. a

Using Vocabulary
(15 points total; 3 points each)

7. e	10. b
8. d	11. c
9. a	

Interpreting and Evaluating
(21 points total; 7 points each)
Answers will vary. Possible answers could include

12. Father:
    used to get sick from pushing car; direct
    never liked the car; direct
    was ignorant and suspicious of old cars; direct
    was eccentric; indirect

13. Roy:
    thought up at least one elaborate scheme to frighten his father; direct
    was creative; indirect
    was mischievous; indirect

14. Mother:
    was terrified of Victrola; direct
    believed Victrola would somehow harm family; direct
    distrusted technology; indirect
    was bewildered by technology; indirect
    was eccentric; indirect

Evaluating and Connecting (16 points)

15. Answers will vary. Possible answers could include
    - Tolerance and patience. Since everyone in the family is eccentric, one would have to be tolerant and patient to get along with and put up with everyone else.
    - A good sense of humor. Without humor, one would be driven mad by the others' eccentricities.
    - Oddness, eccentricity. A completely normal person wouldn't fit in well with the rest of the family.

Answers

- Optimism, confidence. It would require these traits to avoid being influenced by the many goofy fears that people in the family have about things blowing up.

How I Changed the War and Won the Game
Selection Test (page 167)

Recalling and Interpreting
(48 points total; 8 points each)

1. b
2. d
3. b
4. d
5. c
6. c

Using Vocabulary
(12 points total; 4 points each)

7. b
8. b
9. c

Interpreting and Evaluating
(24 points total; 8 points each)
Answers will vary. Model answers follow:

10. Between narrator *and* group of elderly women
11. Exists because narrator wants to play ball but elderly women want her to translate news stories
12. Resolved by narrator's realizing the women will go to church to pray (and leave her alone) when war stories are particularly upsetting

Evaluating and Connecting (16 points)
13. Answers will vary. Students might say that, because the narrator expresses no remorse and her tone is one of gentle humor, her attitude toward her actions is one of
    amusement.
    acceptance.
    good humor.
    pride.

A Marriage Proposal
Selection Test (page 169)

Recalling and Interpreting
(42 points total; 6 points each)

1. c
2. d
3. a
4. a
5. b
6. d
7. c

Using Vocabulary
(12 points total; 4 points each)

8. c
9. b
10. c

Interpreting and Evaluating
(28 points total; 7 points each)
Answers will vary. Possible answers could include

11. Surprises:
    - Chubukov and Natalia surprised by proposal
    - Lomov surprised by nearly everything but especially finding out he's engaged to Natalia
    - audience surprised by engagement because they'd been arguing and Lomov appeared to be dead

12. Exaggeration:
    - exaggeration of character flaws (hypochondria, stubbornness, intolerance)
    - characters' physical movements exaggerated
    - characters overreact to nearly everything: Lomov insists he's dying, Chubukov insists he'll kill himself, Natalia insists her life is over

13. Physical action:
    - characters charge all around, in and out
    - Lomov physically agitated throughout, faints, etc.
    - Chubukov charges around threatening to harm himself
    - Chubukov grabs Lomov and Natalia, forces them to hold hands and kiss

14. Improbable events:
    - Lomov can't get along with Natalia but proposes marriage
    - Natalia insists her life is over if she can't marry the man she can't get along with and just drove from her house
    - second argument breaks out after everyone realizes first one was great mistake
    - Lomov and Natalia get engaged in middle of fight over dogs

Evaluating and Connecting (16 points)
15. Answers will vary. Possible answers could include Traditional ideas about marriage and romance:
    - Natalia and Lomov, who can't get along with each other for two seconds, can't live without each other.
    - They become engaged while Lomov is in the middle of a swoon brought on by his argument with Natalia.

Answers

- Despite a complete absence of the ideals of romance, they will probably be very happy together.

Stubbornness:
- All of the characters are extremely stubborn.
- Their stubbornness causes them to argue constantly and to generally drive each other crazy.

Hypochondria, extreme emotions:
- Lomov's hypochondria just about kills him.
- The other characters' extreme emotions drive them to behave as if the world were coming to an end.

Human nature:
- It is human nature for people to want something only because it is claimed by someone else, and this is shown to be ridiculous.
- It is human nature to think highly of someone who is known to think highly of you. Natalia suddenly becomes desperate to get Lomov back when she hears why he came to the house.

Hot-tempered people:
- All three characters make fools of themselves by letting their tempers get the best of them.
- Temper stands in the way of everything the characters hope to accomplish.

Stupid arguments:
- Each argument is ridiculous.
- Most of the arguments consist largely of "Did too!"/"Did not!" kinds of exchanges.

Pretended affection:
- Chubukov pretends to feel great affection for Lomov while, in reality, he fears a request for a loan.
- Chubukov becomes exaggeratedly fond of Lomov as soon as the purpose of his visit is revealed.

The values of the upper classes:
- Lomov and Natalia argue violently about whose hunting dog is more able, even though neither is used for anything except fox-hunting.
- Lomov, Natalia, and Chubukov argue about land-ownership that, in practical terms, is meaningless to both families.

Theme 1: Transitions

Open-Book Theme Test (page 171)
Answers will vary, depending on students' choices.
Part A. (40 points total; 20 points each)
1. A model answer for Jerry in "Through the Tunnel" and John in "By the Waters of Babylon":

Jerry's transition is brought on by his desire to do what older boys can do, training to swim through the tunnel, conquering his fears, and successfully swimming through the tunnel. John's transition is brought on by his listening to and following his inner voice when it tells him to enter and explore the Place of the Gods even though in doing so he endangers his life and breaks the laws of his people.

These transitions are similar in that both increase the boys' confidence and require the courage to risk one's life. The transitions are dissimilar in that John increases his knowledge of the world, reality, and the past, while Jerry's increases only his knowledge of his abilities and his pride in himself. Also, John's transition will benefit others; Jerry's will not.

2. A model answer for Jing-mei in "Two Kinds" and Mr. Carpenter in "With All Flags Flying":

The happiness of both Jing-mei and Mr. Carpenter depends upon their ability to assert their independence from family members who think they know what is best for them. Jing-mei can only accept herself when she asserts her independence from her mother. Mr. Carpenter can cope with his physical condition only if he is in a situation where he is dependent on strangers, not family.

To assert her independence, Jing-mei refuses to continue playing the piano and rejects her mother's attempts to turn her into a prodigy. She stops trying to succeed and begins deliberately failing. To assert his independence, Mr. Carpenter moves into an old folks' home where he will not have to depend upon his family.

3. A model answer for "Through the Tunnel" and "Chee's Daughter":

In "Through the Tunnel," there is a conflict between Jerry and his mother. Jerry's need to assert his independence and prove himself capable of swimming through the tunnel causes a change in his relationship with his mother. She is forced to allow him to move beyond being a young protected child under her constant watchful eye to being an older child able to conquer new and potentially dangerous situations. His mother realizes he is growing up and needs less daily care and watching.

In "Chee's Daughter," the conflict between Chee and his in-laws, Old Man Fat and his wife, affects Chee's relationship with his daughter. Chee has traditional Navajo values and a lifestyle that Old Man Fat and his wife reject. This conflict makes it difficult for them to compromise on

Answers

the issue of who should raise Chee's daughter. Old Man Fat and his wife use Chee's traditional values against him in order to separate Chee from his daughter.

Part B. (20 points) A model answer for Luis's father in "Catch the Moon":
a. Possession: junkyard
b. Because: he can take pride in it; he hopes to share it with Luis; he hopes to pass it down to Luis; it provides enjoyable, interesting work; it helps him deal with grief and loneliness since his wife's death.

Part C. (20 points) A model answer for Jonathan in "Civil Peace":
a. Disagree
b. How tell: he's a survivor and optimist; considers his family's survival a miracle; would say where there's life, there's hope; spirit can be recovered but life can't.

Part D. (20 points total; 10 points each) A model answer for the picnickers in "What I Have Been . . .":
a. Symbol of independent adulthood and the narrator's feelings about that
b. Why: they seem beautiful, appealing, pleasant, and carefree at a distance; closer, they are not what they seemed—more drab, less appealing; she wants nothing to do with them.

Theme 2: Making Choices
Open-Book Theme Test (page 173)
Part A. (40 points total; 20 points each)
1. A model answer for Sylvia in "The White Heron" and Tom in "Contents of the Dead Man's Pocket":
   Sylvia's choice not to reveal the whereabouts of the heron is admirable for a number of reasons. First, it is the morally correct decision. It's wrong to kill animals (especially rare ones) just for entertainment or display. Second, she is so young and the choice is so difficult. Also, she must keep a secret, must give up reward money that she and her grandmother could really use, and must disappoint the young man, whom she would really like to please.
   Tom's choice to go out on the ledge after his paper is terribly foolish and nearly results in his death. He may be surprised by the trouble he gets into, but the reader isn't. Most people would accept the loss or try to think of a more creative, less risky way to retrieve the paper.

2. A model answer for Juan in "The Censors" and Lise in "The Ring":
   Juan changes in that he loses his individuality, his enjoyment of life, and his moral center as the result of taking a job as a government censor. His superiors' paranoia wears him down so that he comes to believe what they tell him about censorship and anti-government threats. Ultimately, he loses his life.
   Lise loses her happiness, her innocence, her "cocoon" of complete faith in Sigismund and his ability to take care of her, and her self-absorption. The thief takes all of these things from her when he forces her to look him in the face and to see what he represents—poverty, loneliness, sorrow, and death.

3. A model answer for the mother in "Delicious Death" and Tom in "Contents of the Dead Man's Pocket":
   If I were the mother in "Delicious Death," I wouldn't have allowed my son to go hunting. No matter what one thinks about hunting, only a foolish parent would allow a young teen to go off with a bunch of other inexperienced, gun-toting kids. Hunting accidents are very common, mainly because of poor decisions made by inexperienced hunters.
   If I were Tom, I would have tried to think of other, safer ways to get to the paper. I might have tried to get close enough to grab it with some device from a neighbor's apartment. If that didn't work, I'd give up and go to the movies. There's no way that I'd climb out on the ledge of a high rise to retrieve anything except a child.

Part B. (20 points) A model answer for Mr. White in "The Monkey's Paw":
   Seeks: 200 pounds
   Why: curious about wishing on the monkey's paw; son suggests it; would pay off mortgage; is sensible; was warned to seek something sensible
   Risks: pride; embarrassment; possibility of changes occurring in his life
   Results: yes and no; gets the money but his son dies

Part C. (20 points total) A model answer for Carlos's mother, in "Tuesday Siesta":
   Decision: to go out into crowd to put flowers on her son's grave
   Priorities: honoring son's memory; being good role model to daughter; doing what she believes is right

Answers

Part D. (20 points total) A model answer for "The Boar Hunt":

> Event: men are surrounded by thousands of boars that launch what appears to be an organized, personal attack against them
>
> Who: men; readers
>
> Why: wouldn't think that boars would be so organized, intelligent, and capable of seeking vengeance

Theme 3: Twists

Open-Book Theme Test (page 175)

Answers will vary, depending on students' choices.

Part A. (40 points total; 20 points each)

1. A model answer for Monsieur Lantin in "The False Gems" and Linda in "As It Is with Strangers":

   Madame Lantin's death brings many changes to the life of Monsieur Lantin. First, he's emotionally devastated by her death and then he's financially ruined when he can't run his household as well as she did. Discovering that her jewels are genuine and that her devotion to him was false provides another emotional shock.

   Meeting her grown son for the first time takes an emotional toll on Linda. Her excitement, happiness, and nervousness give way after the meeting to intense regret and sorrow.

2. A model answer for the astrologer in "The Astrologer's Day" and Ulrich von Gradwitz in "The Interlopers":

   The astrologer is frightened by a man who's been trying for many years to kill him. The astrologer deserves to be frightened because he had brutally attacked the man and left him for dead.

   Ulrich is trapped by a fallen tree and is about to be killed by wolves. He probably deserves to have something bad happen to him, since he was looking for trouble. However, he doesn't deserve to die at this moment in his life, since he admits his mistakes and befriends his longtime enemy.

3. A model answer for Henry's friends in "The Californian's Tale" and Tiffany in "As It Is with Strangers":

   For nearly twenty years, Henry's friends have gone out of their way each year to help him get through the difficult anniversary of his wife's disappearance. This is especially kind in that they aren't obligated to do it, they've done it for a very long time, and it takes an emotional toll on them, as they also loved his wife. They do it because they care about Henry, want to honor his wife's memory, and believe it's the right thing to do.

Tiffany puts her own concerns aside and goes out of her way to see that the dinner with Jack goes well. She does things that help her mother and Jack deal with the situation, even though they make Tiffany herself uncomfortable—things like wearing a dress, keeping her room clean, making conversation with Jack, and not commenting on her mother's behavior. These actions are especially kind, considering that her mother waits until the day before the dinner to spring the shocking news that Tiffany has a brother.

Part B. (20 points) A model answer for "The Happy Man's Shirt":

> Twist: when happy man is discovered, he's not wearing a shirt
>
> Before: a happy man's shirt would bring happiness to the prince
>
> After: happiness comes from inside, from the heart

Part C. (20 points) A model answer for "Mrs. James":

> Lesson: treat others as you want them to treat you
>
> Communicated: Mrs. James and Mildred begin to get along after Mildred indicates that respect is two-way street

Part D. (20 points) A model answer for the hat in "The Saleswoman":

> Stands for: individuality
>
> How know: phony saleswoman doesn't recommend the hat to the client, discourages her from buying it, but gives in to customer's desire for it

Theme 4: Challenges and Consequences

Open-Book Theme Test (page 177)

Part A. (50 points total; 25 points each)

1. A model answer for Ayah in "Lullaby" and the other little girl in "Winter Night":

   Many awful things happen to Ayah, but I think the worst is losing her two youngest children. They either have tuberculosis or are at risk for developing it, and government workers take them away without adequately explaining the situation to Ayah. The government seems to judge Ayah's home unfit for children, and they are never returned. I don't know whether taking them positively affected their health, but I can see that it had no positive effects on the family. In fact, it seems to have

Answers

destroyed Ayah's life and her relationship with her husband.

In "Winter Night," the other little girl is put into a Nazi concentration camp and separated from her mother. The Nazis may have done this for any number of reasons, but none that would make sense. It's likely that, after much suffering, both the girl and her mother died. There was nothing at all positive in what happened to her.

2. A model answer for Eckels in "A Sound of Thunder" and Noé in "Waltz of the Fat Man":

At first I thought that Eckels was just the stereotypical big-game hunter—a man who is self-centered, ridiculously brave, thrill-seeking, skillful, and athletic. I never expected that he would (a) recognize the possibility of being "out of his league," (b) retreat in the face of danger, (c) panic and lose self-control, (d) whine and beg, and (e) do nothing to prevent Travis from executing him.

At first, I pitied Noé because he seemed to be a pretty nice guy. I also thought it was unfair of the townspeople to avoid him, since he seemed so decent. However, as the story went on and more of Noé's innermost feelings and beliefs were revealed, I began to sympathize with the widows and other people who had to put up with his creepy handshakes and kisses. A man who dances with trees and has a thing for clocks is not someone I'd want to be around. Even though he's a pathetic person, I came to find him revolting as well.

3. A model answer for Prince Prospero in "The Masque of the Red Death":

In Prince Prospero's epitaph, I would be sure to use "abuse of power," "just deserts," and "arrogant." He used his power, not for good or for the benefit of those he ruled, but for his own selfish purposes. I would use "just deserts" because his death is just, since he never shows compassion for those dying from the Red Death and, in fact, throws a huge party during the height of the epidemic. Finally, "arrogant" describes one of the prince's chief qualities, and his arrogance in trying to kill the masked stranger is his downfall.

Part B. (15 points) A model answer for Azucena in "And of Clay Are We Created":
- Remarkable: her situation, that she is buried alive up to her chest
- Effects on her: she's terrified; she dies; she's used by media as symbol of the tragedy

- Effects on others: millions of people see the tragedy; Rolf experiences all the pain he's bottled up for years; Rolf is devastated; Rolf is released from his guilt; Rolf is released from his past; Rolf learns to accept his feelings

Part C. (15 points total) A model answer for the sitting parent in "Winter Night":
Would agree: yes
Reasons:
- doesn't seem to regret having known other girl, just what happened to her
- seems glad to have had chance to be kind to other girl
- has chosen to continue to care for children

Part D. (20 points total; 10 points each)
4–5. A model answer for Da-duh in "To Da-duh, in Memoriam":
Before: proud, satisfied, confident, certain
After: defeated, uncertain, sad, depressed, hopeless
Reasons:
- narrator tells her about Empire State Building
- what narrator tells her suggests that everything she loves is somehow overshadowed by the world she doesn't understand
- what narrator tells her suggests that her view of the world is wrong and that she's ignorant
- world is changing in ways that make no sense to her

Theme 5: Remembering
Open-Book Theme Test (page 179)
Part A. (40 points total; 20 points each)
1. A model answer for Dylan Thomas, the author of "A Child's Christmas in Wales" and Mark Mathabane, the author of *Kaffir Boy*:

Dylan Thomas seems to have been deeply moved by the Christmas holidays of his past. He probably chose to write about them because they meant so much to him and because writing about them was a way of reliving them.

Mark Mathabane's whole life was turned around when his mother forced him to attend school. I imagine he wrote about this because he wanted to share an experience that might help others see how destructive apartheid was, and because he wanted to show respect for his mother and gratitude for her sacrifices.

Answers

2. A model answer for Maya Angelou, the author of "Living Well. Living Good." and Jewelle Gomez, the author of "A Swimming Lesson":

Maya Angelou learns lessons from her aunt's story about her employers, who got to the point where their only pleasure came from watching others have fun. Among other things, Angelou learns that living well is an art that can be developed, that it requires loving life and being able to find pleasure in little things, that life is an adventure, that you can reshape or reinvent your life, that life loves the "liver of it," and that money doesn't buy happiness.

Jewelle Gomez learns many lessons about life from her grandmother's example and her efforts to teach her to swim. These lessons include how to conquer her fears and take control over her life as well as the importance of taking pride in her culture and in her body.

3. A model answer for Mark Mathabone, the author of *Kaffir Boy* and Premila in "By Any Other Name":

Mark Mathabone's decision to attend school reveals that he values his mother's opinions and insights about education and values her love and concern for him and his welfare. After hearing his mother's "lecture," Mathabone understands that lack of education caused many of the problems in their lives and in the lives of many blacks. His decision to attend school shows that he recognizes education as a worthwhile goal in life and as a form of power or control over his life.

Premila makes the important decision to leave her classroom when the teacher insults her and her Indian classmates. This reveals that she values herself, her heritage, her family, her country, and common decency. She reveals these values by refusing to put up with an insult that is directed at all Indians and by refusing to stay in a situation that is so hostile to them.

Part B. (20 points) A model answer for Premila, in "By Any Other Name":

Reacts to: her teacher

Reaction:
- offended
- angry
- disgusted

Judgment: very reasonable

Reasons:
- no one should put up with such insults
- teacher is racist and cruel

- Premila's self-respect is too important to sacrifice in this way
- there are other ways and places to get an education

Part C. (20 points) A model answer for *Farewell to Manzanar*:

Central challenge: maintaining dignity under terrible living conditions

Rating: difficult

Reasons:
- people identified by numbers rather than names
- staff had little understanding of Japanese-American culture
- living conditions at the camp were terrible
- little if any privacy
- dirty, crowded conditions
- insufficient supplies
- for warmth, everyone had to dress in surplus clothing that didn't fit
- just being confined to such a camp is a challenge to one's dignity

Part D. (20 points) A model answer for "Living Well. Living Good.":

Event: employers ask Aunt Tee if they can watch her and her friends having fun

Why:
- expected employers to complain about noise, ask Aunt Tee to do something, or want to join in instead of just watching
- on the surface, the employers are much better off than Aunt Tee and her friends
- expected wealthy people to have more pleasure in their lives
- most people have something better to do than to watch others having fun

Theme 6: Quest and Encounters

Open-Book Theme Test (page 181)
Answers will vary, depending on students' choices.

Part A. (40 points total; 20 points each)

1. A model answer for "I've Seen the Promised Land":

King's "quest" to lead all Americans to the Promised Land is so difficult that we still haven't arrived. It's difficult for many reasons. People may be too selfish and narrow-minded to allow everyone to get to the Promised Land together. How a person was brought up can also cause problems. People who were raised to hate other races can't get to the Promised Land without a lot of hard work. And, unfortunately, no one can get there without everyone's cooperation. There is also the fact that many of those who have led us toward the Promised Land, such as King, have been killed because of their efforts.

2. A model answer for *A Match to the Heart:*

   The "encounter" between Ehrlich and lightning is fascinating mainly because she did a good job of describing it and because she survived both the lightning strike and the medical care she received. She made me understand what it would be like to be hit by lightning. Her description is also fascinating because she was certain that she was dying and shares all her thoughts about that experience.

3. A model answer for A *Match to the Heart:*

   I'd want to ask Ehrlich about her relationship with her husband and her feelings about returning to live in such a remote place after her experience. I want to know more about her relationship because her husband just seemed to abandon her, and she's so matter-of-fact about it. How could she stay married to someone who treated her this way, and what became of their marriage after he returned from his trip? I'd also like to know how she could go back to living so far away from civilization. I don't understand why a person would want to live so far from others—especially someone who almost died because she lived so far from help and good medical care.

Part B. (20 points) A model answer for Eiseley, the author of "The Angry Winter":

   Observed: conflict between him and his dog over bone
   Learned:
   • he and dog are more like early human and wolf than he had believed
   • modern humans are sophisticated and civilized, but ancient instincts remain part of him

Part C. (20 points) A model answer for Thomas, the author of "The Tucson Zoo":
   The place:
   • pathway between two artificial ponds at zoo
   • public
   • unusual
   • artificial

• educational
Feelings:
   • delight
   • joy
   • amazement
Reasons:
   • beavers and otters are adorable and marvelous
   • Thomas is "coded" to react favorably to beavers and otters
   • Thomas's instinct makes him "hanker for friends"

Part D. (20 points) A model answer for the old woman who faints in "Pizza in Warsaw, Torte in Prague":
   Person: woman who faints in shop
   Feeling: despair
   Toward: sausages in shop
   Reasons:
   • there are twenty kinds
   • she's never seen such abundance
   • she's suffered her whole life from want of food
   • probably all her loved ones have always suffered from want of food
   • everyone wants their suffering to have meaning
   • no reasonable explanation for shop to have twenty kinds of sausages when, in past, it was lucky to have one

Theme 7: Loves and Losses
Open-Book Theme Test (page 183)
Part A. (40 points total; 20 points each)
1. A model answer for "Simile" and "The Glory of the Day Was in Her Face":

   Several things seem to have been lost by the people in "Simile." Their most important losses appear to be trust and faith in each other, confidence in their relationship, and a sense of comfort and ease with each other. The speaker suggests that these losses are the result of words that passed between them ("What did we say to each other / that now we are as the deer"). Now, as a result, the speaker and the other person are uneasy with each other; they don't trust each other, and they are fearful of further loss.

   In "The Glory of the Day Was in Her Face," a loving relationship is lost for reasons that are not shared with the reader. The speaker's beloved has either left him by

Answers

choice or has died. As a result, the speaker is devastated and feels cut off from the natural world.

2. A model answer for "Well, I Have Lost You; and I Lost You Fairly" and "Those Winter Sundays":

I admire the expression of love in "Well, I Have Lost You; and I Lost You Fairly" for a number of reasons. It is refreshingly straightforward and honest; nothing about the beloved or the relationship seems exaggerated or idealized. The speaker's determination to avoid the temptation to hold on to the relationship at any cost is also admirable; she understands that she although life without her beloved will be painful, life without her self-respect and moral center is impossible. Finally, her feeling of gratitude toward the beloved is admirable in that most people in her situation would feel at least somewhat bitter and betrayed.

There are many reasons to admire the expression of love in "Those Winter Sundays." The poem pays tribute to the love of a father who was distant, difficult to know, and impossible for a child to understand or appreciate. The father seems not to have been an emotionally demonstrative man, but he showed his love with quiet favors and kindnesses that were, the speaker now regrets, taken for granted and never adequately returned.

3. A model answer for "Eldorado" and "First Lesson":

In "Eldorado," a knight devotes his life to finding Eldorado, a land of riches that doesn't exist. At the end of his life, he is a broken man who has nothing to show for his efforts. His experience has many lessons to teach. I think the most important lesson is that "A full life is far more important than a full wallet."

In "First Lesson," the speaker's efforts to teach the daughter to float on her back convey other more important lessons of life. I think the most important of these is that "Survival requires the ability to have faith in what is truly dependable."

Part B. (20 points) A model answer for "Shall I Compare Thee to a Summer's Day?"
Comparison: "But thy eternal summer shall not fade"
Compares the beloved to summer
Communicates:
• beloved's beauty
• how lasting the beloved's beauty and gentleness are
• speaker's feeling of appreciation for beloved
• unchanging nature of beloved

Part C. (# points) A model answer for "A Blessing":
Element: ponies
Reaction:
• thrilled
• grateful
• overwhelmed
Reasons:
• ponies are very friendly
• ponies are overjoyed at his coming
• a pony nuzzles him
• pony's ear feels so soft and delicate
• ponies make him feel at one with nature

Part D. (20 points) A model answer for "Horses Graze":
Beloved: horses
Loves and/or admires their
• simplicity
• lack of awareness
• living in the moment
• gentleness
• satisfaction with life
• way of life
• appreciation of life
• optimistic viewpoint

Theme 8: Issues of Identity
Open-Book Theme Test (page 185)
Answers will vary, depending on students' choices.
Part A. (40 points total; 20 points each)
1. A model answer for the speaker in "We Are Many" and the old woman on the bus in "A Bus Along St. Clair: December":

The speaker in "We Are Many" is an interesting character because he has so many sides to him or different parts of his personality. He doesn't seem to know who he really is, and he wants more or better things from himself than he is able to count on. He's appealing because he's honest and funny and has a good imagination, and he's likely to embarrass himself at any moment.

The old woman on the bus is interesting because, first of all, she seems to represent nature or a supernatural force and, therefore, isn't even human. Second, she's powerful and dangerous, which is not what one expects an old woman to be. In short, in her case, appearances can be deceiving.

Answers

2. A model answer for the speakers of "Ex-Basketball Player" and "The Floral Apron":

 The speaker of "Ex-Basketball Player" seems strongly influenced by Flick Webb's past as a star athlete in high school. Although it's hard to say exactly who the speaker is or why Flick interests him so much, he (or she) recalls vivid details about Flick's playing basketball and describes him, back then, as "the best" and his skillful hands as "wild birds." Now, there are just flickers of that past in the way he dribbles an inner tube, handles a wrench, and gets his "applause" from boxes of candy in a diner. The speaker sees Flick as a pathetic man who has never fulfilled his potential.

 In "The Floral Apron," the speaker is strongly influenced by the older woman who taught her important things about her heritage and culture. These lessons have stuck with the speaker for a long time because they were interesting and worthwhile, and the speaker saw the truth and value in them.

3. A model answer for "My Mother Pieced Quilts" and "What We Believe":

 The mother in "My Mother Pieced Quilts" is celebrated specifically for her handiwork because it was artistic and because it played a role in keeping the family comfortable and in recording the family's history. The mother's arranging of pieces of fabric and the quilting process fascinated the speaker; the quilts make her feel warm and safe and bring good memories.

 In "What We Believe," the culture and the beliefs of the people in the poem are celebrated. The speaker's main reason for celebrating the people is that they are her people; and their beliefs, traditions, and stories naturally mean a great deal to her.

Part B. (20 points) A model answer for the speaker of "Making a Fist":
Reacts to feeling sick during long car trip
Reaction: innocent, fearful, overly dramatic
Rating: somewhat reasonable
Reasons:
- speaker is very young
- reaction not unusual for young child
- children don't understand serious illness and death

Part C. (10 points) A model answer for "To Satch":
- Subject: Satchel Paige

- Image: Satchel's pitching stars for strikes across the heavens
- Theme: Satchel Paige was one amazing pitcher.

Part D. (30 points total; 15 points each)
A model answer for the speaker of "Miss Rosie":
Embraces
Support:
- doesn't let what happened to Miss Rosie depress her or shatter her faith
- refuses to accept what happened to Miss Rosie as inevitable
- suggests she'll fight against suffering fate similar to Miss Rosie's

Theme 9: Observations and Expressions

Open-Book Theme Test (page 187)
Part A. (50 points total; 25 points each)

1. A model answer for "let my spirit fly in time" and "Jazz Fantasia":

 The speaker of "let my spirit fly in time" expresses strong feelings of appreciation, admiration, and pleasure in response to the jazz music she listens to. Its sound is so smooth and wonderful that she is filled with pleasure and her spirit is carried far away from its earthly concerns.

 In "Jazz Fantasia," the speaker expresses a number of strong feelings, including excitement, pleasure, mellowness, and nostalgia. All of these feelings are a response to, or an anticipation of, the expressive jazz music he is listening to.

2. A model answer for "Reapers" and "For Poets":

 I found "Reapers" very disturbing, mainly because of the shocking image of the wounded field rat and the matter-of-fact attitude taken toward the rat's pain. The cruelty really bothered me, especially because it doesn't seem to bother anything or anyone in the poem. The blade just keeps going, cutting down everything in its path.

 On the other hand, I found "For Poets" to be quite pleasant. I was inspired by the poet's advice, cheered by his images, and delighted by many of his word choices as in the phrase, "the very hero of birds."

3. A model answer for images from "For Poets" and "Constantly risking absurdity":

Answers

In "For Poets," the image of a poet poking his or her head out of a hole in the ground is effective. It suggests to me the idea that poets shouldn't spend too much time holed up by themselves, brooding, writing, and reading, but should be out in the world, observing, experiencing, and feeling.

In "Constantly risking absurdity," the image of a poet performing "above the heads / of his audience" is effective. It communicates the ideas that poetry involves risk and that it's the responsibility of poets to entertain, educate, inspire, and bring fresh insights to their readers.

Part B. (20 points) A model answer for the first tanka:
Observed: willow tree after spring rain
Learned:
- raindrops on willow tree look like string of pearls
- rain on willow tree is quite lovely

Part C. (30 points total; 15 points each)
A model answer for "Night Clouds":
Metaphor: "the tiger sun will leap upon you and destroy you / with one lick of his vermilion tongue"
Compared: tiger *and* sun; tiger's tongue *and* ray of sunlight
communicates:
- sun's strength
- sun's power over clouds, day over night
- bright colors seen in sunlight versus paleness in moonlight

Theme 10: Loyality and Betrayal
Open-Book Theme Test (page 189)
Answers will vary, depending on students' choices.
Part A. (40 points total; 20 points each)
1. A model answer for Brutus in *Julius Caesar*:
Brutus, in *Julius Caesar,* is loyal to a cause. The cause is the Roman republic, which he feels he must defend against the threat of Julius Caesar's tyranny. Brutus demonstrates his loyalty by agreeing to participate in Caesar's assassination, by doing so, and by going to war against Antony and Octavius.

Brutus could also be seen as guilty of a betrayal. By supporting the cause he supports, he is forced to betray his friend and leader, Julius Caesar, who trusts him and feels affection for him. The act of betrayal is murder.

2. A model answer for Raquel in *The Ring of General Macías*:
I would want to play Raquel in *The Ring of General Macías*. Although she's arrogant, she's also a sympathetic character, which would make the role interesting. She goes through some real changes during the play, feels a great variety of strong emotions, and must make a very difficult decision. Raquel has a good speech when she muses about what she would do if her husband were killed, but she also has the opportunity to ham it up as the offended wife of the general while the Federalist captain is in her home.
3. A model answer for Antigone:
Antigone follows the advice to write, if necessary, in blood. She writes in her own blood by taking an action that she knows full well may lead to her death. The action she takes requires bravery and strength of purpose, which seems to match the idea expressed by the metaphor. In addition, when her burial of Polyneices is undone, she repeats it, determined to make the results of her behavior permanent, which also seems to fit the feeling of "writing in blood."

Part B. (20 points total; 10 points each)
A model answer for Julius Caesar:
- Good qualities: leadership, courage, trust in his friends
- Tragic flaw: hunger for power
- Forces: opposition of the conspirators, some motivated by greed and their own desires for power, others by idealistic loyalty to the Roman republic
A model answer for Creon in *Antigone*:
- Good qualities: loyalty to Thebes, strength of purpose
- Tragic flaw: inflexibility
- Forces: Antigone's opposition; Haimon's love for Antigone; opposition of gods

Part C. (20 points) A model answer for Cleto in "The Ring of General Macías":
- Plot: puts human face on political conflict; warns Andrés, hides in closet; drinks poisoned wine
- Major characters: allows Raquel to demonstrate cleverness in protecting him, sympathy for cause, protectiveness about youth
- Play as whole: provides sympathy for cause; sense of conflict; understanding of characters' feelings

Answers

Part D. (20 points) A model answer for Brutus and Portia in *Julius Caesar*:
- Conflict: moral doubts about murder
- Partner's efforts: tries to find out source of conflict, shows loyalty, shows love and concern
- Good relationship: yes and no, good in terms of mutual love, bad in terms of complete imbalance; Brutus doesn't take Portia's needs or concerns into account, doesn't make use of her advice or help, and what he does (on his own) kills her as well as him

Theme 11: Heroism

Open-Book Theme Test (page 191)

Part A. (40 points total; 20 points each)
1. A model answer for Buffalo Calf Road Woman in "Where the Girl Rescued Her Brother" and Sir Launcelot in *Le Morte d'Arthur*:

   Buffalo Calf Road Woman is admirable because her heroism is accomplished without resorting to violence and is motivated by love. She rescues her brother from certain death on a battlefield without harming anyone else. Also, she acts quickly and courageously.

   I don't find Sir Launcelot all that admirable because he can't seem to do "good" without shedding a lot of blood. What he does best is fight, and I'm not too impressed by characters (or real people) whose ability to fight and kill is their major claim to fame. He also seems way too full of himself.

2. A model answer for "The Passing of Arthur" and "Arthur Becomes King":

   "The Passing of Arthur" communicates the insight that humans tend to question and even rebel against things that don't make sense to them. Bedivere would give his life to protect Arthur, and yet he can't make himself obey Arthur's simple instructions to throw Excalibur into the lake. The sword just seems too valuable, for several reasons, to be thrown away.

   An insight I found in "Arthur Becomes King" is that the desire for power can be corrupting, even in people who are mainly good. Kay wants so much to be king that he steals Wart's thunder and lies to his father about who pulled the sword out of the anvil. He does back down, because he's unwilling to continue lying to his

beloved father, but it was interesting to me that this basically decent person's first inclination was to lie to someone he loved and cheat someone else he loved in order to obtain power.

3. A model answer for Nana Triban in *Sundiata* and Wart in "Arthur Becomes King":

   Nana Triban experiences a dramatic change in her situation when she manages to escape from her evil sorcerer husband, Soumaoro. She escapes through her own efforts by wisely discovering his flaws and figuring out how to use them to her advantage.

   Wart's situation changes dramatically after he frees the sword from the anvil. He goes from being a happy, ordinary kid to a much less happy "future king." He becomes the future king because he pulls the sword out of the anvil, something that can be done only by the "Rightwise King Born of England." So, I guess this change is the result of both fate (his secret royal birth) and magic (which got the sword stuck in the anvil in the first place and which allowed Wart to free it).

Part B. (15 points) A model answer for Sir Bedivere in "The Passing of Arthur":

Ordinary:
- fails to follow orders
- is logical
- is led astray by beauty
- lies in order to do things his own way
- worries about his friend and king
- must struggle to carry Arthur to edge of lake
- feels confused, insecure, and unsure of what to do next

Extraordinary:
- knight of Round Table
- only one of Arthur's men to survive battle
- very strong in being able to carry dying Arthur across rough, slippery landscape
- last person in world to see and talk to King Arthur

Part C. (15 points) A model answer for Kay in "Arthur Becomes King":

Action: lies about freeing the sword
Motivations:
- greed, selfishness
- desire for power, fame, fortune, respect
- immaturity, foolishness

Answers

Part D. (15 points total; 15 points each)

A model answer for "The Passing of Arthur":

Value: loyalty

Revealed by

- Bedivere's reluctance to leave Arthur's side
- Arthur's expectations of Bedivere
- Arthur's anger when Bedivere doesn't follow orders
- Bedivere's gazing after Arthur's boat long after it leaves shore

Theme 12: Comic Perspectives

Open-Book Theme Test (page 193)

Answers will vary, depending on students' choices.

Part A. (40 points total; 20 points each)

1. A model answer for "A Marriage Proposal" and "How I Changed . . .":

   "A Marriage Proposal" was the funniest to me. It contains both verbal humor and physical humor. The dialogue was funny, and I could practically hear each character's tone of voice. At the same time, it was easy to picture how ridiculously the people were behaving. I liked the way the playwright made fun of the characters and their situation without being really cruel, and I liked the fact that everyone in the play was a victim of the playwright's wit.

   On the other hand, I didn't much appreciate "How I Changed the War and Won the Game." Part of the problem, I think, is that the situation is presented realistically but isn't very believable. The women can't read English, but they aren't stupid. Didn't they notice that the child just tore open the paper and rattled something off? Also, I thought it was cruel and selfish of the narrator to behave as she did.

2. A model answer for the mother in *An American Childhood* and Lomov in "A Marriage Proposal":

   The mother in *An American Childhood* would be a good person to be stuck in an elevator with because she'd be very likely to get that elevator un-stuck. Since she has absolutely no tolerance for boredom or for mechanical imperfection, she'd get the elevator working or find us some way out. If she couldn't, she'd probably manage somehow to keep us both entertained.

   Being stuck in an elevator with Lomov would be a truly horrible experience. With his hypochondria, he'd probably spend the whole time whining, hyperventilating, yelling, and doing all sorts of other annoying things. The best I could hope for would be for him to pass out and stay that way until we were rescued.

3. A model answer for " "What Is and Ain't Grammatical":

   Most of "What Is and Ain't Grammatical" is completely ridiculous. It is the level of absurdity that makes the essay as funny as it is. It is ridiculous to pretend that English has only two rules of grammar, that Jefferson deliberately misspelled words in the Declaration of Independence, that Americans speak and write the way they do because of rebelling against English grammar rules, and so on. Also, Barry's two rules of grammar are both very ridiculous and very funny. (If only I could get a break from, like, certain teachers. Oops, I mean, if only the undersigned could get a break from, like, certain teachers.)

Part B. (20 points) A model answer for the grandfather in "The Car We Had to Push":

- Struggle: to get the family to bury Zenas
- Win? No
- Reasons:
   Zenas died long ago
   Zenas was buried long ago
   what he wants is impossible

Part C. (20 points) A model answer for the author of "Let's Sweat!":

Realization: It's to her advantage to learn about sports.

Effects:

- she isn't embarrassed anymore by being ignorant
- she can compete with her family in this area
- she spends more time reading about sports
- she's not so bored when she travels
- it makes her happy

Part D. (20 points total; 10 points each)

A model answer for "What Is and Ain't Grammatical":

Pokes fun at people who pretend to know things they don't know ·

Accomplishes this by

- stating ridiculous rules of grammar
- defining an infinitive completely inaccurately
- having a tone of great superiority while clearly being full of nonsense
- making up funny facts about history but presenting them as if they were true